Rethinking Public–Private Partnerships

The global financial crisis hit the world in a remarkable way in late 2008. Many governments and private sector organizations who had considered Public–Private Partnerships (PPPs) to be their future were forced to rethink their strategy in the wake of the crisis, as a lot of the available private funding upon which PPPs relied was suddenly no longer available to the same extent. At the same time, governments and international organizations, like the European Union, were striving to make closer partnerships between the public sector and the private sector economy a hallmark for future policy initiatives.

This book examines PPPs in the context of turbulent times following the global financial crisis (GFC). PPPs can come in many forms, and the book sets out to distinguish between the many alternative views of partnerships: a project, a policy, a symbol of the role of the private sector in a mixed economy, or a governance tool – all within a particular cultural and historical context.

This book is about rethinking PPPs in the wake of the financial crisis and aims to give a clearer picture of the kind of conceptual frameworks that researchers might employ to now study PPPs. The crisis took much of the glamour out of PPPs, but theoretical advances have been made by researchers in a number of areas and this book examines selected new research approaches to the study of PPPs.

Carsten Greve is Professor at the Department of Business and Politics, Copenhagen Business School, Denmark. His research focuses on public–private co-operation and partnerships, and public management in a comparative perspective. He has contributed to or published many books in these areas, including *Contracting for Public Services* (2007, Routledge).

Graeme Hodge is Professor at Monash University, Australia. He is the Director of the Monash Centre for Regulatory Studies in the Law Faculty. He has published extensively in areas such as privatization of public sector enterprise, outsourcing of government services and public–private partnerships.

Routledge Critical Studies in Public Management
Edited by Stephen Osborne

The study and practice of public management has undergone profound changes across the world. Over the last quarter century, we have seen:

- increasing criticism of public administration as the overarching framework for the provision of public services;
- the rise (and critical appraisal) of the 'New Public Management' as an emergent paradigm for the provision of public services;
- the transformation of the 'public sector' into the cross-sectoral provision of public services; and
- the growth of the governance of inter-organizational relationships as an essential element in the provision of public services.

In reality, these trends have not so much replaced each other as elided or coexisted – the public policy process has not gone away as a legitimate topic of study, intra-organizational management continues to be essential to the efficient provision of public services, whilst the governance of inter-organizational and inter-sectoral relationships is now essential to the effective provision of these services.

Further, whilst the study of public management has been enriched by the contribution of a range of insights from 'mainstream' management literature, it has also contributed to this literature, in such areas as networks and inter-organizational collaboration, innovation and stakeholder theory.

This series is dedicated to presenting and critiquing this important body of theory and empirical study. It will publish books that both explore and evaluate the emergent and developing nature of public administration, management and governance (in theory and practice) and examine the relationship with and contribution to the overarching disciplines of management and organizational sociology.

Books in the series will be of interest to academics and researchers in this field, students undertaking advanced studies of it as part of their undergraduate or postgraduate degree, and reflective policy, makers and practitioners.

Rethinking Public–Private Partnerships

Strategies for turbulent times

Edited by Carsten Greve and Graeme Hodge

Routledge
Taylor & Francis Group

LONDON AND NEW YORK

First published 2013
by Routledge
2 Park Square, Milton Park, Abingdon, Oxon OX14 4RN

Simultaneously published in the USA and Canada
by Routledge
711 Third Avenue, New York, NY 10017

Routledge is an imprint of the Taylor & Francis Group, an informa business

British Library Cataloguing in Publication Data
A catalogue record for this book is available from the British Library

Library of Congress Cataloging-in-Publication Data
Rethinking public-private partnerships : strategies for turbulent times / edited
by Carsten Greve and Graeme Hodge.
p. cm. – (Routledge critical studies in public management ; 10)
Includes bibliographical references and index.
1. Public-private sector cooperation. I. Greve, Carsten. II. Hodge, Graeme A.
HD3850.R44 2013
658'.042–dc23
2012029097

ISBN: 978-0-415-53959-3 (hbk)
ISBN: 978-0-203-10813-0 (ebk)

Typeset in Times New Roman
by FiSH Books Ltd, Enfield

Contents

Contributors

Rob Alexander is Assistant Professor at the Department of Political Science, James Madison University, Virginia, USA

Anna A. Amirkhanyan is Assistant Professor at the Department of Public Administration and Public Policy, American University, Washington DC, USA

Tony Bovaird is Professor of Public Management and Policy, Institute of Local Government Studies, University of Birmingham, UK

Cierran Connoly is Senior Lecturer in the Management School, Queens University, Belfast, Northern Ireland

Marc Esteve is a PhD candidate at ESADE Business School, Ramon Llull University, Spain

Carsten Greve is Professor of Public Management and Governance at the Department of Business and Politics, Copenhagen Business School, Denmark

Mark Hellowell is Lecturer in Economics, Public Policy and Health Care Reform at the School of Social and Political Science, University of Edinburgh, Scotland

Graeme Hodge is Professor and Director of the Centre for Regulatory Studies, Faculty of Law, Monash University, Australia

Stephen Jeffares is a researcher at the School of Government and Society, University of Birmingham, UK

Francisco Longo is Professor and Director of the ESADE Business School, Ramon Llull University, Spain

Sarah Pettijohn is a PhD candidate at the Department of Public Administration and Public Policy, American University, USA

Eoin Reeves is Senior Lecturer at the Department of Economics, University of Limerick, Ireland

Sophie Sturup is a researcher at University of Melbourne, Australia

Helen Sullivan is Professor and Director of the Centre for Public Policy, University of Melbourne, Australia

Kit Van Gestel works as a researcher at the Public Management Institute, KU Leuven, Belgium

Veronica Vecchi is SDA Professor in Public Management and Policy at the Bocconi University, Italy

Koen Verhoest is Professor at the University of Antwerp, Belgium

Joris Voets works at the Public Management Institute, KU Leuven and is Assistant Professor at the Faculty of Economics and Business Administration, Ghent University, Belgium

Tony Wall is Senior Lecturer at the Department of Accounting, University of Ulster, Northern Ireland

Tamyko Ysa is Associate Professor at the ESADE Business School, Ramon Llull University, Spain

Preface and acknowledgements

Has the era of visible public–private partnership (PPP) popularity now passed into history? How has our thinking about PPPs changed as we have experienced a serious global credit crisis and heightened distrust of private financial markets? And how might we now build upon the best of what we have learned about PPPs and avoid their past excesses, in order to meet future challenges? This book focuses on ways to rethink (PPPs) in the turbulent times ahead and aims to highlight strategies that countries, organizations and individual actors use to address these conditions.

PPPs have been a research topic for the editors of this book for a considerable time. We both started out analysing 'privatization' in its various forms, and gradually moved on (as the world did) to focus on how the public sector and the private sector intersect in various forms of partnerships. The label of PPP therefore applies to both an object of study as well as a study area ('PPP Studies'). Scholars study PPPs from many different academic disciplines. In this book we want to highlight the study area and enable researchers from many different fields to contribute to knowledge about not only how the crisis affected PPPs, but what strategies and theories are available to understand the phenomenon.

Many of the chapters have been presented at the annual International Research Society for Public Management (IRSPM) conference. Since 2008 we have organized a panel on PPPs at this conference. For the first two years, the panel was organized by Carsten Greve and Erik-Hans Klijn from Erasmus University. Since 2010 the panel has been organized by Carsten Greve and Graeme Hodge. The panel has been held at the IRSPM conferences in Brisbane, Copenhagen, Bern, Dublin and Rome. We approached the authors of the most relevant and exciting recent papers for the 'turbulent times' theme. We also took the opportunity to contact additional authors where we felt the book needed extra insight, for example on the role of non-profit organizations.

We want to thank a number of people for their participation: the authors for responding positively to our request for including their papers in this volume; both the former and current president of IRSPM, Stephen Osborne and Erik-Hans Klijn; everyone at Routledge who helped with the book; Magnus Paulsen Hansen at the Department of Business and Politics at Copenhagen Business School for keeping track and managing the manuscript; Michael Hodge for his research assistance; and Katherine Fullagar for her editorial help. Carsten Greve would like to acknowledge the support of the SONIC (Sources of National Institutional Competitiveness) project, which is directed by Ove K. Pedersen at Copenhagen Business School. We also want to extend a big thank you to colleagues throughout the university world with whom we have discussed PPP themes. Finally, we want to thank our families for being there and for accepting that a new book was on its way.

Carsten Greve and Graeme Hodge
Copenhagen and Melbourne, July 2012

1 Introduction

Public–private partnership in turbulent times

Graeme Hodge and Carsten Greve

Introduction

One of the paradoxes of the last few decades has been the continuity and even growth of infrastructure public–private partnerships (PPPs) despite the loud voices of critics and harsh judgements of some academics. Indeed, there is little doubt about the success of PPPs on the basis of global interest, the frequency of use in countries such as the UK and Australia or by the spectacular delivery of timely new infrastructure. There has been substantial work undertaken to date on the multiple meanings of PPP more generally, the multidisciplinary languages spoken by commentators, and on the evaluation challenges faced by those interested in assessing PPPs as projects or activities. Whilst acknowledging the considerable advocacy and assertions of those pushing such reforms, there has been less work undertaken on the theory of PPPs. There is a real need to articulate the potential causal factors behind why PPPs may be capable of producing superior performance compared to traditional arrangements. It is to this purpose that this book is dedicated. This chapter focuses in particular on meanings given to how PPP might be judged as successful by implementing governments, and it tries to bridge the gap between what analysts purport to 'know' and how advocating political actors behave. The specific aim of the chapter is to explore the notion of success – what constitutes success for PPP? The criteria appear to be both varied and multifaceted, while also mirroring the very goals of government in society. A recent contextual factor has been the global financial crisis (GFC) that hit the world in 2008, catapulting PPP into 'turbulent times'. So how might the aftermath of the GFC affect PPP success?

The chapter is divided into three parts. Part one examines the variety of forms and levels of PPP. Part two details the theoretically-based criteria for 'success', taking inspiration from some of the recent literature on 'policy success'. Part three explores what the GFC and the turbulent times that have followed it may mean for PPPs. The structure of the book is then presented and finally, a conclusion on how to theorize about success of PPPs is offered.

Public–private partnerships: a variety of forms and levels

PPP has been defined as 'cooperation between public–private actors in which they jointly develop products and services and share risks, costs and resources which are connected with these products and services' (Van Ham and Koppenjan 2001: 598, quoted in Hodge and Greve 2005). Moreover, authors such as Weihe (2005) and Hodge and Greve (2007) have defined partnerships as encompassing several different families of activities; and the desire to articulate public–private partnership continues. Thinking about infrastructure partnerships, for example, a recent OECD (Organisation for Economic Co-operation and Development) report defined PPP as 'an agreement between government and one or more private partners (which may include the operators and the financiers) according to which the private partners deliver the service in such a manner that the service delivery objectives are aligned with the profit objectives of the private partners and where the effectiveness of the alignment depends on a sufficient transfer of risk to the private partner' (OECD 2008: 17). While this definition has some advantages, it does not include the non-profit sector where voluntary organizations co-operate with the government, and is therefore limited.

In the United Nations, PPPs are defined as 'voluntary and collaborative relationships between various parties, both state and non-state, in which all participants agree to work together to achieve a common purpose or undertake a specific task, and to share risks and responsibilities, resources and benefits (UN General Assembly 2005: 4; cited in Bull 2010: 480). Such partnerships can include those oriented towards resource mobilization, advocacy and policy goals, as well as long-term operations.

There are several crucial concepts here. One concept is 'risk'. In almost all definitions, sharing of risks in an explicit way is mentioned as one of the key aspects of PPP. This differs from earlier ideas on risk sharing through contracting out/outsourcing arrangements where this was more implicit.[1] Another key concept is 'innovation': the public sector and the private sector have to come up with new solutions and 'work together or achieve a common purpose'. More is expected of PPPs than just 'ordinary' collaboration. There is usually a sense of hope that the relationship is a long-term one – and desirably longer than the temporary relationship achievable through traditional 'contracting out' of services. Additionally, many partnerships entertain the notion of a certain degree of power sharing whilst working together jointly.

As witnessed in the last few decades, PPPs come in many shapes and sizes. Perhaps the most visible form of recent partnership has been the long-term infrastructure contract (LTIC) partnership. The LTIC partnership is organized around a design, finance, build, own, operate, transfer model and involves private-sector financing and private-sector project management capabilities. Historically, too, the urban development and downtown renewal experience of the US from the 1960s onwards saw close redevelopment partnerships as a visible and important PPP form (Bovaird 2010: 50). Another is the widespread co-operation between governments and non-profit organizations. This has been a tradition in some countries, especially in the USA where non-profit sector organizations run many public services (Amirkhanyan 2010; Kettl 2009). In the UK, there has been a debate on the 'big society' since Prime Minister David Cameron took office. Recently, the 'big society' has also been suggested as a guide for research efforts, though universities express misgivings about that (*The Guardian*, 27 March 2011). There are also other newer forms of partnering where the public sector and the private sector team up in new innovative formats to solve common challenges. 'Gate21' is a current example of a partnership on environmental issues. What began as a sustainable future forum by local government quickly spread as relationships were forged with other local governments, private sector companies and non-profit organizations as well as universities and housing associations (www.gate21.dk).

PPPs are, moreover, found at various levels of government, from regional partnerships between local governments and local private sector companies or associations, to national governments that team up with national companies or associations, to international organizations that team up with multinational companies (Skanska) or associations (the Red Cross). There are, of course, a number of combinations possible within that framework (Donahue 1989). Some challenges arise when local governments try to deal with global partners or when national governments want to form partnerships with multinational companies.

PPPs are also, clearly, more than projects (the building of a hospital or bridge). PPPs are now also associated with policies on how the government should interact with the private sector in order to improve public services or create innovation (the recent Danish government's 'Strategy for public–private partnerships and markets' is an example of this). At the UN level, there is a PPP policy (Bull 2010). At an even broader level, PPP could be a metaphor or a brand for how governments want their interaction with business and society viewed, or, alternatively, how they want the role of government in the economy viewed. And at a broader level still, the UN's Millennium Declaration (and the subsequent establishment of the Millennium Development Goals, MDGs) saw partnership being used in the context of developed countries having a role in aiding developing countries; Goal 8 here was to achieve a 'global partnership for development' through various means.[2]

Perhaps it makes sense to view PPP as being understood at many different levels. Hodge (2010b) formulated it in this way:

> PPPs can be understood as (1) a specific project or activity, (2) a management tool or organizational form, (3) a policy, or statement as to the role of the government in the economy, (4) a governance tool or symbol, or (5) an historical context and a cultural set of assumptions.

A conceptual model of the PPP phenomenon

So PPP may indeed mean different things to different people. If this is the case, how might we build on this idea and develop a conceptual model in order to contribute to multiple jurisdictions and PPP debates around the globe?

Considering just the infrastructure family of PPPs for the moment, we might view LTIC-type PPPs to provide infrastructure through a series of lenses: from a narrow lens at one extreme to the broadest lens at the other.[3] We might view PPP as a specific infrastructure project; as a management or project delivery reform; as a government policy or a symbol of a strong and capable private sector role in a mixed economy; or, more broadly again, as a tool in a modern governance task, as shown in Figure 1.1. Also shown is the underlying notion that all four of these perspectives of PPP exist within the context of a broader national history and set of cultural assumptions.

At the narrowest level, A, PPP is viewed as a single project. At level B, PPP is viewed as a specific type of infrastructure delivery mechanism involving the use of contracted private finance to initially fund all works. It is, under this view, a project delivery tool, and one in which private financing incentives encourage excellent project performance and early delivery. This view is typical of the engineering and project finance disciplines, but despite being common, its narrowness is rarely acknowledged.

The next conceptual level, C, takes this project tool one step further and sets the private finance delivery of PPP infrastructure as a policy preference for a

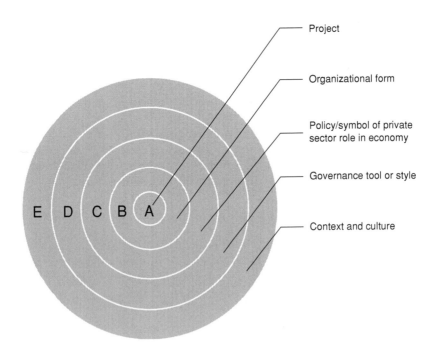

Figure 1.1 Dimensions of the public–private partnership phenomenon
Source: Adapted from Hodge (2010b)

jurisdiction. It may also operate at a wider policy level and recognizes explicitly that there is, in reality, not one single PPP type but a wide variety of alternative project delivery options available to governments, all of which use differing arrangements of public and private sector skills. The OECD list of acronyms is a manifestation of this: the breadth available here[4] is therefore essentially a policy statement that the private sector has a valid – and indeed major – role to play in today's mixed economy, whichever technical delivery option is chosen.

Broader again in this conceptual model, level D represents the inherent political or governance dimension PPP has always had. For example, the use of huge private contracts with a consortium for the delivery of high-profile government projects is a strong regulatory tool in governing.[5] Large economic incentives can be employed to ensure that the promise of early achievement of government objectives is met – even for complex projects and in controversial circumstances. PPPs can also function as a broader governance tool and mark a particular style of governance. For instance, the Labour government in the UK throughout the 1990s struggled to develop its relationship with the City of London. But as Hellowell (2010: 310) points out, PPP provided the incoming Tony Blair and his 'New Labour' government with advantages. Indeed, the use of private finance had the 'crucial [political] advantage that borrowing undertaken through it did not score against the main calculations of national debt', and borrowing was thus essentially 'invisible' to public sector borrowing and investment measurements. Blair's rebranding of the Private Finance Initiative (PFI) scheme as a public–private partnership policy was a further masterful political move under the 'third way' banner. Importantly, this PPP policy not only assisted New Labour in establishing a stronger relationship with the City of London, but also international promotion of PPP ideas then enabled this relationship to be cemented (Hellowell 2010). Both of these political characteristics of PPP suggest that it continues to have an inherently political, and thus governance, context in addition to any functional engineering or economic meaning.

In this model, each of the inner perspectives of PPP exist within the context of others. The notion that a PPP is simply a project delivery tool, for instance, carries with it many assumptions: the role of the private sector in the economy, how governance might occur in a country, as well as broader historical and cultural assumptions of that country. These dimensions are, to a strong degree, inherently bound together.

In this conceptual framework it is important to recognize that the PPP phenomenon exists within any one single cultural/historical tradition at each of the four levels A, B, C and D. In Victoria, Australia, for example, the Bracks/Brumby governments (2000–10) branded a specific set of infrastructure delivery arrangements using private financing as PPP.[6] A broader and less partisan view of partnership would acknowledge that the latest PPP policy is simply the most recent step in a long developmental process in which the delivery of large infrastructure projects through the private sector has been progressively changing over the past three decades. The governments also branded their PPP policy as different to the PFI policy of the UK. This Australian PPP branding might be contrasted against the modern use of PPP terminology by a country such as the People's

Republic of China. The huge Beijing Line 4 construction project has been labelled as a PPP, but the reality is that it most likely has public ownership of just above 92 per cent[7] and would, by western analysts, be regarded essentially as a public–public partnership.[8] Notwithstanding, this arrangement clearly signals new directions in terms of institutional, contractual, professional and project delivery dimensions for China. PPP here implies the use of increasingly professionalized project management methodologies in which new commercial, financing and institutional arrangements are being trialled in preference to traditional methods of the public bureaucracy. In this sense, PPP in China represents an important symbolic move to innovate, to commercialize and to professionalize. PPP represents change.

In our conceptual model, therefore, each of the four levels of PPP meaning exist within a broader historical and cultural context (E). The above examples suggest that this level is an important additional part of understanding the legitimate use of the PPP label as well as other dimensions covering the more technical-, institutional- or governance-related aspects.

In summary, we have noted that there are a number of interpretations of what a partnership is, and that partnerships can be differentiated according to level of government, form (project, policy etc.) or involvement with the profit sector, the non-profit sector or both together with government. These ideas are summarized in Table 1.1 where examples of various different forms of PPP are presented.

Theoretical criteria for PPP success

How do we measure when PPP is 'successful'? In this section we will first look at different understandings of 'success' that have been discussed in some of the literature on PPPs specifically and collaboration more broadly. We will then discuss how 'success' can be linked to the different forms of PPP described in the previous section.

In concept, success can be judged at each of the four levels of PPP meaning indicated in Figure 1.1. In this section we contemplate success from the narrowest of these perspectives (project level), to a broader (organizational) level, through to the perspective of government and the broadest levels of societal change and benefit.

At the narrowest end, the literature is full of claims of success based at the project level. We all enjoy brand-new facilities, whether they are hospitals, schools, courts, tunnels or roads; and given that the very specifications of PPP contracts indicate the need to deliver a project according to particular engineering, timing and financial standards, viewing success in this manner is hardly surprising. When a major infrastructure project is delivered according to the contracted standards, this is success. It may also have come in on time and on budget. A major attraction of declaring success at this level is its certainty, its visibility and its appeal to a common-sense judgment. Indeed, once visible new infrastructure is provided, it is difficult to argue against its 'success' (and, by implication, the success of the government's policies that led up to its provision).

Table 1.1 Examples of forms of partnership (public–private) and dimensions of the PPP phenomenon

	Government–private company	*Government– non-profit*	*Government–private company–non-profit*
Project/activity	Hospital project, school project	Public sector employees 'opt out' to form own non-profit project	Gate21 in DK, a partnership on climate change issues
Organizational form	PFI organizational form	Red Cross running refugee camps on behalf of government	Networked partnership across multiple organizations
Policy/symbol	UK Treasury PFI policy Canadian PPP policy Victoria, Australia PPP policy European Commission PPP policy across directorates from 2010	'Big society' agenda in UK	World Bank policy in private sector involvement
Governance tool or style	EU on the role of government in the European economy	Role of non-profits in delivery of specific services in the US because of pressing policy issues	Millennium goals in the UN
Historical context of public–private relations	Can market economy continue the same way after the financial crisis?	Associations' integral use in the building of the administrative state	UN global compact between developed and developing world

However the reasons for governments adopting PPP ideas are more sophisticated than simply delivering a project – they have been doing that for centuries. If we trace back over the explicit (and implicit) reasons for adoption, they are manifold.[9] The initial rationale under John Major's UK government was to get around restrictions on formal public sector debt levels. Private financing promised a way to provide infrastructure without increasing the Public Sector Borrowing Requirement (PSBR). This was followed by the promise that PPPs would 'reduce pressure on public-sector budgets'.[10] The third promise of PPPs was that this delivery mechanism provides better value for money (VfM) for taxpayers. This is a policy promise most worthy of examination and one that has also formed the primary PPP rationale in countries such as the UK and Australia. In addition to these three initial promises have been many more – some explicit such as: reduced risk to government from projects, better accountability, better on-time and on-budget delivery, and greater innovation; and some implicit such as: encouraging a more innovative public sector, improved business confidence, improved palatability for user funding for infrastructure, provision for long-term infrastructure life-cycle costs, and boosted sales of professional PPP services abroad. To these 13 PPP objectives we might nowadays also add two more objectives following the recent credit market failures and stock market downturns. It may well be that two new implicit objectives for PPPs will be: the desire for governments to broadly support businesses and preferentially adopt the PPP mechanism in difficult market circumstances (the objective of business assistance), or the broader societal objective of economic development. Additional objectives, too, are also possible, but the point here is clear. There have been many separate objectives set for PPPs, ranging from narrow financial objectives such as project value for money and delivery goals, such as timeliness, to much broader efforts to change culture or implement policy, as well as better governing and the pursuit of economic development. These are shown in Table 1.2 below. Furthermore, these objectives have also altered over time, and today still remain slippery in the rough-and-tumble of government policy speak.

Table 1.2 Objectives – both explicit and implied to date

Objective	Number	Objective/promise made by government
Financial	1	Provide better VfM for taxpayers
	2	Reduce pressure on public sector budgets
Project delivery	3	Provide better on-time delivery
	4	Allow better on-budget delivery
Cultural change	5	Allow greater infrastructure (project) innovation
	6	Encourage a more innovative public sector
Policy	7	Enable provision of infrastructure without appearing to increase public sector borrowing
	8	Support businesses in difficult global market conditions (business assistance/subsidy)
	9	Improve political feasibility to impose user fees
	10	Reduce risks to government from infrastructure projects
Governance	11	Be a symbol of new (third way) government
	12	Help put infrastructure issues onto the public policy agenda
	13	Improve business confidence
	14	Improve government budget credentials
	15	Improve accountability
Economic	16	Provide a crucial tool to underpin the broad societal objective of economic development
	17	Boost sales of professional PPP services abroad
	18	Enable the full life-cycle costs of infrastructure to be provided

Source: Adapted from Hodge (2010a)

It is also clear that these objectives form a series of promises at the level of project delivery mechanism (or organizational form); at the policy level and at the level of governance. Whilst there is no neat one-to-one correspondence, and categories overlap, governments clearly expect PPP to deliver benefits across a far wider base than is often discussed. So, returning to our thoughts about defining PPP success, how might we determine, for example, if PPP has been successful in delivering projects more 'on time' (as promised as a delivery mechanism), encouraging a more innovative public sector (promised at the policy level), or improving business confidence and underpinning economic development (as implied at the governance level)?

A major contribution here has been the work of Jeffares *et al.* (see Chapter 9 in this book) and Skelcher and Sullivan (2008), which builds on earlier work by Skelcher and Sullivan. Jeffares *et al.* have been concerned with how it is possible to measure the performance of partnership. Instead of taking the usual private sector route, and only asking if a partnership contributes to economic success, Jeffares *et al.* and Skelcher and Sullivan pointed to the need for a theory-based evaluation of partnership performance. In their work, Jeffares *et al.* talk about 'performance domains' that are linked explicitly to acknowledged bodies of theory. These performance domains (and the associated theoretical arenas) include: *democracy* (democratic theory); *policy* goal achievement (network theory); *transformation* to produce new public sector behaviours (institutional theory); *connectivity* to stimulate innovation (innovation theory, network theory); *co-ordination* to achieve synergies (resource dependency); and *coalition* to achieve sustainable partnerships (discourse theory). Each of these alternative dimensions is valuable and each brings different PPP values into the spotlight.

Crucially, Jeffares *et al.* acknowledge the need for a 'theoretically informed' evaluation framework and for any PPP assessment to consider 'performance' in a range of ways. However, they also are clear about 'the politically-loaded nature of PPPs as public policy instruments'. As they quite rightly state: 'PPPs are as much political as they are managerial entities'. Importantly, Jeffares *et al.* also articulate both a 'narrow' and a 'broad' definition of partnership performance.

Narrow definition

'Partnership performance could be narrowly conceived as concerned with the achievement of particular service or outcome targets as set out in the partnership agreement (strategy, contract, business plan) and assessed in relation to other factors such as the cost of the partnership's operations' (Chapter 9 by Jeffares *et al.*). In this narrow definition, partnership is therefore concerned with 'goal-based evaluation'; that is to evaluate success through criteria officially set out. This could be through Parliament and legislation, but often it is through the specific goals and objectives that were formulated by government or by the partners themselves prior to setting the partnership forth. It should then be relatively easy to be able to determine if a partnership was successful or not by going back to the 'original documents' and seeing what the objectives were. Of course, often this is not so clear-cut, and explicit policy documents detailing the 'purpose' may not exist.

Wider definition

> Alternatively, partnership performance may be more broadly conceived and include consideration of the longer-term relationship that might exist beyond the delivery of a particular project or programme, the wider benefits to particular individuals or partner organizations or indeed to citizens and service users.
>
> (Chapter 9 by Jeffares *et al.*)

In the wider definition, there is clearly more work for those doing the evaluation to assess the degree to which 'success' has been achieved.

A further finding of the Jeffares *et al.* research was the articulation of a preliminary list of elements in an 'ideal partnership'. These elements were developed from eight partnership 'toolkits' made by various organizations (consultants and public organizations). Jeffares *et al.* identified the 12 composite partnership principles, the implication of which was twofold: first, that partnerships could be assessed across all dozen domains; and second, that an ideal PPP would presumably score well on all counts.

Others have also followed this desire for a tool to assess the extent to which PPPs are performing well (or, in other words, 'successfully') (OECD 2008: 133–4); and have, for example, produced a heuristic listing of 10 'good practices in the public–private partnership process' as their guidance.

Added to this work has been that of Huxman and Hubbert (2009), along with other colleagues. Huxman and Hubbert picked out five types of success. They saw success as: (1) achieving outcomes, (2) getting the process to work, (3) reaching emergent milestones, (4) gaining recognition from others, and (5) acknowledging personal pride in championing a partnership. Of these types of success, perhaps the most well known from other parts of the literature are the first two. 'Achieving outcomes' is often considered to be the final decision on whether a project or a policy is judged a success or not – 'mission accomplished' could be another expression for this. The second criteria is 'getting the process to work'. Many network analysts argue that it is not the output or outcome that is important to a reform and change effort, but more what the process brings with it. New and innovative elements can be discovered in a partnering process. If the process itself runs smoothly and helps create new ideas and satisfaction among participants, then the process could be a success criterion. The third point, 'reaching emerging outcomes', is about the content of that innovation that a smooth process can bring about. New goals and objectives may have risen because of a well-structured process, and a success factor could be that an invention is being discovered. The two remaining factors mentioned by Huxman and Hubbert relate to personal investment and the point of view of the actor making the change. If a partnership ensures 'recognition from others' and 'acknowledgment of personal pride' then that, in Huxman and Hubbert's view, also counts as a success factor.

Skelcher (2010) writes about PPP success from another angle – that of the governance of PPP. Acknowledging the existence of a wide range of PPP families, he writes about four different types of governance: legal, regulatory, democratic and corporate. In his view, the corporate governance aspect has been the least examined aspect of PPPs, with few studies having focused on the relationship between the board and the director, and the governance structures surrounding them. There has been some focus on legal governance and also regulatory governance, for example the regulatory framework of entering partnerships in the European Union (EU) (Tvarnø 2010).

At the broadest level, too, there are different kinds of criteria for 'success', which are associated with more disciplinary perspectives. Economists tend to look at economic factors concerning PPPs, political scientists and public policy scholars are likely to see if the political mandate is being fulfilled, while sociologists want to know the difference PPPs make at a broader societal level, including being clear about who the winners were as well as the losers. And in the world of auditing, there is now talk of the 'five Es' as opposed to the 'three Es' in the New Public Management (NPM) era. The five Es are economy, efficiency, effectiveness, equity, and environmental. While economists typically care about economy, efficiency and effectiveness, and political scientists and public policy people care about both effectiveness and equity, sociologists and other groups are increasingly beginning to focus more on environment (see, for example, the world famous sociologist Anthony Giddens' recent book on climate change).

The straight technical challenge to assess the relative success of a PPP is not insignificant. Hodge (2010a), for example, defines six serious infrastructure PPP evaluation challenges: the challenge of defining the evaluand; of multiple PPP objectives; of multiple discourses and disciplines; of the evaluator's role; of evaluative rigour for an individual PPP; and of accurately summarizing multiple evaluation studies. He notes 15 infrastructure PPP objectives discernible at that point in time, one of which is VfM. And for this single VfM objective, he then also presents the mixed results of some 28 evaluations and reviews from the past decade. These are shown in Appendix A of this chapter.

So, at this broadest level of societal existence, how should PPP 'success' be seen? And knowing that PPP is as political a task as it is a technical or policy goal-oriented one, how can we think about judging the success of PPP at the highest level? Put another way, what precisely do governments mean when they view PPP as successful or not successful?

Like talk of 'good' governance and 'better' regulation, 'success' in government policy is an attractive linguistic. It is, as McConnell (2010) says, comforting and pleasing to everyone. We all desire success. It is clear that success is not an issue of 'all or nothing', and that governments, for example, may achieve success to a degree across many fronts. McConnell suggests that one major distinction in thinking about success from a theoretical perspective has been between the foundationalist and anti-foundationalist positions. In the first instance, success is seen as a matter of fact, because success can be assessed against identifiable standards. The rationale here is that when government meets its objectives, such as building a road, delivering a piece of infrastructure or effecting a policy reform on target, it achieves success. Objectives are met and the desired outputs are achieved. In other words, successful execution is regarded as policy success. The opposite position is that of the anti-foundationalists. To them, success is purely a matter of interpretation. In this case, there are no identifiable standards for success because objectives and outcomes are supported and opposed by different actors. A road through a local community who does not want it can be seen as a failure, whilst the government perceives it as a success – but this is simply their view.

McConnell's 'realistic' definition of success acknowledges a midway position between these two extremes. To the realists, a policy can indeed be judged a success 'insofar as it achieves the goals that proponents set out to achieve'. He adds, however, that 'only those supportive of the original goals are liable to perceive, with satisfaction, an outcome of policy success. Opponents are likely to perceive failure, regardless of outcomes, because they did not support the original goals.' In other words, their definition of success accommodates the important, but thus far unstated, question – 'Success for whom?'. It also begins to delve into the dual worlds of success viewed from the utilitarian goals and objectives perspective, on the one hand, and the more fluid world of politics on the other, where the words are the fundamental currency for framing meaning in the polity. The title of Edelman's 1977 book said it all: *Political Language: Words that Succeed and Policies that Fail.*

Importantly, McConnell (2010: 29) observed that despite several strands to the literatures on policy success (including much literature on 'failure'), 'the phenomenon of policy success is rarely tackled directly and systematically'. Moreover, to his mind, 'the academic world has barely begun to dig beneath the surface of this key policy phenomenon and the rhetoric that surrounds it'.

He acknowledges, though, that policy has to date been about process, about programmes and about the political dimension. As a consequence, he suggests that these three main dimensions provide a foundation for interpreting success, as shown in Table 1.3.

McConnell (2010: 54) put it well when he noted that governments *do process* (defining issues as problems, examining options, consulting, and so on), they *do programmes* (using a wide variety and combinations of policy instruments), and they *do politics* (engaging in activities that can influence electoral prospects, maintaining capacity to govern and steering policy direction).[11] Clearly, 'success can reside in each of these three spheres'.[12] These insights are, in our minds, crucial in our discussions of PPP success. And McConnell's framework neatly ties together some of our thoughts in this paper.

Other commentators such as Bebbington and McCourt (2007) have also observed the achievement of 'success' at the highest levels of societal change, and in the context of developing countries. Their work adopted the normative definition of success as 'the enhancement of human capabilities, in particular for the people who have the greatest capability deficits'. And whilst their work analysing development success was clearly a more complex undertaking, their analysis of eight (southern) case studies had something to offer theories of 'success' in the north.

Table 1.3 The three main dimensions of policy success

Dimension	Elements
Process	• Preserving policy goals and instruments • Conferring legitimacy • Building a sustainable coalition • Symbolizing innovation and influence
Programmes	• Meeting objectives • Producing desired outcomes • Creating benefit for target groups • Meeting policy domain criteria
Politics	• Enhancing electoral prospects/reputation of governments and leaders • Controlling the policy agenda and easing the business of governing • Sustaining the broad values and direction of government

Source: McConnell (2010: 46)

They suggested that success was achieved through seven stages:[13] 'an initial upsurge in social energy' (to lay popular roots); 'generates a policy idea...or highlights an existing idea'; 'around which a coalition assembles'; this then 'throws up a leader who gets the idea on the policy agenda'; 'and overcomes opposition from supporters of the old dispensation'. The coalition is then 'institutionalized, empowering beneficiaries and deflecting patrons and rent-seekers'; and 'the policy is consolidated through feedback to adapt it to changing circumstances'. The importance of their contribution relates to the 'sociology of knowledge and the politics of ideas in policy processes' along with the 'multifarious membership of policy coalitions' (Bebbington and McCourt 2007: 241). And as they put it, understanding success is crucial not only for the practice of development but also in order to examine the role that governments can play. Perhaps PPP success in the north has owed much of its success to the power of the fundamental partnership ideal as well as to the more obvious policy coalitions hard at work?

Importantly, we have now mapped the terrain covered by two slippery concepts – the PPP phenomenon, and the idea of 'success'. Clearly, both of these domains remain complex; and whilst they do not fit into any single, neat meta-framework for evaluating PPP success, we at least now have some broad dimensions that would seem central to any analysis of PPP, its current success and its future. Indeed, irrespective of how one looks at the issue of PPP (from its narrowest conception as an activity or a project through to the broadest conception of partnership as symbolism and part of governance), the three broad success dimensions (process, programmes and politics) would seem to apply. And for all types of PPP, this success framework suggests that issues of legitimacy, sustainability and innovation matter; utilitarian notions of meeting policy objectives, achieving outcomes and delivering benefits to target groups matter; and issues of enhancing one's own electoral prospects and sustaining the broad values of government also matter. In other words, PPP success would seem from these arguments to be as much about politics and the business of governing strongly and legitimately as it is about policy objectives and technical issues such as VfM.

Public–private partnerships in turbulent times

PPPs have been affected by the financial crisis that hit the world in late 2008. Like other areas, however, it is not certain how serious and severe the consequences will be for PPPs. PPPs, at a minimum, are living through 'turbulent times' and there is no easy answer as to what will happen to PPPs in the long run. What is certain is that, as Flinders (2010) remarked, the whole politics of the PPP debate has

> to a great degree been recast, or has at the very least taken on new emphasis, as a result of the global financial crisis from 2008 onwards. Assumptions regarding the dominance and superiority of the market that had become almost uncontested towards the end of the twentieth century are now receiving renewed attention, and this may have important ramifications for the future utilization of PPPs.

This could also have influence on the topic of 'success' discussed in this chapter.

Judging from an impression of the literature and commentary so far, we might contemplate two different scenarios or interpretations as to the future: (1) a sceptical, technical and pessimistic interpretation, and (2) an optimistic, holistic and political interpretation.

A sceptical and technical interpretation

In a sceptical interpretation, PPPs have been affected hard by the financial crisis. Looking at PPPs from a North American perspective, Boardman and Vining (2010) write:

> ...in the latter part of the decade, between late 2007 and early 2010, the dominant trend has been a reduction of private sector sources of capital for infrastructure stemming from the global financial meltdown and an increase in cost of capital from remaining lenders. Foreign (non-North American) banks who were major sources of financing for Canadian P3s have reduced their long-term credit facilities. The Macquarie Group (and the Royal Bank of Scotland) have undergone major restructuring. Other commercial banks have failed, resulting in consolidation.
>
> (pp. 354–5)

According to the OECD in 2010, the financial crisis had an 'immediate negative impact on the volume of PPP projects in member countries'. The overview of the OECD ran like this:

As credit markets dried up, debt capital became next to impossible to acquire by SPVs [special purpose vehicles, the PPP company formed when the public sector and private sector enter a partnership], and new projects that had not already been finalized largely came to a standstill. In response to these developments, a number of countries made efforts to unclog the PPP pipeline by making financing available in different forms. The United Kingdom chose to do this by setting up a unit within the Treasury that acts like a private sector bank: the Infrastructure Finance Unit. France and Portugal chose to set up a guarantee scheme, and other countries such as Korea and Mexico set up special PPP initiatives as part of their stimulus plans.

(OECD 2010)

The events in the UK have also been examined by Connoly and Wall – the British banks' and the British government's responses to the financial crisis, and the practice of setting up a temporary bank within the Treasury (see Chapter 2 of this book). The result of this, for the time being, has therefore been a 'public–public partnership', as the Treasury as a public organization is financing the building of public sector organizations such as schools or hospitals.

An optimistic and political perspective

The partnership ideal in which we aim to get the best of the government (in defining common interests) and the best of the private sector (to generate wealth) will not go away. There will be even more demand for PPPs in various forms in the future. The policy challenges are, increasingly, becoming too great for any one organization to cope with alone (Kettl 2009), which is also reflected in the broader 'collaborative governance' movement (O'Flynn and Wanna 2009). In the EU, the Commission is shifting its attention towards PPPs in a broader policy perspective. The Commission wants PPP to be a defining feature that will cut across many of the other policy areas. Instead of just being a policy that is relevant to the transport or infrastructure sector, a PPP policy is more about the role of European governments in the economy (European Commission 2011). The EU is therefore turning up the volume on what a PPP can be, and in our terminology here the EU is shifting focus from project and organizational form levels to a policy level. Of course, the future reality in any country will depend on local circumstances, but it is also most likely to be somewhere along the continuum between these two extremes.

The future of the post-GFC PPP terrain is also likely to be influenced by several other trends and dynamics in the way that PPP success is being discussed currently. These include:

- *A change from projects and organizational forms to policy*: There appears to be a move away from only focusing on individual projects. In the beginning of the PPP literature, there was much focus on individual projects in the UK or North America. The evaluations were about the initial rounds of project experiences, and they were examined by individual researchers or by leading auditing institutions such as the National Audit Office in the UK. There has since been a move towards focusing more on broader policies that governments or international organizations form. Both Australia and the UK, for example, have been spearheading the formulation of PPP policies. Other countries have followed, often by establishing PPP units that could support such policies. International organizations are also formulating PPP policies, such as the United Nations and the OECD. The European Commission has recently proposed a shift in the EU from looking only at projects and specific sectors to making PPPs a general policy priority across different departments in the EU, with the aim of ensuring a greater role for European governments in the running of the economy. PPP policy has, in some ways, therefore come of age and become part of broader discussions about a mixed economy.

- *A change from economic success criteria and political criteria to broader social criteria*: There appears to be a move away from only assessing 'success' as economic or financial for individual projects. This was very much the case in studies of specific projects in the UK and Canada. Now the focus is on broader success criteria, and moving towards broader 'programme' success criteria. 'Process' success criteria, such as user involvement or innovative practices, and the 'politics' success criteria of establishing ways of dealing with often competing values of government and private sector actors are also being considered.

- *A change from a sceptical to an optimistic view on partnerships in the long run, towards 'emerging' partnerships*: The GFC certainly put a damper on the economics-based families of the PPP phenomenon for a time. The 'partnership idea' is hard to suppress, however, and attention has shifted towards other types of partnerships, notably to partnerships with the non-profit sector (as currently witnessed by the advent of the 'big society' idea in the UK, although many observers think it is bogus). New ways to partner with private sector organizations are also being explored. This buzz can be found in new or rising policy areas, such as environment and climate issues, and in more enduring policy challenges such as urban development or town planning. The current interest in collaborative governance or 'nodal governance' can be aligned with the partnership discussion in the wider definition of the term. Emerging partnerships are likely to emphasize multiple partners rather than two, and new policy areas are also appearing through collaborations in the information and communication technology (ICT) arena.

In short, there is a movement underway from looking at 'established' PPPs such as long-term infrastructure contracts, which are often dependent on private finance, towards what we will here term 'emerging partnerships', because they are emerging around new and evolving public policy issues. These emerging partnerships cross organizational borders as well as countries, and can be expected to be found at the local level, the national level, the international level or some combination of these.

Studies of 'success' should therefore look to theories that can capture the advent of the emerging partnerships, and be sure to capture a broader view of their 'success'. In all likelihood this cannot be captured in only economic terms, but also requires a combination of process, programme and politics dimensions to understand partnership 'success' from a theoretical and empirical perspective.

Structure of the book

The chapters in this book examine the theme of turbulent times and of theoretical approaches and strategies to cope with PPPs. The next three chapters look at 'the era of turbulence'. In Chapter 2, Cierran Connoly and Anthony Wall investigate the impact of the GFC and look at the UK example. Their chapter is particularly relevant as the UK is seen by many as being the 'lead' country of infrastructure PPP policy, with over 700 projects being undertaken. The chapter discusses how many organizational relationships have been changed during the GFC as the UK Treasury has had to step in and take over some of the less-successful projects. In Chapter 3, Mark Hellowell and Veronica Vecchi discuss the price of equity capital in PPPs. This may seem like a very technical area, but the detailed financial aspects of many PPP projects are quite important for the future prospects of PPP policy. Hellowell and Vecchi discuss if new regulations from governments are needed to limit excessive profit-making by private organizations. In Chapter 4, Eoin Reeves studies the key feature of VfM and accountability mechanisms in PPPs. Using illustrations from Ireland, which was also seen as an advanced PPP country at a time, Reeves examines how the accountability mechanisms have now been challenged by the new economic and financial realities that followed from the GFC. The next section in the book discusses various theoretical approaches and strategies in relation to PPPs. In Chapter 5, Tamyko Ysa, Marc Esteve and Francisco Longo focus on innovation processes in PPPs. They examine a case study of a blood bank in Spain and point to the importance of the role public managers can play in the innovation process. In Chapter 6, Anna Amirkhanyan and Sarah Pettijohn give a detailed and nuanced view into the world of the non-profit sector, and they argue for a role of the non-profit organizations in the literature on PPPs. They discuss both the historical development and the current challenges in bringing non-profit organizations closer to the public service delivery system. In Chapter 7, Sophie Sturup examines three PPP cases in Australia and views them as mega-projects. She calls for greater use of the theoretical lenses used by Foucault and others in the study of PPP mega-projects. In Chapter 8, Rob Alexander examines public management strategies in PPP projects in brownfield clean-up and development projects. In the US, the term PPP is often used for urban (re)development projects and Alexander gives a systematic insight into the different strategies public managers can pursue when they engage with a variety of stakeholders in PPP projects. Alexander highlights the role managers can play as does Ysa and colleagues in Chapter 5. In Chapter 9, Stephen Jeffares, Helen Sullivan and Tony Bovaird take on the task of establishing a theory-based way to properly evaluate PPPs. As discussed in this introductory chapter, various ways of measuring 'success' are notoriously difficult in PPPs. Jeffares, Sullivan and Bovaird provide a new method of how to understand the performance of PPPs in turbulent times. In Chapter 10, Koen Verhoest, Joris Voets and Kit Van Gestel present a theoretical framework that helps to grasp how the dynamics of complexity and control can be conceptualized and analysed. They use case studies from the infrastructure of sport facilities in Belgium to illustrate their point. In Chapter 11, Carsten Greve and Graeme Hodge sum up the main arguments of the book and reflect on the contributions from the different chapters. They discuss how there is a need to rethink PPPs, what we have learned about the turbulent times, and how new strategies have emerged to address these.

Conclusions

In this chapter we have discussed different ways to view PPP 'success'. A brief discussion on the concept of partnerships focused on the idea that PPPs both include government partnerships with private sector organizations, with non-profit organizations, and with a combination of government, private companies and non-profit organizations. We identified PPP to exist at different levels: project, organizational form, policy, and governance symbol or tool, and located in a broader historical context what constitutes 'public' and 'private' in a given society. We then examined different theoretical approaches to determining success. Definitions of success depended on whether one viewed success from: on high (at the societal level) and including political matters, programme (utilitarian) matters and process (legitimacy) matters; at the project or activity level (where it was more straightforward to judge goals and deliverables); or in terms of how the organizations combined to innovate, collaborate and transform in order to deliver outcomes. No single view of success provided a meta-framework and all were helpful in their own way. Narrow and wide definitions of success were possible, as well as the more traditional views of the disciplines (such as economics, accounting, sociology, political science and public policy). McConnell's success framework was supported as one way of ensuring that future ideas of success included not only technical matters but also an integrated sense of what matters across a range of lenses from the political, through the programme to the process.

In conclusion, we argued that despite the recasting of the PPP debate following the GFC, it is possible, paradoxically, that PPP may have a bright future. And whilst there will no doubt be increased attention on the many technical issues central to our continuing assessments of success, it will be the power of the PPP ideal as well as the political drivers of PPP success that will continue to capture the hearts of elected representatives. These drivers, as well as the breadth and inherent flexibility of the PPP phenomenon itself, will enable PPP to adapt to the needs of a turbulent future.

Notes

1   See Montiero (2010) who sees risk explicitly at the centre of the OECD definition of PPP performance. In the OECD's words, 'the effectiveness of the alignment depends on a sufficient transfer of risk to the private partner'.

2   Whilst the UN's use of 'partnership' in the context of the MDGs, strictly speaking, calls on developed countries to assist developing countries, it is essentially a call for the wealth (both private and public) of developed countries to play a role in solving the common problem of poverty across developing countries.

3   This conceptualization of the PPP phenomenon might alternatively be seen in terms of the ontology of PPP or the idea of the PPP 'space'. These parallel the ideas of Linder's (1999) 'multiple grammars', the notion of 'regulatory space' from Hancher and Moran (1989) or Dubnick's (2011) ontology of accountability and his idea of accountability as 'social space'.

4   The recent National Audit Office (NAO) (2009) review for the UK Parliament formally confirmed the breadth of the PPP idea, stating that 'we have mainly concentrated on the widely used PPP model called the Private Finance Initiative (PFI)... which has been adopted in the UK for more than £28 billion worth of projects.' They then noted that 'there are also hundreds of other types of PPPs, ranging from small joint ventures to the London Underground PPPs, which have a capital value of £18 billion'.

5   Braithwaite *et al.* (2007) suggested that the 'regulatory work' of government was increasing. They argued that work of governments broadly included three functions: providing, distributing and regulating. They observed that whilst the government's role in directly providing services is currently decreasing (through, for example, outsourcing and privatization), and their role in distributing (or redistributing) wealth will continue unabated through time, the government's role in regulating is increasing through a myriad of ways. The modern sense of regulation adopted here is broad and is construed as 'involving a sustained and focused attempt to alter the behaviour of others according to defined standards or purposes with the intention of producing a broadly identified outcome or outcomes' (Black 2002). Central to notions of how governments regulate, too, is the work of Freiberg (2010) who lists six different modes of regulating: through economic tools; through contracts (or grants); through authorization; through information; through structural means; and through law.

6   Thus the Bracks/Brumby Labor governments established their PPP policy platform in 2000 and through this action, implied that PPPs had essentially not existed prior to the year 2000. Whilst this is technically nonsense, given that the private funding of infrastructure had occurred at various points over the previous two decades, the political power of this PPP symbolism was also indisputable.

7   Paper presented by G. Hodge to the China–Australia Governance Program, Guizhou Workshop, 28–29 April 2010, entitled 'Towards Service Oriented Government through Public–Private Partnership: Some Reflections and Directions for China'.

8   Of course, labels rarely tell the full story. 'Medibank Private' is an Australian government private health insurer. Established in 1976, it is Australia's largest health insurance provider. It was established through the Health Insurance Commission (now known as Medicare Australia) and currently operates commercially as a Government Business Enterprise. It is, despite its name, 100 per cent government owned (Source: http://en.wikipedia.org/wiki/Medibank_Private).

9   At the outset, of course, different stakeholders clearly have differing objectives for the delivery of a PPP. We focus simply on the objectives of government in this paper.

10 We might reflect that the private financing of a long-term infrastructure does not strictly reduce the call on the budget. A mechanism through which governments may turn a large, one-off capital expenditure into a series of smaller, annualized expenditures has simply been provided. And like any domestic credit card or mortgage

arrangement, this does not reduce pressure on the family budget, because all debts must be repaid in the end, at, hopefully, minimum interest rates to ensure efficiency. The one important exception to this is the case where a government enters an infrastructure deal requiring users or citizens to pay directly, such as tolls on a new road. Here, such an arrangement does reduce pressure on public sector budgets, because government has essentially purchased the infrastructure through the promise of funds from future (private) road users rather than using its own resources.

11   While most commentators are aware of both government 'programmes' (with a utilitarian emphasis) and government 'politics' (emphasizing electoral prospects), the additional thread of 'process' is useful. McConnell gives an example for each of these three threads. For the instance of government (utilitarian) 'programme', flood control in the Netherlands is cited. Programme success here has been demonstrated by the effective capacity to hold back the North Sea (as well as other bodies of water) so that one quarter of the land mass and the 11 million citizens living below sea level are not adversely affected, so that thousands of citizens do not die and so that the Dutch economy is not decimated. The key criterion here is clearly safety, and this programme has, to date, been successful in avoiding a repeat of the 1953 Zeeland floods that killed 1,800 people. The case cited for the dimension of 'politics' was an episode in Australia's treatment of its Aborigines and Torres Strait Islanders. A shocking part of Australia's history was the forced removal, over the period 1910 to 1970, of between one tenth and one third of these children from their families. A two-year high-profile report on the scandal in 1997 suggested that a national apology should be undertaken as a first step, but the Howard government at the time refused, saying it could not say 'sorry' for something that was the responsibility of previous governments. The election in 2007 of a Labor government saw Prime Minister Kevin Rudd give a historic 'sorry' speech at Parliament House for all the pain and suffering caused. This official statement was a huge political success. It saw the government's opinion poll ratings soar, it diffused a sensitive political issue, and it symbolized a new governing direction that was more tolerant, inclusive and respectful of social diversity. The case cited for the third dimension of policy success, that of 'process', involved the electoral system of British Columbia (BC) in Canada. The late 1990s saw the Liberal opposition committing itself to electoral reform after receiving 42 per cent of the vote, whilst the New Democrats party gained the majority of the seats in the legislature after receiving only 39 per cent. When the Liberals were elected in 2001, they established a diverse Citizens Assembly of 160 people, undertook 50 public hearings and extensive e-consultation, and produced a report recommending that the existing system be replaced with a more proportional one. This went to referendum in 2004, but received support from only 58 per cent of voters, just short of the required 60 per cent. A second referendum was then held in 2009 in conjunction with provincial elections, but this received only 38 per cent of voter support. The existing system was not to be reformed after all, but the Liberals were returned to power. This was a case of 'process success' where the government's goal was not closed (but was electoral reform subject to referendum endorsement), where the processes adopted suggested it was legitimate to proceed no further, where the Citizens Assembly initiative was seen an innovative way of tackling a difficult issue, and where these processes symbolized forward thinking and legitimate governance.

12   McConnell also suggests that for each of these dimensions we can assess policy success as being durable, conflicted, precarious or a failure (McConnell 2010: 67). These terms provide a sense of a continuum between clear success and failure, as well as a sense of the durability of relative success over time.

13   See Bebbington and McCourt (2007: 240).

Appendix A

Study	Sample/cases	Country	Type of publication	Better VfM?	Comments/conclusions
Bloomfield et al. (1998)	A Massachusetts correctional facility	USA	Case study	No	• 7.4% more expensive through PPP lease purchasing. • 'Inflated sales pitches' camouflaged real costs and risks to the public, and project was 'wasteful and risky'.
Arthur Andersen and LSE Enterprise (2000)	29 business cases analysed	UK	Initial evaluation	Yes	• 17% cost savings estimated against the Public Sector Comparator (PSC). • Risk transfer accounted for 61% of forecast savings.
Savas (2000: 240)	General observations	USA	Literature review	Yes	• '[The private sector through PPPs] build more quickly and more cost effectively than governments usually can…'.
National Audit Office (2000)	Seven business cases from NAO (2000)	UK	Business cases	Yes	• 10–20% cost savings estimated.
Walker and Walker (2000: 204)	General observations of Australian cases	Australia	Literature review	–	• PPP infrastructure financing deals seen as 'misleading accounting trickery' with eroded accountability to Parliament and the public. • Private project consortium real rates of return were up to 10 times those returns expected for the public.

Study	Sample/cases	Country	Type of publication	Better VfM?	Comments/conclusions
Teisman and Klijn (2001)	General observations	Four EU countries	Review of strengths and weaknesses	–	• PPPs have strengths and weaknesses.
Department of Transport (2002)	250 London Underground projects	UK	Unknown	–	• Cost overruns averaging 20% were found (1997–2000).
Mott Macdonald (2002)	39 traditional projects and 11 PFI projects	UK	Multiple cases reviewed	Yes	• Traditional 'public' infrastructure provision arrangements were on time and on budget 30% and 27% of the time, but PFI-type partnerships were on time and on budget 76% and 78% of the time respectively.
Pollock et al. (2002)	Three NHS hospitals and eight trusts	UK	Review and re-analysis	No	• The PFI justification is a 'sleight of hand'.
Pollitt (2002)	10 major PFI cases	UK	Review of NAO cases	Yes	• The best deal was probably obtained in every case, and VfM was probably achieved in eight of the 10 cases.
Audit Commission (2003)	10 traditional and eight PFI schools were compared	Scotland	Audit report	No	• 'We found no evidence that PFI projects delivered schools more quickly than projects funded in more conventional ways'. • 'The public sector comparator has lost the confidence of many people…'.

Study	Sample/cases	Country	Type of publication	Better VfM?	Comments/conclusions
Greve (2003)	Case study of Farum Municipality	Denmark	Case analysis	No	• PPP assessed as 'the most spectacular scandal in the history of Danish Public Administration'. • It resulted in raised taxes for the citizens of Farum, higher debt for citizens and a former mayor currently on trial in the courts.
Fitzgerald (2004)	Eight PPP cases from Victoria	Australia	Report to government	Uncertain	• The superiority of the economic partnership mode over traditional delivery mechanisms was dependent on the discount rate adopted in the analysis. • Opposite conclusions were reached when using an 8.65% discount rate at one extreme (where the PPP mechanism was 9% cheaper than traditional delivery) compared to an evaluation adopting a 5.7% discount rate (where the PPP mechanism was 6% more expensive).
Edwards et al. (2004)	Eight cases from roads and 13 case studies from hospitals	UK	Case reviews and interviews	No	• Contracts reviewed three years in. • 'PFI is an expensive way of financing and delivering public services…' • 'The chief beneficiaries are the providers of finance and some of…the private sector service providers…'

Study	Sample/cases	Country	Type of publication	Better VfM?	Comments/conclusions
Ghobadian et al. (2004: 300)	General observations	UK	Literature review	–	• 'We have no firm evidence that the current PFIs would deliver on their long-term objectives…'
Grimsey and Lewis (2004: 81, 245)	Global observations across several sectors	Several countries	Literature review	Yes	• 'Preliminary evidence does seem to indicate strongly that PPPs offer one solution to the public procurement problem…' • 'There is not one "model" of a PPP…'
Pollitt (2005)	General observations of UK cases plus five cases	UK	Literature review	Yes	• 'It seems difficult to avoid a positive overall assessment'.
Shaoul (2005)	General observations of UK cases	UK	Literature review	No	• PFI has turned out to be very expensive with a lack of accountability. • Suspects that PFI policies 'enrich the few at the expense of the majority and for which no democratic mandate can be secured'.
Boardman et al. (2005: 186)	Five North American cases across several sectors	Canada and USA	Case reviews	No	• Unless contracts both compensate the private sector for risks and then ensure that they actually bear it, 'P3s will not improve allocative efficiency'.

Study	Sample/cases	Country	Type of publication	Better VfM?	Comments/conclusions
Hodge (2005: 327)	General observations of UK cases plus three cases	Australia	Literature review	Uncertain	• There have been no rigorous and transparent evaluations of all Australian PPPs. • The few available assessments suggest mixed performance to date. • Government has moved away from its traditional stewardship role to a louder policy advocacy role. It now faces multiple conflicts of interest (as advocate, developer, steward, elected leader, regulator, contract signatory and planner).
Auditor-General of New South Wales (2006)	Construction of 19 schools in New South Wales	Australia	Audit report	Yes	• Between 7 and 23% cheaper. • Auditor saw as 'persuasive' the business case for these two PFI contracts.
Pollock et al. (2007)	Re-analysis of Mott Macdonald and other reports	UK	Academic paper	No	• 'There is no evidence to support the Treasury cost and time overrun claims of improved efficiency in PFI'. [Estimates being quoted are] 'not evidence based but biased to favor PFI…' • 'Only one study compares PFI procurement performance, and all claims based on [this] are misleading'.

Study	Sample/cases	Country	Type of publication	Better VfM?	Comments/conclusions
Allen Consulting Group (2007)	Sample of 21 PPPs and 33 traditional projects	Australia	Consulting report	Yes	• PPPs reported as being 11% cheaper than traditional projects. • Research project funded by Australia's infrastructure suppliers.
Blanc-Brude *et al.* (2006)	227 new road sections across 15 EU countries, of which 65 were PPPs	EU	31 regression analyses	Not tested	• *Ex ante* construction costs of PPPs were 24% higher than traditional procurement. • This is a similar magnitude to the traditional cost over-runs. • Whether PPPs deliver lower overall life-cycle costs remains unknown.
Leviakangas (2007: 211)	A Finnish toll-road case study	Finland	Financial models	No	• The hypothesis that private finance enabled welfare gains to be achieved was not confirmed.
Vining and Boardman (2008a)	10 cases across several sectors	Canada	Case studies	Un-certain	• In these 10 case studies, exactly half were judged as economic 'successes', whilst the other half were judged as 'not successful'. • Those projects judged as not successful were generally bigger projects.

Study	Sample/cases	Country	Type of publication	Better VfM?	Comments/conclusions
Vining and Boardman (2008b)	London Underground (Metronet)	UK	Case study	No	• This case 'illustrated the difficulty of risk transfer even though this was a major initial rationale for the P3 contracts'. • Metronet 'did nothing more than secure loans . . . [largely] underwritten by the public purse, at an inflated cost – the worst of both possible worlds'. • 'Overall transaction costs were . . . extremely high'. • Gordon Brown was seen as a 'desperate customer' to bankers.
Hellowell and Pollock (2009)	Financial viability of NHS organizations analysed	UK	Case study	No	• PFI funding of capital investment is highly problematic. • It is associated with reduced capacity in England's healthcare system.
Jupe (2009)	Rail transport in the UK	UK	Case study	–	• Nationalization and PPPs both represent imperfect solutions for transport. • PPP risk transfer and VfM are difficult to achieve and cannot be left to the market discipline of bankruptcy.

Study	Sample/cases	Country	Type of publication	Better VfM?	Comments/conclusions
Vecchi *et al.* (2010)	14 new and refurbished hospitals and support services	Italy	Academic paper, financial analysis	No	• 'Excess returns are being made by the investors in these projects... projected rates of returns... were very much higher than we would expect to find in a properly functioning and competitive market'. • A 'very low level of systematic risk' was taken in PPP contracts by investors.
Sarmento (2010)	'SCUT' highway project	Portugal	Academic paper, economic analysis	No	• 'If traditional procurement had been used, it would have been far less expensive ... EUR 2 billion or EUR 3 billion less'. • The government was judged as being incapable of properly negotiating with private bidders in this case study.

References

Allen Consulting Group (2007) *Performance of PPPs and Traditional Contracting Out in Australia.* Final Report to Infrastructure Australia, 30 November.

Amirkhanyan, A. (2010) Monitoring Across Sectors: Examining the Effect of Non-Profit and For-Profit Contractor Ownership on Performance Monitoring in State and Local Contracts. *Public Administration Review* 70(5): 742–55.

Arthur Anderson and LSE Enterprise (2000) *Value for Money Drivers in the Private Finance Initiative.* London: UK Treasury Task Force.

Audit Commission (2003) *PFI in Schools.* London: Audit Commission.

Auditor-General of New South Wales (2006) *The New Schools Privately Financed Project.* Auditor-General's Report Performance Audit, March, Sydney, p. 53.

Bebbington, A. and McCourt, W. (eds) (2007) Explaining (and Obtaining) Development Success, in *Development Success: Statecraft in the South*, edited by A. Bebbington and W. McCourt, pp. 211–45.

Black, J. (2002) Critical Reflections on Regulation. *Australian Journal of Legal Philosophy*, 27: 1–35.

Blanc-Brude, F., Goldsmith, H. and Valila, T. (2006) Ex Ante Construction Costs in the European Road Sector: A Comparison of Public–Private Partnerships and Traditional Public Procurement. Economic and Financial Report. 2006/01. European Investment Bank, pp. 49.

Bloomfield, P., Westerling, D. and Carey, R. (1998) Innovation and Risks in a Public–Private Partnership: Financing and Construction of a Capital Project in Massachusetts. *Public Productivity and Review*, 21(4): 460–71.

Boardman, A., Poschmann, F. and Vining, A. (2005) North American Infrastructure P3s: Examples and Lessons Learned, in *The Challenge of Public–Private Partnerships: Learning from International Experience*, edited by C. Greve and G. Hodge. Cheltenham: Edward Elgar, pp. 162–89.

Boardman, A.E. and Vining, A.R. (2010) Assessing the Economic Worth of Public–Private Partnerships, in *International Handbook on Public–Private Partnerships*, edited by G. Hodge, C. Greve and A. Boardman. Cheltenham: Edward Elgar.

Braithwaite, J., Coglianese, C. and Levi-Faur, D. (2007) Can Regulation and Governance Make a Difference? *Regulation and Governance*, 1(1): 1–7.

Bull, B. (2010) Public–Private Partnerships: The United Nations Experience, in *International Handbook on Public–Private Partnerships*, edited by G. Hodge, C. Greve and A. Boardman. Cheltenham: Edward Elgar, pp. 479–95.

Connoly, C. and Wall, A. (2012) The Impact of the Global Financial Crisis on Public–Private Partnerships. Chapter 2 in this book.

Department of Transport (2002) Public Sector Comparators Factsheet (http://www.railways.dtlr.gov.uk).

Donahue, J. D. (1989) *The Privatization Decision: Public Ends, Private Means.* New York: Basic Books.

Dubnick, M. (2011) The Space Between: Reconceptualizing the Role of Accountability in Governance Settings. Paper presented to the Public Management Research Conference, Maxwell School of Syracuse University, 2–4 June.

Edwards, P., Shaoul, J., Stafford, A. and Arblaster, L. (2004) *Evaluating the Operation of PFI in Roads and Hospitals.* London: Certified Accountants Education Trust.

European Commission (2011) *Public–Private Partnerships: The Implementation of the Commission's Communication.* Presentation by Elias Messaoudi for the Audit of

Public–Private Partnership seminar arranged by the Bundesrechnungshof in Bonn, Germany, 9–11 February 2011 (http://bundesrechnungshof.de/the-audit-of-ppp-key-speeches).

Fitzgerald, P. (2004) *Review of Partnerships Victoria Provided Infrastructure*. Melbourne: Growth Solutions Group.

Flinders, M. (2010) Splintered Logic and Political Debate, in *International Handbook on Public–Private Partnerships*, edited by G. Hodge, C. Greve and A. Boardman. Cheltenham: Edward Elgar, pp. 115–31.

Freiberg, A. (2010) *The Tools of Regulation*. Sydney: The Federation Press.

Ghobadian, A., Gallear, D., O'Regan, N. and Viney, H. (2004) The Future of Public–Private Partnership, in *Public–Private Partnerships: Policy and Experience*, edited by A. Ghobadian, D. Gallear, N. O'Regan and H. Viney. London: Palgrave Macmillan.

Greve, C. (2003) When Public–Private Partnerships Fail: The Extreme Case of the NPM-Inspired Local Government of Farum in Denmark. Paper for the EGPA conference, 3–6 September, Oeiras, Portugal.

Grimsey, D. and Lewis, M. (2004) *Public–Private Partnerships: The Worldwide Revolution in Infrastructure Provision and Project Finance*. Cheltenham: Edward Elgar.

Guardian/Observer, 27 March 2011: Academic Fury over Order to Study the Big Society.

Hancher, L. and Moran, M. (1989) Organizing Regulatory Space. Chapter 10 in *Capitalism, Culture, and Economic Regulation*, edited by L. Hancher and M. Moran. Oxford: Clarendon Press.

Hellowell, M. and Pollock, A.M. (2009) The Private Financing of NHS Hospitals: Politics, Policy and Practice. *Economic Affairs*, 29(1): 13–19.

Hellowell, M. (2010) The UK's Private Finance Initiative: History, Evaluation, Prospects, in *International Handbook on Public–Private Partnerships*, edited by G. Hodge, C. Greve and A. Boardman. Cheltenham: Edward Elgar.

Hodge, G. (2005) Public–Private Partnerships: The Australian Experience with Physical Infrastructure, in *The Challenge of Public–Private Partnerships: Learning from International Experience*, edited by G. Hodge and C. Greve. Cheltenham: Edward Elgar, pp. 305–31.

Hodge, G. (2010a) Reviewing Public–Private Partnerships: Some Thoughts on Evaluation, in *International Handbook on Public–Private Partnerships*, edited by G. Hodge, C. Greve and A. Boardman. Cheltenham: Edward Elgar, pp. 81–112.

Hodge, G. (2010b) On Evaluating PPP Success: Thoughts for Our Future. Key note address to the Finnish Association of Administrative Sciences, Helsinki, November 2010.

Hodge, G. and Greve, C. (eds) (2005) *The Challenge of Public–Private Partnerships: Learning from International Experience*. Cheltenham: Edward Elgar.

Hodge, G. and Greve, C. (2007) Public–Private Partnerships: An International Review. *Public Administration Review*, 67(3): 545–58.

Huxman, C. and Hubbert, P. (2009) Hit or Myth? Stories of Collaborative Success, in *Collaborative Governance*, edited by J. O'Flynn and J. Wanna. Canberra: ANU Press.

Jeffares, S., Sullivan, H. and Bovaird, T. (2012) Beyond the Contract: The Challenge of Evaluating the Performance(s) of Public–Private Partnerships. Chapter 9 in this book.

Jupe, R. (2009) New Labour, Public–Private Partnerships and Rail Transport, *Economic Affairs*, 29(1): 20–5.

Kettl, D. F. (2009) *The Next Government of the United States: How Our Institutions Fail Us and How to Fix Them*. New York: W.W. Norton.

Leviakangas, P. (2007) *Private Finance of Transport Infrastructure Projects: Value and Risk Analysis of a Finnish Shadow Toll Road Project.* ESPOO, VTT Publications: 624.

Linder, S. (1999) Coming to terms with the public–private partnership: a grammar of multiple meanings. *The American Behavioural Scientist*, 43(1), 35–51.

McConnell, A. (2010) *Understanding Policy Success: Rethinking Public Policy.* Basingstoke: Palgrave Macmillan.

Montiero, R. S. (2010) Risk Management, in *International Handbook on Public–Private Partnerships*, edited by G. Hodge, C. Greve and A. Boardman. Cheltenham: Edward Elgar, pp. 262–91.

Mott Macdonald (2002) *Review of Large Public Procurement in the UK*, London: Mott Macdonald.

National Audit Office (2000) *Examining the Value for Money of Deals under the Private Finance Initiative.* London: The Stationary Office.

National Audit Office (2009) *Private Finance Projects.* A Report to the House of Lords Economic Affairs Committee.

O'Flynn, J. and Wanna, J. (eds) (2009) *Collaborative Governance.* Canberra: ANU Press.

OECD (2008) *Public–Private Partnerships: In Pursuit of Risk Sharing and Value for Money.* Paris: OECD.

OECD (2010) Third Annual OECD Symposium on Public–Private Partnerships (www.oecd.org).

Pollitt, M. (2002) The Declining Role of the State in Infrastructure Investment in the UK, in *Private Initiatives in Infrastructure: Priorities, Incentives and Performance*, edited by Berg Sanford V., M. G. Pollitt and M. Tsuji, Aldershot: Edward Elgar.

Pollitt, M. (2005) Learning from the UK Private Finance Initiative Experience, in *The Challenge of Public–Private Partnerships: Learning from International Experience*, edited by G. Hodge and C. Greve. Cheltenham: Edward Elgar, pp. 207–30.

Pollock, A., Price, D. and Playe, S. (2007) An Examination of the UK Treasury's Evidence Base for Cost and Time Overrun Data in UK Value-for-Money Policy and Appraisal. *Public Money and Management*, 27(2): 127–34.

Pollock, A., Shaoul, J. and Vickers, N. (2002) Private Finance and Value for Money in NHS Hospitals: A Policy in Search of a Rationale? *British Medical Journal*, 324: 1205–8.

Savas, E. S. (2000) *Privatization and Public–Private Partnerships.* New York: Chatham House Publishers and Seven Bridges Press.

Sarmento, J. M. (2010) Do Public–Private Partnerships Create Value for Money for the Public Sector? The Portuguese Experience. *OECD Journal on Budgeting*, 10(1): 93–119.

Shaoul, J. (2005) The Private Finance Initiative or the Public Funding of Private Profit, in *The Challenge of Public–Private Partnerships: Learning from International Experience*, edited by G. Hodge and C. Greve. Cheltenham: Edward Elgar, pp. 190–206.

Skelcher, C. (2010) Governance of Public–Private Partnerships, in *International Handbook on Public–Private Partnerships*, edited by G. Hodge, C. Greve and A. Boardman. Cheltenham: Edward Elgar.

Skelcher, C. and Sullivan, H. (2008) Theory driven approaches to analyzing collaborative performance. *Public Management Review*, 10(6): 751–77.

Teisman, G. and Klijn, E.-H. (2001) Public–Private Partnerships in the European Union: Official Suspect, Embraced in Daily Practice, in *Public–Private Partnerships: Theory and Practice in International Perspective*, edited by S. Osborne. New York: Routledge, pp. 165–86.

Tvarnø, C.D. (2010) Law and Regulatory Aspects of Public–Private Partnerships: Contract

Law and Public Procurement Law, in *International Handbook on Public–Private Partnerships*, edited by G. Hodge, C. Greve and A. Boardman. Cheltenham: Edward Elgar, pp. 216–36.

Van Ham, H. and Koppenjan, J. (2001) Building Public–Private Partnerships: Assessing and Managing Risks in Port Development. *Public Management Review*, 4(1): 593–616.

Vecchi, V., Hellowell, M. and Longo, F. (2010) Are Italian Healthcare Organizations Paying too Much for their Public–Private Partnerships? *Public Money and Management*, 30(2): 125–32.

Vining, A. and Boardman, A. (2008a) Public–Private Partnerships in Canada. Theory and Evidence. *Canadian Public Administration*, 51(1): 9–44.

Vining, A. and Boardman, A. (2008b) Public–Private Partnerships: Eight Rules for Governments. *Public Works Management and Policy*, 13(2): 149–61.

Walker, B. and Walker, B. C. (2000) *Privatisation: Sell Off or Sell Out? The Australian Experience*. Sydney: ABC Books.

Weihe, G. (2005) *Public–Private Partnerships, Addressing a Nebulous Concept*. Working Paper No. 16. International Center for Business and Politics, Copenhagen Business School.

2 The impact of the global financial crisis on public–private partnerships

A UK perspective

Cierran Connoly and Tony Wall

Introduction

HM Treasury (HMT) (2000) claims that PPPs bring the public and private sectors together in long-term partnership for mutual benefit, asserting that the PPP label covers a wide range of different types of partnership including (p. 8):

- the introduction of private sector ownership into state-owned businesses, with sales of either a majority or a minority stake;
- arrangements where the public sector contracts to purchase services on a long-term basis so as to take advantage of private sector management skills incentivized by having private finance at risk. This includes concessions and franchises, where a private sector partner takes on the responsibility for providing a public service, including maintaining, enhancing or constructing the necessary infrastructure; and
- selling government services into wider markets and other partnership arrangements where private sector expertise and finance are used to exploit the commercial potential of government assets.

In many cases, PPPs use a private company to design, build, finance and operate (DBFO) a new development such as a hospital or school over a contract period of 20–30 years. Throughout this period, payments are recouped from the public sector, which is ultimately responsible for the delivery of these services. When first introduced in the UK by the Conservative government in 1992, the PPP initiative[1] was met with relative scepticism and, although Labour opposed the scheme in opposition, it embraced PPP when it came to power in 1997. Since then the volume of PPPs, not only in the UK but throughout the world (Grimsey and Lewis 2004), has increased significantly. Despite widespread criticism, the use of PPPs showed no sign of abating. However, the GFC that began in 2007 has significantly reduced the availability of private finance, and has therefore had a detrimental impact upon PPPs.

There are a number of well-documented reasons behind the GFC. One of the principal factors was the sharp rise in the number of subprime mortgages sold in the United States (Krinsman 2007; Brunnermeier 2009) and the subsequent ramifications in other countries, including the UK (Hall 2008a). Uncertainty over the magnitude of the crisis has meant that banks have been reluctant to lend, with even the largest companies finding it difficult to obtain finance due to default and insolvency fears (Hall 2008a). In the UK, the desire to safeguard existing PPPs and future infrastructure projects led, at the time, to government initiatives and increased borrowing from the European Investment Bank (EIB). Since then, concerns over sovereign debt levels have also emerged in many countries within the European Union (EU) (for example Greece, Italy, Spain and Portugal) as well as elsewhere (Japan and USA). These concerns have exacerbated financial nervousness. Whilst Burger *et al.* (2009) provide some general statistics for how the GFC has affected PPPs in a number of countries, this chapter examines approximately 630 PPPs in the UK, a key user of this procurement method, to assess the impact of the GFC on the programme.

In terms of the format of the chapter, the next section reviews the literature associated with PPPs and risk. The effect of the GFC on PPP funding is then considered, together with several of the initiatives designed to safeguard existing and future projects. The methodology is then outlined before the research findings are presented and conclusions drawn.

Public–private partnerships

The introduction of PPPs was in response to concerns about the need to provide public infrastructure despite the high level of public debt, which grew rapidly during the macro-economic dislocation of the 1970s and 1980s. As a consequence, pressure mounted to change the standard model of public procurement. In essence, a PPP is a contract between government and a consortium of private companies (referred to as a Special Purpose Vehicle (SPV)) under which the latter is required to DBFO an asset in return for payment over a number of years for both the cost of construction and the operation of the related service. Such payments may be based on either direct user charges (e.g. toll roads) or a unitary payment from a public authority, or a combination of both (Grimsey and Lewis 2004).

The original objective of PPPs in the UK was to enable new infrastructure to be provided outside of the public sector borrowing requirement; however, when Labour came into power in 1997 the emphasis shifted towards the achievement of value for money (VfM). This change in focus was in response to an amendment of Financial Reporting Standard (FRS) 5, which stated that the purchaser (the public sector) was required to demonstrate that the involvement of the private sector offered VfM when compared with alternative ways of providing the services (Accounting Standards Board (ASB) 1998). This VfM calculus was achieved by valuing the transfer of risk from the public to the private sector, with VfM being assessed through a comparison of the Public Sector Comparator (PSC) – the hypothetical cost of undertaking a project under conventional procurement – with the cost of procuring via PPP. VfM was deemed to be achieved when the price established under the PSC exceeded the price offered by the most competitive private bidder.

Since its conception, PPP has been heavily criticized. Some critics argue that the transfer of risk to the private sector is inappropriate, overvalued or does not take place at all. This criticism is on the basis that PPPs are rarely terminated, often due to potentially high litigation and counterclaims by contractors (Hencke 2003). Furthermore, as essential public services must continue to be delivered even if the contractor fails, this risk cannot be transferred. Edwards *et al.* (2004), for example, raised concerns over the level of risks actually being transferred, and questioned whether those who are not best able to manage the risks are bearing them nonetheless, with the public sector being left with risks that are not easily quantified. Broadbent *et al.* (2008) also found that with regard to 17 PPP health projects, certain items could be made invisible, whilst others that were either deemed more significant or possibly easier to monitor were given unprecedented attention. Moreover, Pollock and Price (2008: 176) suggested that 'the government's central justification for PPP in terms of risk transfer remains largely unevaluated' due to a lack of oversight in this area by government, and reported that out of 622 PPP contracts signed up to October 2007, 'only 10 financial inquiries into central government operational PFIs had been undertaken by the NAO [National Audit Office] by 2006, and of these only three examined the relationship between risk transfer and risk premiums' (p. 177).

The risks posed by the GFC and today's continuing market turbulence on PPPs stem from the interaction of threats and vulnerabilities. Burger *et al.* (2009: 10) identify the follows threats (i.e. the likelihood of a negative event occurring in the future):

- the risk of an increase in interest rates leading to increasing costs, liquidity problems and project feasibility considerations for private partners and the possible postponement of projects by the government or it having to inject cash to support the SPV;
- the risk of credit being unavailable leading to the termination of existing projects, existing projects failing to reach financial close and capital injections from government;
- the risk of a decline in stock market prices leading to banks having reduced capital, which affects their ability to lend and causes reduced investment in new and existing PPPs;
- the risk of exchange rate depreciation making new investments that rely on external borrowing less attractive, with private partners being tempted to export their services thus reducing the pool of domestic bidders; and
- the risk that there is a slump in domestic demand leading to liquidity problems for private partners and lower domestic revenue for governments, meaning lower investment for new and existing PPPs.

PPP vulnerabilities (i.e. the preparedness of the partners to either prevent a threat or cope with its impact) to market turbulence can be project-specific or extend more widely. The former includes overly optimistic revenue projections (e.g. with respect to toll roads) while the latter may be related to the institutional framework. The institutional context is fundamental to managing PPPs to secure their benefits whilst containing the risks, which can be can be classified in a number of ways.

The ASB (1998) identified six main risks: demand; residual value; design; performance/availability; potential changes in relevant costs; and obsolescence. Moreover, a distinction may be made between commercial, macro-economic and political risk. Macro-economic risks entail aggregate demand risk, interest rate risk, liquidity risk and exchange rate risk. The materialization of macro-economic risk can, in turn, cause other risks. For instance, interest rate or demand risk can cause credit risk. Risk may also be categorized as exogenous and endogenous, with the latter being those risks that can be actively managed by changing behaviour. The risk-management philosophy underpinning VfM has long asserted that risk should be allocated to the party best suited to carry, or manage, that risk. In principle, this should incentivize each party to act in a manner that manages the risk allocated to them and therefore improves the overall efficiency of the PPP.

To best allocate risk, two questions need to be answered (Organisation for Economic Co-operation and Development (OECD) 2008): first, which party is best able to prevent an adverse occurrence, and thereby ensure that the actual outcome conforms as closely as possible to the expected outcome; and second, in the case where no party can prevent an adverse occurrence (an exogenous risk), which party is best able to manage its outcome. Different parties carry different types and amounts of risk, and not all are affected in the same way. This may alter the attractiveness of PPPs for the parties most affected and reduce their interest in participating in PPPs unless they are compensated. As such they may not want to enter into new PPPs; refinance debt in existing PPPs; or continue operating under an existing agreement. Risk can be managed in several ways including through (OECD 2008): risk avoidance – the risky activity is not undertaken, for example, when a public body forgoes an investment; risk prevention – action is taken to reduce vulnerabilities; for example, when a PPP consortium borrows in domestic currency to avoid exchange rate risk; and risk transfer – risk is transferred to another party through a contractual arrangement, such as minimum traffic guarantees.

The notion of 'risk transfer' plays an important role in justifying PPPs. Firstly, it is a key element in Eurostat's definition of whether the debt is treated as being on or off the government's balance sheet. Secondly, it is used, especially in the UK, to justify the use of PPPs that do not demonstrate that they are better value than the public sector option. This occurs when the aforementioned PSC is compared with a PPP bid and the latter is made less expensive by factoring in risk. However, transferring risk is not free. While it is possible to create contracts that transfer the risk of construction delays to the contractor, such contracts cost about 25 per cent more than conventional contracts (Hall 2008b). Risk transfer is not necessarily the best policy option, either, and it needs to be subjected to a cost–benefit analysis. For example, a theoretical analysis of risks and PPPs concluded that it is most efficient for demand risk to remain with governments (Engel *et al.* 2011). The International Monetary Fund (2004: 14) warns that governments may 'overprice risk and overcompensate the private sector for taking it on, which would raise the cost of PPPs relative to direct public investment'. It is argued that this may have occurred in the UK as no attempt appears to have been made to monitor if risk transfer happens in reality, or how much benefit it really brings (Pollock and Price 2008).

The impact of the GFC on PPPs

The value of PPPs in Europe (excluding the UK) rose sharply during the period 2004–6 to approximately €18 billion per annum (European PPP Expertise Centre (EPEC) 2010). The total value of PPPs signed by the end of 2006 was €31.6 billion, of which €23.6 billion was signed between 2004 and 2006. Moreover, at the start of 2007, projects valued at €67.6 billion were in procurement (Hall 2008a). In the UK, the annual PPP programme increased from nine projects valued at £667 million in 1995 to 65 projects valued at £7.6 billion in 2002 (HMT 2003). In addition, it was estimated that a further 200 projects with a total value of £26 billion would be closed between 2005 and 2010 (HMT 2006). However, the value of PPP transactions reaching financial close fell sharply across Europe in 2008 and 2009 (from a high of approximately €30 billion in 2007) and, whilst returning to the 2004–6 levels in 2010, it remains well below the record years of 2005–7 (EPEC 2010). In terms of the *number* of transactions, the UK remains by far the most active market across the European Union, with 44 PPP deals reaching financial close in 2010 (EPEC 2010) and 20 during the first half of 2011 (with a total value of approximately €1.8 billion) (EPEC 2011a). In value terms, Spain was the largest PPP country in 2010 (with 13 deals totalling approximately €4.4 billion) (EPEC 2010), with France being the largest during the first half of 2011 (with eight deals totalling approximately €8 billion). Regardless of the improvement in 2010 and the first half of 2011, reflected in the figures above, the numbers and value of PPP transactions remain considerably less than those observed prior to 2008. To put the extent of this reduction in context, while the value of all European PPP deals for 2007 was approximately €30 billion, this figure had fallen to €18.3 billion in 2010 (recovering from just over €15 billion in 2009); this represents a decline of 39 per cent. Figure 2.1 illustrates this new subdued funding level and shows the financial details of European PPPs between 2003 and 2011a. Moreover, few large deals closed in the UK in 2010 and the first half of 2011 (EPEC 2010 and 2011a).

PPPs are normally funded by 90 per cent debt finance and 10 per cent equity finance. Equity is higher risk as it will be lost first if the project company fails. Therefore, such shareholder loans are seen as junior to the external debt, known as senior debt, which is repaid first (NAO 2010). Between 1995 and 2002 the use of both index-linked and wrapped bonds in the financing of PPPs grew (see Kirk and Wall 2002 for a fuller explanation). However, following the 2007 housing market decline, the monoline industry, (which guaranteed bond repayment if an

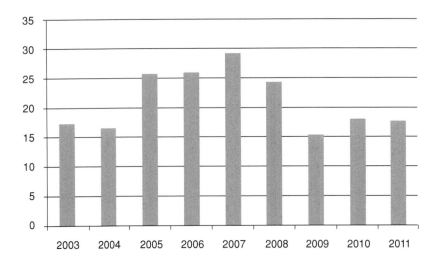

Figure 2.1 European PPP market 2003–11 by € billion
Source: EPEC (2011b)

issuer defaulted), collapsed, resulting in the closure of the wrapped bond market (BBC 2009). Consequently, the only viable source of finance for infrastructure projects was banks. However, the demise of Lehman Brothers in September 2008, widely accepted as the tipping point for the GFC, meant that the global interbank lending market dried up as banks stopped trusting each other. At the height of the crisis, banks were unable to fund themselves at the wholesale money market reference rates and there were suggestions that those rates had become unrepresentative. This constraint on liquidity meant:

- less debt available for any given project and the need for a consortium of banks for all but the smallest of projects;
- a higher price of debt, making it harder for privately financed deals to beat the PSC;
- a shorter term for debt leading to refinancing risk and hedging issues; and
- greater conditionality relating to the debt during the procurement phase.

A global review by PricewaterhouseCoopers (2008) reported that interest rates for lending to infrastructure projects had risen between 1.5 and 2 per cent above the lowest rates obtainable by governments, causing difficulties for both existing and future PPPs. Indeed, the NAO (2010) found that loan margins (i.e. above the interbank rate) for UK PPP projects had increased to around 2.5 per cent on average, with some complex projects facing margins of 3 per cent. EPEC (2010) reports similar commercial debt pricing. With respect to existing PPPs, loan repayments become more difficult, refinancing problematical due to the reluctance of banks to provide funding and, for concession-type PPPs such as toll roads, forecasted earnings unlikely to be achieved due to a slump in domestic demand (Hall 2009). Consequently, as reported above, the flow of new PPPs has slowed down.

Standard and Poor's (2008) warned that some Spanish public authorities may have their credit rating revised downwards unless expenditure on employment and services is reduced because of the inflexible burden of PPP debt coupled with declining tax revenues due to the GFC. Ironically, this will increase the cost of debt and further reduce uncommitted income. In other countries there is also evidence that PPPs are being cancelled because of the GFC. For example, in Ireland, six social housing PPPs have been cancelled, a planned prison PPP was postponed indefinitely (Hall 2009) and a metro PPP has been deferred (Department of Transport, Tourism and Sport 2011). In Australia, despite its extensive use of the PPP model, there has also been a renewed questioning of overinflated traffic forecasts (Ferguson 2009; KPMG 2009a) following the failure of a number of projects.

The GFC has also had a significant impact on PPPs in the UK, with only 34 deals being signed in 2008 (Hall 2009), which was approximately half that of 2007 and the lowest level of activity for over a decade (Kapoor 2008). Although, as noted above, EPEC reports that this has recovered slightly to 44 deals in 2010 (albeit the value of such deals is much lower). The NAO (2010: 9) highlighted that as well as charging higher margins, banks are adopting a more cautious approach to lending following the credit crisis and are, as a result, lowering the proportion of debt in projects; requiring the private sector to inject equity earlier; and placing more onerous conditions on when the private investors can withdraw cash from the project. Hence, UK public service programmes that currently rely on PPPs may suffer. Moreover, the GFC led to the collapse of land and property values, which contributed to the failure of businesses, declines in consumer wealth, substantial financial commitments incurred by governments and a significant decline in economic activity. This impacted upon PPP deals, which involved disposal of land as part of the financing, and may have contributed to the termination of the Defence Training Review programme (see Case studies) (Defence Policy and Business 2010). Further issues include increased government guarantees, greater state involvement in some UK banks and direct HMT lending (see below), which makes the achievement of VfM more difficult. This increased public sector risk coincides with substantial strain being put on public finances, arguably due to the measures taken by the previous Labour government to protect the fragile economic recovery, support growth and job creation and provide reassurance to capital markets (Ostry *et al.* 2010). Consequently, the coalition government has reversed a number of policies implemented by the previous Labour government, including the Building Schools for the Future (BSF) programme (see Case studies) (Richardson 2010). Given these difficulties, the UK and other countries have sought to introduce measures to assist PPPs struggling to reach financial close. Some of these are now outlined.

UK initiatives

Four main approaches were being trialled in the absence of traditional financial approaches in the UK; they were mini-perm structures, HMT lending, the non-profit distributing model and the prudential borrowing framework. Each of these is now briefly explained.

Mini-perm structures

Broadly speaking, a mini-perm is a short-term financing tool, usually payable in three to five years and typically used to pay off income-producing construction or commercial properties. The term 'perm' is short for 'permanent', alluding to permanent financing, albeit for a short period of time, as indicated by the word 'mini'. Mini-perm financing might be used by a developer until a project has been completed and can therefore start producing income and establish an operating history. In other words, this type of financing is used prior to being able to access long-term financing or permanent financing solutions. The interest payable on a mini-perm will usually be higher than longer-term financing options, often with a balloon payment at the end of the term in anticipation that the loan can then be easily refinanced due to the fact that the asset now has an operating history on which to successfully obtain less-expensive permanent financing. They can be split into two distinct types: hard and soft (KPMG 2009b). The former has a relatively short maturity, typically five to seven years, at which point the bulk of the loan remains outstanding. Arguments for hard mini-perms are that they force refinancing, which would be at prevailing market prices, and they allow the lenders to price on a short-term basis. In contrast, soft mini-perms have a longer maturity, for example 26 years of a 28-year contract. Nevertheless, two features encourage early refinancing. Firstly, incremental step-ups of 25–50 basis points at certain dates result in the cost of borrowing being more expensive if the loan is not refinanced. Secondly, a cash sweep at a certain date is used to repay the outstanding debt rather than distribute rewards to shareholders. In 2009 it was reported that two large PPP projects and one small one had been financed using a mini-perm. However, it was felt that these projects had caused affordability issues for the public sector and increased the private sector's risk exposure (KMPG 2009b). Therefore, it is doubtful that such structures will prove to be much of a solution, particularly with their emphasis on refinancing, which is less likely due to the GFC. An example of a large project using a soft mini-perm structure would be London's Riverside waste-to-energy £570 million PPP, which reached financial close in July 2008.

HMT lending

In 2009, the Labour government announced its intention to lend to PPPs, which were unable to raise sufficient finance (HMT 2009). The aim was not to replace banks or capital markets but to provide additional funding, with the private sector and EIB continuing to supply the majority of finance. To qualify for HMT lending, there must have been a failure to secure finance following a competitive process and any funding offered must have been unrepresentative of market terms. These loans would still bear interest and be repaid over the life of the project. However, HMT hoped that if favourable market conditions returned, the loans could be sold prior to maturity at a profit. These loans were to be issued by HMT's own finance unit known as The Infrastructure Finance Unit (TIFU), which was established with the aim of supporting PPP schemes in procurement, thereby safeguarding £13 billion of public investment (HMT 2009). These included the Greater Manchester waste project (see Case studies), the M25 widening, Merseyside Waste, Building Schools for the Future (see Case studies) and a number of hospital projects. However, TIFU only provided lending for the Greater Manchester waste project (see Table 2.5) and was subsequently placed under the umbrella of Infrastructure UK, which has a much wider role in reducing the cost of infrastructure projects (NAO 2010). As with mini-perms, TIFU loans were seen as a short-term solution until the project could obtain more conventional finance.

Non-profit Distributing model (NPD)

Although similar to PPP, the main difference is that the NPD provides economic or social infrastructure financed 100 per cent by debt (90 per cent senior and 10 per cent junior). This differs from PPP deals, which normally consist of 90 per cent debt and 10 per cent equity. Under an NPD, SPV shareholders receive a capped return on their capital, with any surpluses remaining at the end of the contract being passed to a designated charity as opposed to being paid out as dividends. Subsequently, the dividend opportunity is removed, which is considered to flatten out overall risks when compared to equity-based PPPs or public procurement. NPDs are therefore still attractive to banks, but not as popular with investors or bidders as they do not obtain the same returns (Hellowell and Pollock 2009). This model was piloted in Scotland in the Argyll and Bute Council's schools project, which reached financial close in September 2005. Since then, two more schools' projects (in Falkirk and Aberdeen) reached financial close in May and December 2007 respectively. Moreover, the National Health Service in Tayside has used this model for a PPP and the Borders rail link project, which was announced in 2008, will also use NPD.

Prudential Borrowing Framework (PBF)

Although it could be argued that the PBF was not initiated in response to banks' reluctance to lend, it does provide an alternative to PPP. Indeed, as it excludes the private sector from all aspects of the project apart from construction, it is closer to traditional procurement. Under the Local Government Act 2003, local authorities were given greater freedom over their capital expenditures; therefore whilst most of their revenue still comes from central government, it now has less say over how this money is spent. Therefore local authorities are no longer forced down the PPP route by central government. However, whilst Hood *et al.* (2007) believe that the PBF has benefits, they feel it is not as robust as PPP regarding the treatment and allocation of risk. One UK local authority spent £11 million on a programme of highway structural work via the PBF, which they calculated would not only deliver a better long-term solution but would also deliver savings of £1 million from the highways maintenance budget and reduce future liabilities by a further £1.9m. Moreover, the resurfacing work would increase the operational life of the road and reduce the number of insurance claims and litigation from potholes created by adverse weather conditions. Had they gone down the PPP route they would have had to deal with the substantial running costs of such projects, complex contractual arrangements and extended contractual periods, all of which contribute to a heightened risk profile (Hood *et al.* 2007).

Other initiatives

PPPs in France have never been equivalent to PPPs elsewhere from a legal perspective, but recent financial turmoil has prompted financial reforms there too. In order to alleviate the problems with the financial markets, several measures have been introduced (Hall 2009). These include a government guarantee for all PPP bank loans; tax allowances; allowing the government to advance to a bank the majority of the loan required by the private partner (thus enabling the bank to pass on lower interest rates obtainable by government); and allowing PPPs to be signed on the basis of 'adjustable financing' without finalizing a deal with banks so that it can proceed on the basis of government advances while waiting for improved conditions in the financial market. PPPs have been widely promoted in developing countries for many years by the World Bank and other donors and development banks. However, the International Finance Corporation (IFC), the World Bank's private sector arm, believes that the GFC will make it even harder to finance PPPs. It estimates that projects totalling $110 billion may be delayed or cancelled, and that $70 billion of existing PPPs are at risk because of increased financing costs (IFC 2008). Therefore, the IFC has created a global equity fund and a loan financing trust to support PPPs.

It can be seen therefore that the financial threats highlighted by Burger *et al.* (2009) have impacted on the PPP initiative. Interest rates have increased, credit has become less available, there has been a slump in domestic demand and increased borrowing from the EIB could expose the UK public sector to exchange rate risk. But have these dynamics affected the time taken for PPPs to reach financial close, and the types of financing arrangements being put in place? It is to these questions that we now turn.

Methodology

The data used for this research was obtained from two primary sources: HMT (2011) statistics for both signed projects (698) and those still in procurement (61) at 16 March 2011, and Partnerships UK's (PUK) (2011) project database.[2] The

HMT signed projects list is revised on a six-monthly basis to reflect the updates HMT receives from departments at budget and pre-budget review. The list of projects in procurement is also updated regularly. The PUK database holds details of 920 projects that have all achieved financial close. In compiling this database, PUK liaise with HMT, government departments, the Welsh Assembly and the Northern Ireland (NI) and Scottish Executives. The main reason for the difference between the HMT signed list of 698 projects and the PUK database of 920 is that the latter also contains non-PPP projects. Furthermore, with respect to the HMT list of both signed projects and those in procurement, the same amount of information is not provided for each project. Accordingly, for the purposes of this research, 570 (82 per cent) signed projects and 57 (93 per cent) of those in procurement were deemed useable.

In order to ascertain whether the GFC has led to delays in projects being closed, the length of time between the appearance of the project in the *Official Journal of the EU* (OJEU) and financial close was measured. The EU public procurement directives require all public sector bodies to publish details of tenders and contract opportunities in the *OJEU* and financial close is deemed to be when both the bidder and the purchaser have reached agreement on all the contractual documents, all relevant technical issues, and all matters affecting the unitary charge. The only remaining issue is for the bidder to fix the interest rate on the debt taken out to finance the project. Comparisons were then made between the length of time from the *OJEU* notice to financial close for projects signed since the beginning of the PPP scheme in 1992 and those in procurement at 16 March 2011. It was expected that these latter projects would have been delayed due to the reluctance of banks to lend.

Three case studies are also presented to demonstrate some of the difficulties that projects have had in obtaining finance and the attempts to overcome these.

Findings

Table 2.1 presents a list of both signed projects (570) and those in procurement (57) by government department. As can be seen, the average number of months from the *OJEU* date to financial close for signed projects was 33.9. If departments with three or less projects are excluded, the time to financial close ranges from 25.8 months (HMRC) to 40.6 months (Health and MoD). Table 2.1 also indicates that, on average, it is estimated that projects in procurement will reach financial close in 42.1 months (which is approximately eight months longer than for signed projects). However, while this difference in the time to reach financial close may not appear that significant in the context of the GFC, the following points need to be considered. Firstly, the figure for projects in procurement is only an estimate, and in a number of cases this has been exceeded. Secondly, the signed projects list takes into account all projects since the scheme was launched in 1992. Therefore one would expect the earlier projects to have taken longer as the process was new to all parties. Thirdly, as the average figure only provides an overall perspective, it is necessary to examine each department separately.

Table 2.1 UK PPP projects signed and in procurement at 16 March 2011 by government department

Department	Number of projects		Average months – OJEU to financial close	
	Signed	In procurement	Signed	In procurement
Business, Innovation and Skills	1	–	20.0	–
Communities and Local Government (CLG)	50	14	39.3	47.1
Culture, Media and Sport (CMS)	15	1	35.9	50.3
Education	118	11	26.6	48.8
Environment, Food and Rural Affairs (EFRA)	22	11	35.7	39.8
Foreign and Commonwealth	1	–	48.6	–
Government Communications Headquarters (GCHQ)	1	–	36.7	–
Health	102	5	40.6	30.6
HM Revenue and Customs (HMRC)	6	–	25.8	–
HMT	1	–	58.1	–
Home Office	22	2	34.4	24.8
Ministry of Defence (MoD)	28	–	40.6	–
Ministry of Justice (MoJ)	19	–	33.4	–
NI Executive	32	5	35.4	38.5
Scottish Government	81	–	30.4	–
Transport	45	8	30.2	40.3
Welsh Assembly Government	23	–	36.2	–
Work and Pensions	3	–	40.8	–
Overall	570	57	33.9	42.1

   Comparing signed projects with those in procurement, it is estimated that the latter projects in CLG, CMS, Education, EFRA, the NI Executive and Transport will take longer to reach financial close than those already signed in the same departments; whereas it is predicted that projects in procurement in only Health and Home Office will close more quickly than those already signed. However, as will be seen later in the chapter, four projects across three of the departments named above (Education, Transport and the NI Executive) have missed their predicted financial closure date at 16 March 2011 and will take longer still. In addition, as later illustrated in Table 2.4, while 29 of the 57 projects in procurement at 16 March 2011 were due to reach financial close by 31 October 2011,[3] only six had done so by this date; thus 23 (79 per cent) missed their predicted date of financial close.

If the information in Table 2.1 is analysed by project category, it is found that the average time for signed projects to reach financial close ranges from 20.9 (Information Technology (IT)) to 52 months (Housing: Housing Revenue Account (HRA)). HRA housing refers to subsidized or 'council' housing, and the long time taken to reach financial close is perhaps not surprising as the system has been under review since 2009 due to concerns over how the scheme is financed (Bury 2010; Wilson 2011). In October 2010 it was announced that the HRA system is to be reformed from April 2012 to give local authorities that own housing stock full control of their housing income and expenditure and allow them to make their own decisions on how and in what way they invest in tenants' homes. If they wish they will even be able to build new homes using surplus rental income (Wilson 2011). If single projects are excluded from the analysis, the estimated time to reach financial close for projects in procurement ranges from 24.8 months (Police) to 51.8 months (Housing (HRA)).

While the overall averages for signed projects and those in procurement (33.9 months and 42.1 months respectively) by government department and project category will be identical, analysing any differences in length by the type of project gives a clearer idea of those taking longer to come to financial close. Projects in procurement, in seven of the 12 project categories, in Housing (non-HRA) (5), Libraries (1), Roads and Highway Maintenance (4), Schools (BSF – 11; non-BSF – 1), Street Lighting (4) and Waste (14), which account for 40 (70 per cent) of the 57 projects in procurement, are taking longer than those already signed. Two project categories are taking approximately the same time (Fire and Housing (HRA)) and three are estimated to take less (Health, IT and Police). There is naturally a link between some of the projects in procurement that are estimated to take longer to reach financial close than similar signed projects and the equivalent position referred to above with respect to departments (Table 2.1) (for example: CLG – Housing; Education – Schools; EFRA – Waste; and Transport – Roads and Street Lighting).

In February 2001, the Labour government launched a review of PPP called Gateway, which sought to cut delays to PPP contract negotiations (HMT 2001). In order to ascertain whether the length of time to financial close was subsequently reduced, the data was analysed in the following time-frames: 1993 (the first *OJEU* date) to 2000; 2001 to 2006; and finally 2007 onwards (post-GFC). Table 2.2 displays projects by department with an *OJEU* date between 1993–2000 and 2001–6. It can be seen that the earlier projects took 34.8 months on average to reach financial close, whereas the later ones took approximately two months less (32.9 months). Of the 13 departments represented in both periods, eight reached financial close more quickly in 2001–6 than in the period 1993–2000 (CMS, Education, Health, Home Office, MoJ, Scottish Government, Transport, and Work and Pensions). These eight departments accounted for 188 (74 per cent) of the 254 cases in 2001–6. The five departments taking longer to reach financial close in 2001–6 than in 1993–2000 were CLG, EFRA, MoD, NI Executive and the Welsh Assembly Government. These five departments accounted for 66 (26 per cent) of the 254 cases in 2001–6.

Table 2.2 Signed PPP projects with *OJEU* dates 1993–2000 and 2001–6 by government
department

Department	Number of projects		Average months – OJEU to financial close	
	1993–2000	*2001–6*	*1993–2000*	*2001–6*
Business, Innovation and Skills	1	–	20.0	–
CLG	22	26	33.4	45.1
CMS	4	10	41.9	35.8
Education	46	70	27.7	25.6
EFRA	11	11	31.2	40.2
Foreign and Commonwealth	1	–	48.6	–
GCHQ	1	–	36.7	–
Health	58	44	44.7	35.1
HMRC	6	–	25.8	–
HMT	1	–	58.1	–
Home Office	16	6	34.6	33.9
MoD	21	7	38.5	47.1
MoJ	18	1	34.1	20.0
NI Executive	13	19	34.3	36.2
Scottish Government	46	35	31.8	28.5
Transport	20	21	31.1	28.5
Welsh Assembly Government	20	3	33.0	57.4
Work and Pensions	2	1	48.3	25.8
Overall	307	254	34.8	32.9

An analysis of the information in Table 2.2 by project category reveals that of
the 20 project categories represented in both periods, only eight reached financial
close more quickly in 2001–6 than in 1993–2000 (Defence (Education and
Training and Other), Health, Leisure Centres, Prisons and Secure Training
Centres, Schools (non-BSF), Street Lighting and Water). However, these eight
project categories accounted for 175 (73 per cent) of the 239 comparable cases
(i.e. excluding 15 BSF schools cases in 2001–6, for which there were no projects
in 1993–2000 (see Case studies)). Overall, therefore, it is clear that projects
reached financial close more quickly following the Gateway review.

Due to the problems with regard to bank lending it could be reasonably
expected that projects that had an *OJEU* date from January 2007 onwards would
take longer to come to financial close. However, perhaps surprisingly, as can be
seen from Table 2.3, which displays projects by department and project category
with an *OJEU* date between 2007 and 16 March 2011, it was actually quicker
(30.6 months). However, these figures must be put into context as they only refer

to nine projects with a lower estimated average capital value[4] (£59 million) than other signed projects (£76 million) and projects in procurement (£122 million). Moreover, the extremely low number of projects signed between 2007 and 2011 when compared with the previous periods is in itself an indication of the impact of the GFC. It should also be noted that the reduction in PPP projects post-2006 is partly due to the unpopularity of the scheme in Scotland. As a result, those projects already signed have been allowed to continue; for those not yet in procurement the NPD model has been adopted (Scottish Government 2008).

Prior to the GFC, it was estimated that projects would close more quickly than in the past due to all parties gaining more experience with the processes involved. This would appear to be confirmed by an initial analysis of the 57 projects in procurement at 16 March 2011 (see Table 2.1), which reveals that only four (7 per cent) had missed their estimated financial close date by 3.4 months on average. However, whilst this appears quite positive at first sight, further analysis of the projects in procurement at 16 March 2011 provides a different interpretation. Table 2.4 provides an analysis of the estimated financial close dates of projects in procurement at 16 March 2011. This indicates that the aforementioned four projects, which had missed their estimated financial close date, were the only projects that were due to close by this date. Of the 29 projects in procurement at 16 March 2011, which were due to reach financial close by 31 October 2011, only six (21 per cent) had actually closed by this date (not shown in tables); suggesting that a growing number of projects are having difficulties achieving financial close as originally expected.

Whilst the analysis above has focused on the length of time taken for PPP deals to come to financial close, it could be reasonably argued that this in itself does not confirm that PPPs have been affected by the financial crisis. The increase in time could be the result of a number of process issues such as the size or complexity of a project. Moreover, as with Scotland and some UK local authorities, delays

Table 2.3 Signed PPP projects with *OJEU* date between 2007 and 16 March 2011 by government department and project category

Department	Project category	Number of projects	Average months – OJEU to financial close
CLG	Fire	1	28.3
CLG	Joint service centres	1	28.6
CMS	Leisure centres	1	12.4
Education	Schools (BSF)	2	32.9
Transport	Street Lighting	4	35.2
Overall		9	30.6

Table 2.4 Analysis of the estimated financial close dates of projects in procurement at 16 March 2011

Estimated date of financial close	2010	1 January 2011 to 16 March 2011	17 March 2011 to 31 October 2011	1 November 2011 to 31 December 2011	2012	2013	Total
Number of projects	2	2	25	5	18	5	57

could be down to a general dissatisfaction with PPPs as a method of procuring infrastructure. Likewise, on coming to power in 2010, the UK coalition government exhibited caution over the use of PPPs due to concerns over VfM. However, as the case studies in the following section illustrate, a lack of funding has clearly led to project delays. Furthermore, it is perhaps a little ingenuous to assume that factors apart from financing have been the major cause of the slow down in PPPs when the falling number of projects directly coincides with the timing of the GFC. Additionally, Labour was still in power in the UK when the GFC began and its appetite for PPPs had shown no signs of diminishing.

Case studies

Defence Training Review (DTR)

The DTR aimed to deliver military technical training on a defence basis rather than separately by the Royal Navy, Army and Royal Air Force, and originally consisted of two separate PPPs, termed Package 1 and Package 2. The first, estimated to cost £12 billion, covers technical training, including aeronautical engineering, and communications and information systems. The second was to include logistics, personnel administration, security, languages, intelligence, and photography. DTR involves considerable infrastructure investment as well as the sale of large amounts of MoD property. A consortium called Metrix, consisting of QinetiQ, the MoD's privatized former research and development agency, and Land Securities Trillium (LST) as equity partners, was set up to finance and manage the project (Hansard 2007).

In January 2008, funding issues forced MoD to retract Package 2, with LST withdrawing from Package 1 in December 2008 over financing concerns (Defence Management 2009). In 2009, two years after the DTR was awarded to the Metrix consortium, major questions remained over the affordability of this project. This was brought about by the collapsing property market as the project was to be financed largely from the sale of vacant MoD land; but declining property prices meant Metrix's original projections for financing the deal were no longer appropriate. Norton-Taylor (2009) reported in February 2009 that, according to the MoD, the DTR was in trouble as a result of increases in the cost of borrowing and other areas of cost growth that have arisen as a consequence of the GFC. The MoD stated that the project had been 'more difficult and prolonged than expected' and could fall victim to the 'abnormal market environment' – a reference to its dependence on banks affected by the GFC (Norton-Taylor 2009). Furthermore, in July 2009, Smith (2009) reported that the government had provided £44 million to keep the project going, in addition to 'contingent liability' funding of about £50 million. It was widely accepted that the future of the DTR was uncertain following the election of the coalition government (Public and Commercial Services Union 2010) and the project was eventually terminated in October 2010 due to affordability issues as a result of falling asset values and increases in borrowing costs against a backdrop of already fragile UK public finances.

Greater Manchester Waste Disposal Authority (GMWDA)

An analysis of Table 2.1 by project category indicated that waste projects in procurement are estimated to take longer to reach financial close than those already signed, and a waste project was one of four that missed the estimated date of financial close at 16 March 2011.

The GMWDA project provides an interesting example of issues faced by large projects in general and waste projects in particular. GMWDA was given permission for a £640 million waste disposal and recycling project. This was the largest of its kind in Europe and involved the development of a network of state-of-the-art recycling facilities, comprising 36 plants on 23 sites across Greater Manchester, capable of handling 1.3 million tonnes of waste per annum. Shifrin (2009) identified the GMWDA project as a prime example of a PPP that had suffered serious delays due to banks' reluctance to finance large and complex projects and reported that although interest rates had reached a record low, the costs of financing PPPs was higher than ever. Financial close was due in June 2008, but a lack of funding meant that this deadline was missed. Although the outlook for the project remained somewhat uncertain, PUK's chief executive expressed confidence that even if they had to hold out for credit from existing banks or introduce new ones, they were reasonably confident that they would hit their 2013 completion target. However, the final financial package (see Table 2.5) demonstrates the reliance of the scheme on non-conventional sources.

As can be seen from Table 2.5, only one UK bank committed finance to the project, and that is partially owned by the UK government. Banks from outside the UK contributed £290 million (37 per cent of the total), which could expose the government to exchange rate risk, and £347.5 million (44 per cent) came directly from public sector sources. Eventually it took approximately 50 months for this project to reach financial close, which is much higher than the average of 36.6 months for signed waste projects.[5] Pinsent Masons (2009), who advised the construction company Viridor Laing, stated that 'completing a transaction of this size and complexity in the face of the credit crunch provided a great challenge for the sponsors and their advisers'. A spokesperson from GMWDA (2009) also

Table 2.5 Funding for Greater Manchester waste project

Funder	Amount (£m)	Comment
PFI credits	124.5	Grant from UK government
TIFU	120	Loan from UK government
GMWDA	103	Two thirds equity and one third loan facility
European Investment Bank (EIB)	100	Non-UK bank
Bank of Ireland	95	Non-UK bank
Viridor Laing consortium	90	Equity stake
Banco Bilbao Vizcaya Argentaria	55	Non-UK bank
Lloyds Banking Group	55	Partly owned by UK government
Sumitomo Mitsui Banking Corporation	40	Non-UK bank

stated that the project had 'been secured during a period of unprecedented financial turbulence', underlining how the GFC had led to delays. Whilst the eventual funding of this project may be categorized as innovative and flexible, others may see it as highly risky on the part of the public sector. None of the debt is being forwarded by a conventional UK bank and thus the purchaser is primarily borrowing from overseas or public sector sources. This raises issues about the higher levels of risk being retained by the public sector, which could potentially jeopardize the achievement of VfM. Moreover, the NAO (2010) estimated that the increase in the financing charges of this project added 12 per cent to its annual contract price.

Building Schools for the Future (BSF)

Another project category that is estimated to take longer to close than existing signed projects is BSF schools (48.8 months versus 36 months[5]). BSF, which was launched in February 2004, was a long-term strategic investment programme by the Labour government intended to transform the delivery of secondary school education (Partnerships for Schools (PfS) 2010). It involved the rebuilding and renewal of 3,500 secondary schools in England and transforming them into a standard fit for twenty-first century education. In late 2008, the Labour government announced that it would continue to invest in public services such as schools and hospitals; but the announcement of a review of three key education programmes, including the £45 billion BSF initiative, which almost inevitably meant a cut in investment, undermined these promises. The NAO (2009) revealed in January 2009 that BSF was £10 billion over budget and two years behind schedule. While reports in February 2009 (Anon 2009) confirmed that more than six banks were interested in providing financial backing for BSF, in previous years this figure was as high as 30. With an estimated £1.2 billion needed for the programme, there was concern that the funding committed by the banks would be insufficient. In March 2009 it was announced that the EIB was in talks with PfS over the possibility of doubling the £300 million it had already made to BSF. Many individual projects had already suffered significant delays, notably in Salford and Wigan, where the £350 million developments were already 15 months behind schedule and were expected to be further delayed because of financing difficulties (Richardson 2009). A House of Commons Select Committee warned that the reliance placed on private funding by the BSF scheme meant it was severely under threat and could be one of the 'first major casualties' of government spending reductions (Curtis 2009).

On 5 July 2010, Secretary of State for Education Michael Gove announced that the BSF programme was to be abandoned and that BSF projects that had not achieved financial close would not proceed, meaning that 715 school refurbishments already signed up to the scheme would not now go ahead (Richardson 2010). The 706 schools that had reached financial close will continue; however, officials have been charged with seeing how savings can be made within them.

The UK policy environment

It is difficult to draw any robust conclusions about changes to the UK's attitude to PPPs, and in particular PPP funding, when less than two years after the first real impact of the GFC there was a change of government. However, despite an initial indication that the new coalition government would be more circumspect over the use of PPPs, like many new governments it has accepted that the private sector can play a major role in infrastructure development beyond purely design or construction. Notwithstanding, it can be argued that prior to the GFC, financiers saw PPP projects as less risky than other investments due to factors such as implicit government guarantees (Asenova and Hood 2006; Edwards *et al.* 2004), the passing on of risks to sub-contractors and the long-term returns on offer (Asenova and Beck 2010). Consequently, there was a tendency for PPP projects to be driven by private sector consortia that could transform a government wish-list of desirable projects into concrete propositions. Raising finance was not a problem during the boom period of the late 1990s to the onset of the GFC and therefore the UK government, as with the governments of many other countries, could be seen to be actively rebuilding the nation's infrastructure and concurrently creating and maintaining jobs across a range of sectors.

When the bond market collapsed and the banks became increasingly reluctant to lend, the Labour government, now under the premiership of Gordon Brown, took on what some would describe as a post-Keynesian (Holt and Pressman 2001) approach to stimulating the economy by seeing the role of government as driving demand. However, the short-term solutions offered by HMT lending or encouraging the use of mini-perms were not overly successful and thus initiatives such as quantitative easing (the printing of extra money to repurchase government debt) were introduced to encourage banks to begin lending again. As has been seen in this chapter, although the PPP market did not come to a complete halt, the number of projects reaching financial close decreased and those that proceeded became increasingly reliant on non-conventional lending. More recent announcements by the Chancellor of the Exchequer, George Osborne (at the time of writing), have emphasized the role that private finance still has to play in infrastructure development (BBC 2011). Therefore it would be naive to think that a new era has begun when the UK government has become so sceptical of the advice that it receives from the financial sector that it eschews increasing private involvement in the public sector. Indeed, it is likely that right-of-centre thinking will dominate and that the private sector will move into a number of new areas. For these reasons the dominant position held by the financial sector prior to the GFC is likely to remain in the UK regardless of pressure from the EU, and, despite different approaches in certain parts of the country and government rhetoric about caution, the private finance element of PPPs will continue.

Conclusions

This chapter does not claim the GFC is the only factor leading to project delays; indeed reasons such as project size, project complexity and policy learning leading to a general dissatisfaction with PPPs as a method of infrastructure development could all be contributing factors. However, it is proposed that the GFC is clearly having an adverse effect on the PPP initiative. This assertion is supported by Asenova and Beck (2010), who state that PPPs create profit opportunities for finance capital and that financiers apply strict risk–return criteria when making key investment and procurement decisions. They also felt that financiers had a preference 'for the relatively safe long-term returns offered by PFI projects' (p. 4). Therefore, if the risk–return ratio for PPPs remains unchanged, one reason why less PPPs are reaching financial close must be a lack of this capital. Prior to 2007, the impact PPPs were having on public infrastructure in the UK was significant. With 641 signed projects worth just over £64 billion and the number and value of PPPs steadily increasing between 2004 and 2007 (HMT 2006), it appeared the momentum was set to continue, despite its many critics. However, the banking collapse that led to the GFC affected the private finance upon which PPPs were reliant. As a consequence of the GFC, banks were unable to fund themselves at the wholesale money market rates, which had become too high. This led to the subsequent constraint on liquidity in debt markets and, as the securing of finance is crucial to PPPs, the lack of funding was a contributing factor to half the usual number of projects being signed in 2008.

Therefore, whilst this research has shown that some recent projects have come to financial close relatively quickly, a far greater number are exceeding their estimated targets. Out of 57 projects in procurement at 16 March 2011 (Table 2.1), 29 had an estimated date for financial close on or before 31 October 2011. However, 23 of these projects (79 per cent) had not reached financial closure by this date. As the remainder of those projects in procurement at 16 March 2011 have estimated closure dates after 31 October 2011, whether these projects will close as predicted remains uncertain. The first case study demonstrated that whilst factors such as project complexity may have originally led to a delay, the impact of the GFC has also had an impact, and that due to falling asset values and the higher cost of borrowing, the DTR project was ultimately terminated. The second case study illustrated that whilst certain projects do eventually obtain funding, this is often not from traditional sources. The increasing reliance on the EIB as a source of PPP funding, and borrowing from foreign banks, exposes the UK to exchange rate risk (Burger *et al.* 2009). Furthermore, as the government is financing this and other projects, either directly or through banks in which it has a major share, it makes a mockery of the 'private' in PPP and completely undermines the claims of its proponents that it spreads the cost of projects and transfers the risk of borrowing away from the state and on to private firms. This has implications for the achievement of VfM.

It is clear that significant improvements are required in the economic circumstances, together with a greater availability of finance, before PPPs will become as substantial as they were prior to the GFC. The data provided by EPEC (2011) show that whilst large amounts of money are still being raised for PPPs, the totals remain considerably lower than they were before the crisis. However, a return to what may be termed 'normal lending conditions' may not be enough to resurrect PPPs as a major means of improving the UK's infrastructure. Indeed, there should be no presumption that continuing the use of private finance at current rates will achieve VfM (NAO 2010). Moreover, the abolition of the BSF scheme highlights the fact that the coalition government is prepared to abolish flagship PPP programmes introduced by the previous Labour government. What has also become clear since the change of government in 2010 is that there is a much greater emphasis on what is appealingly referred to as 'efficiency savings' on projects; however, whether this leads to PPPs being seen as a less attractive proposition for the private sector remains to be seen. Indeed, the financial sector continues to have a dominant position in the UK economy and thus the role of private finance in infrastructure development is unlikely to disappear. What is more likely is a shift from bank lending to more market-based solutions such as pension and wealth funds and investment from insurance companies.

Notes

1   The PPP initiative was initially referred to as the Private Finance Initiative (PFI), and while these terms are not completely synonymous, they are often used interchangeably. The term PPP will be used primarily throughout the remainder of this chapter.
2   PUK has embarked on a process of disposing of its various businesses and is expected to close down during 2011. Consequently, while PUK's website is no longer updated, it can still be viewed, together with the Projects Database.
3   The time of analysing the data presented in this chapter.
4   Capital values not shown in tables.
5   This was revealed by the analysis of Table 2.1 by project category.

References

Accounting Standards Board (ASB) (1998) *Application Note F to Financial Reporting Standard 5: Reporting the Substance of Transactions*. London: ASB.

Anon (2009) Funding worries and more delays shadow building schools scheme. *Publicprivatefinance*, February.

Asenova, D. and Beck, M. (2010) Crucial silences: when accountability met PFI and finance capital. *Critical Perspectives on Accounting*, 21: 1–13.

Asenova, D. and Hood, J. (2006) PFI and the implications of introducing new long-term actors into public service delivery. *Public Policy and Administration*, 21(4): 23–41.

BBC (2009) *Timeline: Credit Crunch to Downturn* (available at: http://news.bbc.co.uk/1/hi/business/7521250.stm).

BBC (2011) *Multi-Billion-Pound Push on UK Economy* (available at: http://www.bbc.co.uk/news/uk-15914145).

Broadbent, J., Gill, J. and Laughlin, R. (2008) Identifying and controlling risk: the problem of uncertainty in the Private Finance Initiative in the UK's National Health Service. *Critical Perspectives on Accounting*, 19: 40–78.

Brunnermeier, M. K. (2009) Deciphering the liquidity and credit crunch 2007–08. *Journal of Economic Perspectives*, 23: 77–100.

Burger, P., Tyson, J., Karpowicz, I. and Coelho, M. D. (2009) *The Effects of the Financial Crisis on Public–Private Partnerships*, International Monetary Fund Working Paper WP/09/144.

Bury, R. (2010) Minister confirms HRA will be scrapped. *Inside Housing*, 5 October (available at: www.insidehousing.co.uk/news/finance/minister-confirms-hra-will-be-scrapped/6511929.article).

Curtis, P. (2009) Cuts to cause 'austere' future for schools. *The Guardian*, 7 January.

Defence Management (2009) *The Training Review at Two* (available at: www.defence management.com/feature_story.asp?id=11161).

Defence Policy and Business (2010) Termination of the Defence Training Review. *Defence News*, 19 October (available at: www.mod.uk/DefenceInternet/DefenceNews/DefencePolicyAndBusiness/TerminationOfTheDefenceTrainingReview.htm).

Department of Transport, Tourism and Sport (2011) Minister Varadkar freezes planning on Metro West. Press Release, 25 September (available at: www.transport.ie/pressRelease.aspx?Id=415).

Edwards, P., Shaoul, J., Stafford, A. and Arblaster, L. (2004) *Evaluating the Operation of PFI in Roads and Hospitals*. London: Association of Chartered Certified Accountants.

Engel, E., Fischer, R. and Galetovic, A. (2011) *The Basic Public Finance of Public–Private Partnerships*, Cowles Foundation Discussion Paper No. 1618 (available at: http://cowles.econ.yale.edu/P/cd/d16a/d1618.pdf).

European PPP Expertise Centre (EPEC) (2010) *Market Update: Review of the European PPP Market in 2010*. Luxembourg: EPEC.

European PPP Expertise Centre (EPEC) (2011a) *Market Update: Review of the European PPP Market. First Semester of 2011*. Luxembourg: EPEC.

European PPP Expertise Centre (EPEC) (2011b) *Market Update: Review of the European PPP Market in 2011*. Luxembourg: EPEC.

Ferguson, A. (2009) Infrastructure rethink needed as PPPs burn participants. *The Australian* (available at: http://www.theaustralian.news.com.au/story/0,25197, 24876607-5014000,00.html).

Greater Manchester Waste Disposal Authority (2009) Greater Manchester's £640m revolutionary recycling deal signed. *News Release*, 8 April.

Grimsey, D. and Lewis, M. K. (2004) *Public–Private Partnerships: The Worldwide Revolution in Infrastructure Provision and Project Finance.* Cheltenham: Edward Elgar.

Hall, D. (2008a) *Economic Crisis and Public Services.* University of Greenwich Business School: Public Services International Research Unit (PSIRU).

Hall, D. (2008b) *PPPs in the EU – A Critical Appraisal.* University of Greenwich Business School: PSIRU.

Hall, D. (2009) *A Crisis for Public–Private Partnerships (PPPs)?* University of Greenwich Business School: PSIRU.

Hansard (2007) *Defence Training Review* (available at: www.publications.parliament.uk/pa/cm200607/cmhansrd/cm070117/debtext/70117-0004.htm).

Hellowell, M. and Pollock, A. M. (2009) 'Non-profit distribution: the Scottish approach to private finance in public services'. *Social Policy & Society UK*, 8: 405–41.

Hencke, D. (2003) *Court Computer Plan Wastes Millions – and Still Doesn't Work* (available at: www.guardian.co.uk/uk_news/story/0,3604,1082416,00.html).

HM Treasury (HMT) (2000) *Public–Private Partnerships: The Government Approach.* London: The Stationery Office.

HMT (2001) *New Government Procurement Technique will Save £Millions for Front Line Services* (available at: http://archive.treasury.gov.uk/press/2001/p15_01.html).

HMT (2003) *PFI: Meeting the Investment Challenge.* London: The Stationery Office.

HMT (2006) *PPP: Strengthening Long-term Partnerships.* Norwich: The Stationery Office.

HMT (2009) *Safeguarding Government Infrastructure Investment* (available at: www.articles.scopulus.co.uk/Safeguarding%20Government%20infrastructure%20investment.htm).

HMT (2011) *Public–Private Partnerships – Statistics* (available at: www.hm-treasury.gov.uk/ppp_pfi_stats.htm).

Holt, R. P. F. and Pressman, F. (2001) What is Post-Keynesian economics, in Holt, R. P. F. and Pressman, F. (eds) *A New Guide to Post Keynesian Economics.* London: Routledge.

Hood, J., Asenova, D., Bailey, S. and Manochin, M. (2007) The UK's Prudential Borrowing Framework: a retrograde step in managing risk? *Journal of Risk Research*, 10, 49–66.

International Finance Corporation (IFC) (2008) *IFC Infrastructure Crisis Facility Fact Sheet* (available at: www.ifc.org/ifcext/about.nsf/AttachmentsByTitle/IssueBrief_ICF/$FILE/IssueBrief_ICF.pdf).

International Monetary Fund (2004) *Public–Private Partnerships* (available at: www.imf.org/external/np/fad/2004/pifp/eng/031204.htm).

Kapoor, M. (2008) Things can only get worse. *Public Private Finance*, November.

Kirk, R. J. and Wall A. P. (2002) The Private Finance Initiative: has the Accounting Standards Board reduced the scheme's value for money? *Public Management Review*, 4: 529–47.

KPMG (2009a) *Financing Australian PPP Projects in the Global Financial Crisis* (available at: www.kpmg.com.au/Portals/0/Infrastructure_PPP-Projects-GFC200905.pdf).

KPMG (2009b) *The Use of Mini-perms.* Dublin: KPMG.

Krinsman, A. (2007) Subprime mortgage meltdown: how did it happen and how will it end? *The Journal of Structured Finance*, 13: 13–19.

National Audit Office (NAO) (2009) The Building Schools for the Future programme:

renewing the secondary school estate. *HC 135, Parliamentary Session 2008–2009*. London: The Stationery Office.

NAO (2010) HM Treasury: financing PFI projects in the credit crisis and the Treasury's response. *HC 287, Parliamentary Session 2010–2011*. London: The Stationery Office.

Norton-Taylor, R. (2009) Credit crisis puts £12bn MoD training project in jeopardy. *The Guardian*, 9 February.

Organisation for Economic Cooperation and Development (OECD) (2008) *Public–Private Partnerships: In Pursuit of Risk Sharing and Value for Money*. Paris: OECD.

Ostry, J., Ghosh., A, Kim, J. and Qureshi, M. (2010) *Fiscal Space*. International Monetary Fund Staff Position Note SPN/10/11.

Partnerships for Schools (2010) *Introduction to BSF and PfS* (available at: www.partnershipsforschools.org.uk/documents/library/BSF-archive/PfS_Factsheet_PfSandBSF.pdf).

Partnerships UK (2011) *Projects Database* (available at: www.partnershipsuk.org.uk/PUK-Projects-Database.aspx).

Pinsent Masons (2009) *Pinsent Masons Advises on £640 Million Manchester Waste Project* (available at: www.pinsentmasons.com/default.aspx?page=2138).

Pollock, A. M. and Price, D. (2008) Has the NAO audited risk transfer in operational Private Finance Initiative schemes? *Public Money & Management*, 28: 173–8.

PricewaterhouseCoopers (2008) *Infrastructure Finance – Surviving the Credit Crunch* (available at: www.pwc.com/en_CZ/cz/verejna-sprava-zdravotnictvi/infrastructure-finance-surviving-the-credit-crunch.pdf).

Public and Commercial Services Union (2010) *Defence Training Review Update* (available at: www.pcs.org.uk/en/ministry_of_defence_group/mod-news/index.cfm/id/9AB9FF44-7A9D-4FED-9F1BA8A86D5800B3).

Richardson, H. (2010) *School Buildings Scheme Scrapped*. 5 July (available at: www.bbc.co.uk/news/10514113).

Richardson, S. (2009) *£300m PFI Schools Rescue Fund to Double* (available at: www.building.co.uk/news/%C2%A3300m-pfi-schools-rescue-fund-to-double/3137125.article##ixzz0TGttGpDn).

Shifrin, T. (2009) Bill for Manchester waste PFI scheme hits £4.7bn. *Public Finance*, April.

Smith, M. (2009) Lenders torpedo £12 billion defence training. *The Sunday Times*, 4 July.

Standard and Poor's (2008) *Autonomous Community of Madrid Outlook Revised to Negative: 'AA+/A-1+' Ratings Affirmed* (available at: www.standardandpoors.com/ratingsdirect).

Scottish Government (2008) *Infrastructure Investment Plan*. Edinburgh.

Wilson, W. (2011) The reform of Housing Revenue Account subsidy. *House of Commons Library Social Policy Section*, SN/SP/4341, 4 August, pp. 1–31.

3 What return for risk?

The price of equity capital in public–private partnerships

Mark Hellowell and Veronica Vecchi

Introduction

This chapter focuses on the United Kingdom's experience with design, build, finance and operate contracts (DBFO), of which more than 700 (with a net present value of £117 billion) have been agreed (HM Treasury (HMT) 2011a). Typically, DBFO projects have a highly geared structure, with debt providing 90 per cent of the capital investment requirement, against 10 per cent equity. This is believed to minimize the Weighted Average Cost of Capital (WACC) for the Special Purpose Vehicles (SPVs) established to deliver projects, thereby minimizing the final cost to the public authority. However, as in many other countries, changes in financial sector regulation and concerns about the quality of assets held by banks have restricted long-term lending to new projects (HM Treasury 2011a), while increasing the cost of loans (Threlfall 2011). In this context, the sustainability of the traditional highly geared DBFO model is being questioned.

The UK government has announced a review of the Private Finance Initiative (PFI), with the aim of reducing the cost of debt by relying less on banks, instead sourcing capital from alternative financial institutions, such as pension funds, sovereign wealth funds and insurance companies (HM Treasury 2011b). However, as in many other countries, institutional investors in the UK will not enter the project finance market unless contracts are modified so as to reduce the risk borne by creditors (Inderst 2009). The high up-front cost, lack of liquidity and long asset length of infrastructure projects require significant investment in dedicated human resources capable of assessing the risks involved – resources that most funds are lacking (Croce 2011). This implies that, in future contracts, risk will need to be reallocated from debt holders to one or both of the other main counter-parties: the public authorities and/or the equity investors.

One option is for governments to underwrite refinancing risk, so that a project's development phase is financed by bank loans, and then refinanced into the capital markets once operational (at which point DBFOs are perceived to offer the cashflow stability required by institutional funds). Another is for governments to guarantee the first loss of debt, raising the credit of the remaining debt to make it more attractive to the capital markets. However, reducing the risk borne by the private sector counter-party diminishes the incentive for good project management and might increase the short-term impact of privately financed investment on official estimates of public spending and debt (EPEC 2011).

As a result, policy-makers have shifted the emphasis of reform away from increasing the scope of state intervention towards a model in which the contribution of equity is increased (House of Commons 2012).[1] A natural question to ask is what effect a reduction in gearing is likely to have on the cost of capital for DBFO projects. Common sense suggests that an increase in the ratio of equity to debt will increase the average cost of capital since, in capital markets, required returns on equities typically exceed those on debt assets such as loans and bonds. However, finance theory holds that the average cost of capital for a project is invariant to changes in capital structure and is simply a function of risk (Modigliani and Miller 1958). In this view, reducing gearing does not increase the average cost of capital. Rather, as equity substitutes for debt, the equity becomes less risky, as lower interest payments to creditors make the cashflows to equity less volatile (Jenkinson 2003).

However, the *debt irrelevance theorem* rests on a number of assumptions. In many jurisdictions, debt interest is tax-deductible and this gives rise to a difference in the post-tax cost of different types of capital (though not necessarily from the perspective of the government – the ultimate payer). In addition, theory dictates that in the presence of transaction costs and/or incomplete contracts (both of which are, *a priori*, likely to be significant in DBFOs because of their long-term and complex nature), the minimum return required by equity holders may exceed the actuarially fair rate (Jensen and Meckling 1976). Given the theoretical ambiguity and the salience of the issue for infrastructure policy, it is important to consider the evidence on the returns targeted by equity investors in relation to the risks they bear. More generally, if equity is going to play a more important role in the capital structure of DBFO contracts, it is important to understand how efficiently it is priced.

Empirical research on this key question has been limited, not least due to the commercially sensitive nature of the data required to identify and evaluate returns. However, in the UK, freedom of information legislation and enhanced powers for public auditors have enabled some preliminary studies to be undertaken. This chapter provides a review of this empirical research – including our own contribution, in which returns to equity investors involved in British healthcare DBFOs have been evaluated using various methods. The studies agree that the returns expected by investors include a risk premium above the actuarially fair rate.

We argue that, because of the inherent complexity and inefficiency of the process by which equity investors are engaged in projects (i.e. the procurement process), eliminating excess returns is unlikely to be achieved without regulatory action by central governments. Finally, we outline the basic parameters of what we believe is the appropriate regulatory model.

A framework for identifying and evaluating the return to equity

The capital asset pricing model approach

In its simplest form, an investment is characterized by an initial outflow of cash (capital expenditure or *capex*) followed by net inflows of cash (the *return*). As it is impossible to predict with certainty the actual cashflows accruing to an investment, the uncertainty around the likely outcomes is expressed as a probability distribution, summarizing the investor's degree of belief about the likelihood of the possible returns. This distribution is often based on the past historical performance of equivalent investments, modified to reflect the features of the project being evaluated. On the basis of the distribution of returns, the mean is calculated (giving the *expected return*) along with the dispersion of the possible return (giving the *variance*). According to this, the conventional *mean-variance approach* (Markowitz 1952), all an investor needs to know about an investment is the mean and variance of the possible returns. Investors prefer a higher expected return to a lower one and less variance to more. They may be willing to accept greater risk (higher variance in the return) but only if this is associated with a proportionally higher expected return.

To illustrate, we can consider the case of an all-equity firm with surplus capital resources. The firm has two options: it can use the cash to finance a new investment, or hand the cash back to the firm's shareholders. In the first case, the expected cashflows will be redistributed as dividends. In the second case, shareholders use the cash to purchase a financial security with the same risk as the investment. The first option increases shareholders' wealth, relative to the second option, only if the expected return on the investment is greater than that offered by securities in the same risk class. This latter return is what is meant by the *cost of capital* – i.e. the return the firm must pay shareholders to persuade them to retain the shares. The firm maximizes shareholders' wealth by investing in all projects with an *Internal Rate of Return (IRR)*[2] above the cost of capital (Hirshleifer 1958).

To undertake this comparison, the firm needs a theory of how expected returns on financial securities are determined in the capital market. In finance theory, risk is normally measured from the perspective of an investor with a diversified portfolio. Computing the variance of a portfolio involves estimating the variance of individual assets and the extent to which they vary together, or co-vary. If the returns tend to move in opposite directions, this reduces the risk of the portfolio. By contrast, if the returns on the assets tend to move in the same direction, portfolio risk is increased. In a perfectly diversified portfolio, the risk on individual investments (i.e. investment-specific risk) is eliminated and the variance of the portfolio reduces to the covariance – i.e. the component of risk that is common to all investments.

The Capital Asset Pricing Model of Sharpe (CAPM) (1964) and Lintner (1965) formalizes this idea. It states that the cost of capital for a firm (assuming that it carries no debt) is calculated by summing the return associated with a zero-variance asset (normally referenced to the return on government bonds) and a premium for the amount of systematic risk, as follows:

$$\overline{r}_i = r_f + \beta_i \, (r_M - r_f)$$

where $\overline{r}_i$ is the expected return on investment i, r_f is the return on a zero-variance asset, β_i measures the covariance of returns on investment i with those of the market portfolio divided by the variance of the latter, and r_M is the return on the market index. Consequently, in standard theory, the cost of capital for equity is determined by the value of *beta* – a measure of the extent to which the returns on the investment are estimated to co-vary with those of the market portfolio (Sharpe 1964). In practice, the key element in the process is the identification of a financial asset that falls in the same class of risk as that of the project being evaluated.

Applicability of the standard approach to the DBFO model

The CAPM is more than just a theory of how assets will be priced in equilibrium; it is also the dominant capital budgeting theory used by corporate financial managers internationally (Graham and Harvey 2002). As such, there is a strong argument for using CAPM as a starting point for considering the efficient return to equity investors. However, there are three reasons to question the validity of the assumptions underpinning the CAPM in the context of DBFOs.

1   There is a general recognition among financial economists that even if the CAPM is the most rational approach to calculating required returns it may not be an accurate description of real decision-making among investment practitioners (Mehra and Prescott 1985; Fama and French 1992; Dimson *et al.* 2002). In particular, agency frictions such as information asymmetries and risk aversion are seen to play a prominent role (Shleifer and Vishny 1997). For example, while a management team responsible for managing an equity investment will be rewarded if the returns on the project exceed the expected return, they may be more than proportionally penalized if returns fall short (Spackman 2001). Therefore, as Arrow and Lind noted (1970), from the perspective of an individual manager's career and income, the variance of returns on a single investment may have significant importance – even if, from a shareholder's point of view, project-specific risk is not a material concern. Relatedly, if, in contrast to the assumptions of the mean-variance approach, the distribution of possible returns around the mean is non-normal (e.g. if returns are *skewed* or *leptokurtic*), this may give rise to a level of risk aversion that is higher than is assumed in the CAPM.[3]

2   Recent audit evidence from the UK suggests that equity investors evaluate projects using *corporate hurdle rates*, based on the *betas* of their core businesses, rather than cost of capital benchmarks appropriate to their specific investments (National Audit Office 2012). Corporate *betas* will normally be higher than is appropriate for DBFO projects because the level of systematic risk associated with their core business activities is higher. Looking at UK construction firms, which generally form bidding consortia, Gregory and Michou (2009) estimated the *beta* for the industry to be 1.05, implying a

level of systematic risk slightly higher than the average for the market index as a whole. As revenues on a DBFO contract are more likely to vary according to endogenous factors, such as the ability of subcontractors to deliver contracted assets to time and to budget, rather than exogenous factors, such as changes in user demand and interest rates or inflation,[4] the systematic risk (and thus the *beta* for pricing the equity) is low. Consequently, a hurdle rate will produce a target return above that implied by the orthodox CAPM theory.

3   Equity returns are strongly influenced by the requirements of debt funders (PricewaterhouseCoopers and Franks 2002). Lenders set minimum requirements for *cover ratios* – effectively the level of free cashflow that a project is required to maintain over and above debt repayments – which have a strong influence on required returns. In some projects, where lenders take a conservative approach to setting cover ratios, this will require higher expected equity returns than is implied by the level of risk borne by investors.

The efficiency of equity returns: evidence from public audit

Identifying the return to equity investors has been an important focus of public audit in the UK. A succession of reports has compared the Equity IRR expected by investors at the point of contracts being signed against that expected after bank loans have been refinanced or equity has been sold to secondary market investors. In many cases, the increase in the expected return following such transactions has been substantial. For example, on the Norfolk and Norwich University Hospital Trust's PFI contract, the expected Equity IRR increased from 18.9 per cent at financial close to 60.4 per cent after investors refinanced their loan – a transaction that lowered the interest rate, reduced required cover ratios (allowing cash to be taken out of the project) and increased the term of the debt (reducing the amount of debt capital to be repaid annually) (National Audit Office (NAO) 2005).[5] Returns to primary investors can also be increased by selling their equity assets. So long as the buyer of the asset is willing to accept a lower return on their money than that expected by the vendor, these sales can result in large capital gains. One recent report found that investors have secured an outturn IRR of up to 40 per cent after selling equity assets (NAO 2012).

In addition, analysis of survey data in the most recent NAO report (2012) provides a comparison of expected and actual (outturn) equity returns in respect of 118 projects showing, in most cases, that equity returns have, so far, exceeded rather than undershot those originally forecasted. In 84 of the 118 contracts, equity investors were forecasting returns that equalled or exceeded those expected at the point that contracts were signed. Investors were forecasting lower returns than those initially expected in 34 of the 118 projects. Some of the forecast changes were substantial. The expected rate of return had increased by at least four percentage points since the contract was awarded on 36 of the 118 projects.

In its 2012 report, the NAO makes use of the prices paid by secondary market investors for equity assets relating to three PFI contracts as a baseline for the evaluation of the returns earned by primary investors, and explicitly takes into account the *project-specific* risks borne. For each contract, the auditors subtracted from the sale price:

1   estimated changes in the value of equity between financial close and the point of sale, due to changes in expected cashflows and the return required by secondary investors;
2   adjustments for the time value of money (i.e. the fact that the secondary market sales took place years later than the initial investment, so the effect of discounting is reduced);
3   an amount to reflect the fact that by the time of sale some of the cashflows had already been distributed;
4   an amount to reflect the fact that primary investors bear certain types of risk (primarily those associated with competitive bidding and building the asset), which the secondary investor does not.

In principle, the sum of the four values should equal the initial stake by the primary investor. Yet the auditors found that for each project the sale price was roughly 10 per cent higher than the initial stake, implying a level of excess return to the primary investors equal to between 1.5 and 2.5 per cent of the annual service charge. These excess returns were identified despite the auditors' adoption of a highly conservative methodology for assessing the level of construction risk, i.e. the main category of risk borne by primary investors and not by secondary market investors.

The NAO report acknowledges that, because most of the construction risk is passed to the construction contractor, the investor's main construction risk is the risk of the contractor defaulting. The auditors therefore estimated the probability of a default and multiplied it by the estimated impact on equity cashflow, by using Standard & Poor's generic investment grade ratings, assuming that the project had a minimum investment grade rating at financial close of BBB, i.e. the minimum investment grade rating. Further, it assumed that the construction contractor had a lower-than-minimum investment grade rating of BB+. Standard & Poor's average one-year global corporate default rates for BB+-rated entities is 0.68 per cent and this was applied to the length of the construction phase to calculate a probability of default. To capture the potential for ratings of contractors to change over the construction phase the auditors' somewhat arbitrarily doubled the estimated probability of default. To calculate the *impact* of insolvency during the construction phase, the auditors assumed a uniform impact over the entire construction period. The size of impact that was adopted was a 15 per cent increase in construction costs and the complete loss of revenue in the first full operational year.

The result of this approach is that, for example, for the Queen Alexandra Hospital PFI project, which had a construction cost of £260 million, the impact of default is estimated at some £78 million and the estimated probability of default at 6 per cent, giving an estimated value of construction risk of £4.7 million. This implies a very high rate of contractor default and a willingness among equity investors to invest substantial amounts of additional capital into struggling projects. As the auditors acknowledge, neither of these assumptions, which serve to significantly increase the estimated value of the risk borne by equity investors, is supported by the experience of actual projects in contractor default. Given the extreme conservativeness of the NAO's approach to risk assessment, and the quality of data to which they (as the supreme audit institution of the UK) had access, its conclusion that there is a non-trivial amount of excess return to equity in the projects studied is significant. Although the number of case studies in the report is small, they add to an accumulation of evidence that equity in DBFO projects represents an element of cost inefficiency for the public authorities involved.

The evaluation of healthcare DBFO projects

Here we outline the methods and results of a succession of studies undertaken by the authors along with colleagues (Hellowell and Vecchi 2012; Vecchi and Hellowell forthcoming; Vecchi *et al.* forthcoming). In each study, a different variant of the CAPM approach (what we have called the 'orthodox', 'opportunistic' and 'hurdle rate' approaches) was applied to construct cost of equity benchmarks with which to evaluate expected internal rates of return on hospital DBFO projects signed by UK National Health Service (NHS) organizations. The small size of the data set relative to the population of contracts (n=10/p=123) reflects the difficulty of accessing financial models (i.e. the documents that contain projected revenues, costs and cashflows and are necessary to calculate the expected Equity IRR). Despite the existence of a Freedom of Information Act in the UK, and the fact that all project revenues are ultimately provided by the taxpayer, these documents are often regarded by public authorities as commercially confidential, and this view is currently endorsed by the Information Commissioner's Office (Hellowell and Vecchi 2012). Table 3.1 shows the base data for the ten projects included in the sample.

The orthodox approach

In Vecchi and Hellowell (forthcoming), reference *betas* were drawn up from a range of comparable sectors, including construction, facilities management, real estate and private healthcare. The form of *beta* available on financial databases is the equity *beta*. This form of *beta* reflects the level of systematic risk that a firm's shareholders face in addition to risks relating to the firm's financial leverage (which will be different to the leverage on the specific project under consideration). Therefore, the equity *betas* of the companies from which the raw data had been extracted were 'unleveraged' to estimate the asset *betas*.[6]

In addition, the estimates took account of the fact that most of the systematic risk borne by investors in the comparator sectors is, in a DBFO project,

Table 3.1 Contract duration, capital expenditure and Equity IRRs for the ten projects

NHS purchaser: project	Contract duration	Capital expenditure (£m)	Blended Equity IRR (%)	Project IRR (%)
North Cumbria I Cumberland Infirmary rebuild	11/1997 to 11/2032	85.42	17.8	9.64
Norfolk/Norwich[a] Acute hospital rebuild	01/1998 to 01/2038	233	18.64	10.72
Durham and Darlington General Hospital rebuild	03/1998 to 03/2031	111.8	14.5[b]	10.7
NHS Lanarkshire Hairmyres Hospital rebuild	03/1998 to 05/2031	86.15	22.58	9.71
NHS Lanarkshire Law Hospital rebuild (Wishaw)	07/1998 to 11/2029	148.4	15.43	10.4
NHS Lothian Royal Infirmary of Edinburgh	08/1998 to 03/2028	267.83	19.72	9.79
Nottingham University Queen's Medical Centre	05/1999 to 12/2035	17.7	14.79	8.21
East/North Hertfordshire Herts and Essex Hospital	05/2001 to 06/2035	14.1	15.86	8.22
Hull/East Yorks Hospitals Castle Hill Hospital rebuild	05/2001 to 05/2031	8.9	13.86	10.05
Sandwell/West Birmingham Ambulatory Care Centre	12/2002 to 12/2038	36.7	12.43	7.22
Total/average	–	1,010/101	16.8	9.5

a Data refers to the actual and projected costs and revenues in the pre-refinancing base case financial model.
b This figure is taken from the summary sheet of the financial model, as the Free Cashflow to Blended Equity cannot be calculated from information in the financial model using a method consistent with other schemes.

Source: Information provided by the relevant NHS authorities under the Freedom of Information Act

contractually allocated away from investors. For example, the risk associated with changes in patterns in the demand for healthcare facilities will be a major determinant of returns in the private healthcare sector, but in a DBFO contract the equivalent demand risks are allocated to the public authority.

Similarly, profitability in the construction sector may be significantly impacted by changes in wages and the cost of supplies, but in a DBFO these are allocated to the investors' operational subcontractors (Yescombe 2008). Therefore, in the study, the reference *beta* was used as a baseline to which adjustments were made in order to estimate the appropriate risk premium for each deal. This process involved a number of steps. First, the specific sources of systematic risk accruing to the project were identified and their relative contribution to the total determined. The allocation of these risks between the different parties involved in the contract was estimated. From this, an asset *beta* for the investors was estimated,

Table 3.2 The cost of the equity under the orthodox approach for the Royal Infirmary of Edinburgh DBFO[a]

Risk type	Contribution to overall risk (%)	Project asset beta	Allocation of risk to SPV (%)	Beta for SPV capital
Demand	40	0.64	2	0.01
Inflation	30	0.64	40	0.08
Residual value	10	0.64	0	0.00
Downturn	20	0.64	80	0.10
Asset *beta* for equity				0.19
Re-leveraged *beta* according to project-specific gearing (equity *beta*)				0.47
Blume-adjusted equity *beta* (= (0.67) × βOLS + (0.33) × 1)				0.65
EQUITY RISK PREMIUM (0.65 × 4.00); 4% is the Market Risk Premium				2.60%
30-year gilt rate (i.e. average in the year of financial close)				5.60%
TOTAL BENCHMARK COST OF EQUITY				8.20%

a The Market Risk Premium was set at 4 per cent, equal to that used at the time of financial close by the UK Competition Commission (2010).

Source: Vecchi and Hellowell (forthcoming)

which was re-leveraged to derive the equity *beta*.[7] This was then adjusted according to a standard statistical technique called *Blume adjustment* (Blume 1971), which reflects the tendency of estimated *betas* to revert to the market mean (i.e. 1) over time.[8]

Table 3.2 illustrates the process applied in this study with the example of the Royal Infirmary of Edinburgh scheme – a major UK hospital DBFO that reached financial close in 1998.

The 'spread' between the cost of equity and the Equity IRR provided the focus of evaluation in the study. On average, across the 10 DBFO projects, the spread between Equity IRR and the benchmark cost of equity was estimated within the range 8.46 per cent.

Opportunistic approach

An alternative approach is provided by Hellowell and Vecchi (2012), in which cost of equity benchmarks are constructed according to the project-specific discount rates actually used by major PFI investors in estimating the net present value of their equity portfolios. These discount rates are constructed on the basis of adding to the risk-free rate an equity risk premium, in accordance with the standard CAPM as outlined earlier (section on framework for identifying and evaluating the return to equity). These project-specific rates are recorded in the

Table 3.3 Risk premia (%) used by major healthcare PFI investors in portfolio valuation (2002–9)

Fiscal year	2002	2003	2004	2005	2006	2007	2008	2009
Gilt rate	4.68	4.60	4.66	4.34	4.11	4.49	4.42	4.30
Company								
AMEC PLC	–	–	5.84	6.06	4.99	–	–	–
Balfour Beatty	–	–	–	5.36	5.39	5.01	4.98	5.10
Carillion	–	–	–	5.56	3.89	3.51	4.58	4.70
Costain	–	–	–	–	–	–	3.58	3.70
HSBC	–	–	–	–	–	2.51	2.98	4.00
John Laing	–	–	–	–	3.09	2.81	2.98	3.60
Kier Group	–	–	–	–	–	2.51	2.58	3.70
PFI Infra Co.	–	–	–	4.96	4.39	–	–	–
Serco	–	3.90	–	–	–	–	–	–
Skanska	–	–	–	5.66	4.89	4.51	5.08	5.20
Average risk premia	–	3.90	5.84	5.52	4.44	3.48	3.82	4.29

Source: Hellowell and Vecchi (2012)

annual reports and accounts published by these companies. By calculating the average of these rates, and subtracting the yield on long-dated government gilts, the authors computed the average equity risk premium estimated by the largest PFI investors to be appropriate for this asset class (Table 3.3). Adjusting these for the specific characteristics of the PFI contractual model in the UK health sector, the authors applied these benchmarks to evaluate projected returns on the 10 DBFO projects.

The study found excess returns to equity on each of the data set projects. On average, the spread between Equity IRR and the benchmark cost of equity was estimated within the range 7.1 to 10.1 per cent (depending on the specific cost of equity benchmark applied).

Hurdle rate approach

Discussion on evaluating the return to equity earlier in this chapter showed that, in practice, it is hurdle rates that establish the minimum equity return acceptable to equity investors. This is both contrary to conventional finance theory and, from a capital allocation perspective, sub-optimal, but may be explicable in the context of agency frictions and the degree of risk aversion among individual decision-makers pursuing managerial utility. It therefore seems reasonable to reflect this reality in constructing an estimate of the appropriate return. This underpins the analytical approach undertaken by Vecchi *et al.* (forthcoming) in a final study of returns on the 10 DBFO projects.

As noted, corporate hurdle rates incorporate a *beta* that is inappropriately high for a DBFO project, and therefore the analytical approach in this study is more likely to underestimate rather than overestimate the amount of excess profitability in these contracts. However, the study may be an illuminating one for policy-makers; for, if it is the case that expected returns exceed even corporate hurdle rates, this is strong evidence of inefficiency in the design of the procurement process and/or an unduly risk-averse approach by senior debt providers, both of which would indicate the need for a comprehensive regulatory response.

A corporate hurdle rate approach focuses on the Weighted Average Cost of Capital (WACC) of the firm making the investment. The WACC is a function of the cost of equity for the company and the yield to maturity of the firm's debt, in addition to the ratio (or *gearing*) between the two sources of finance and the effective tax rate, i.e.:

$$WACC = \left[\frac{E}{E + D} \times K_e \right] + \left[\frac{D}{E + D} \times K_d \times (1 - T\%) \right]$$

where E is the amount of equity in the financing structure; D is the amount of debt; K_e is the cost of capital for equity; K_d is the yield to maturity of the firm's debt and $T\%$ is the effective corporation tax rate. The $(1 - T\%)$. function on the right-hand side of the formula reflects the fact that debt interest is deductible from corporation tax payable in the UK.

In order to estimate the WACC of the equity investors for each project in the sample, the authors collected data about their cost of equity (K_e) and the cost of the debt (K_d). In accordance with the CAPM, the components of the cost of equity capital were estimated as follows:

1   The risk-free rate (r_f) was calculated as the weighted average gross redemption yield[9] on UK government bonds maturing in 15, 20, 25 and 30 years at each contract date.
2   The market risk premium ($r_m - r_f$) was calculated as the arithmetic mean of historical market index returns, obtained through regressing annual returns on the market index (1900–2003).
3   *Betas* were found using different approaches for listed and unlisted companies. *Betas* for listed sponsors were extrapolated from *Bloomberg*, as regressions of sponsors' monthly share returns over market indexes. The Financial Times Stock Exchange UK Index was used as a proxy of UK market performance over time and the regression time period set equal to the decade prior to the signing of each contract. The *betas* were adjusted according Blume theory (see Note 8).

Conversely, *beta* coefficients for unlisted companies were calculated as the average *beta* coefficients of comparable companies, selected according to the nature of the core business, reference market and geographical presence using information released by each company. Levered *beta* coefficients were computed using *Bloomberg*, then de-leveraged to calculate an average *beta* to be applied to the group of unlisted firms. The *betas* were then re-leveraged, using the sponsor's capital structure at the point at which the relevant contract reached financial close.

The cost of debt was calculated as the average yield on corporate bonds maturing in five to seven years from the contract signature date of the projects under assessment, issued by organizations with the same credit rating as that of the equity investors in the data set. For rated companies, the credit rating quoted in *Bloomberg* was used to determine this. For unrated companies, the authors used a proxy creditworthiness merit class between BBB+ and BBB−, reflecting a recent analysis of project finance loan default and recovery rates by one of the main credit ratings agencies (Moody's 2010).[10] The cost of debt was calculated using the GBP Euro Bloomberg Fair Value curve function, as an average of five- and seven-year debt maturities.

As a final step, the authors collected data on the capital structure of each investor. For listed companies, the data were retrieved directly from *Bloomberg*. For unlisted sponsors, an average value of comparable companies' capital structure ratios was applied as a proxy for the typical debt/equity ratio in each of the relevant industries. As noted above, this analysis differs from previous CAPM analyses in comparing the Equity IRR to the cost of equity to the individual investor, rather than the cost of equity to the project overall. The authors estimated the mean difference between the WACC and the Equity IRR, and thus the level of excess return on this measure, at 9.27 per cent.

The results of this approach, together with the results of the other approaches used to evaluate the primary equity return on these 10 NHS PFI contracts through a comparison of IRRs and cost of equity, are shown in Table 3.4. Note that, under the hurdle rate approach, there are numerous costs of the equity benchmarks. Each project sponsor has a different WACC and thus hurdle rate.

Table 3.4 shows that project-specific cost of equity benchmarks are quite similar. Whether the cost of equity is constructed according to the *betas* of comparable industries, or taken from the discount rates applied by major DBFO investors in valuing their portfolios, the benchmark is estimated to be within the range 7.4 to 10.6 per cent. When a hurdle rate approach is applied, based on an estimate of the WACC of individual investors, the range is slightly higher, from 8.5 to 12.3 per cent. This is in line with expectations, given that corporate *betas* will normally be higher than is appropriate for PFI projects because of the higher level of systematic risk associated with the investor's core business activities. However, it is notable that, even on this highly conservative measure, the presence of excess returns is systematic.

Discussion and policy implications

Our analyses and those conducted by the NAO show a consistent pattern of excess profitability for primary equity investors in the UK DBFO market. In our view, the most likely source of excess return is the lack of competition in the market. Therefore, eliminating this source of inefficiency should be the focus of policy. A key policy challenge is the fragmented and unco-ordinated nature of

Table 3.4 Equity IRRs and benchmark costs of equity calculated according to the three methodologies

NHS trust/board	Equity IRR (%)	Cost of equity 'orthodox' (%)	Cost of equity 'hurdle rate' (%)	Cost of equity 'opportunistic' min – max (%)
1. North Cumbria	17.80	8.25	9.55, 11.84	8.09–10.59
2. Norfolk & Norwich	18.64	10.11	8.8, 9.48, 10.90, 11.55, 11.68	8.09–10.59
3. Durham & Darlington	14.50	9.46	9.87, 11.95	8.09–10.59
4. NHS Lanarkshire	22.58	8.20	8.52, 8.80	8.09–10.59
5. NHS Lanarkshire	20.25	8.32	8.62, 15.77	8.09–10.59
6. NHS Lothian	19.72	8.23	9.23, 10.25, 11.90	8.09–10.59
7. Nottingham University	14.79	7.44	10.04, 10.10, 17.62	7.37–9.87
8. Hull & East Yorkshire	13.86	8.25	9.54, 12.15	7.43–9.93
9. East/North Hertfordshire	15.86	7.63	9.59, 12.31	7.49–9.99
10. Sandwell/Birmingham	12.41	10.11	9.34, 9.65	7.54–10.04

Sources: Adapted from Hellowell and Vecchi (2012); Vecchi and Hellowell (forthcoming); and Vecchi *et al.* (forthcoming)

government procurement, however. Although in most developed economies the public sector accounts for a significant proportion of demand within construction, facilities management and project finance (i.e. the industries engaged within DBFO contracts), that demand is fragmented across individual public sector organizations, which often act in an unco-ordinated way. With fragmentation, the market power of suppliers may be hard to address, especially where ministers restrict access to public capital, thus eliminating the potential for alternative financing options.

In addition, by virtue of their multidimensional and long-term nature, DBFOs are complex procurements, so that a procurer's requirements cannot be specified in a simple way. This may lead to high transaction costs associated with searching for and negotiating with bidders, generating high barriers to entry and limited competitiveness (*econ* 2004). Dudkin and Välilä (2005) show that, on a sample of 55 PFI procurements in the UK (drawn from across the public sector), the combined pre-contractual transaction costs for the public sector and the winning bidder were, on average, 7 per cent of the total capital value of the project (split roughly equally between the public sector and the winning bidder). Where a concentration in market share leads to a reduction in the competition for contracts, this may confer substantial advantages on market players when bargaining with purchasers. As has been noted by the NAO (2007), it is the final phase of bidding, incorporating an *exclusive negotiation* between a single bidder and single purchaser, when transaction costs escalate most rapidly. Due to the sunk costs involved (an issue of greater salience for public authorities than for bidders, for whom the costs of losing bids are part of doing business), investors are in an advantageous position *vis-à-vis* the authority, in knowing that they are virtually guaranteed to secure the contract (Lonsdale and Watson 2007).

As the procurement process often fails to moderate the market power of major investors, reforming the process is a natural place to start in addressing excess returns. In the European Union, there is a view that the EU directives have increased transaction costs and barriers to entry by imposing a regulatory require-ment on contracting parties to agree the substantive terms of the bid before entering into exclusive negotiations (EPEC 2012). In the UK, the government has argued for 'an accelerated and cheaper procurement process' for PFIs (HM Treasury 2010). Yet, if the requirement to negotiate the bids in competitive condi-tions is removed, and the substantive negotiations over output specification and contract price take place in bilateral negotiations, this will undermine the contestability of the procurement auction. Indeed, it may be that the inherent complexity of DBFOs – and the need to secure external financing – will always constitute major obstacles to the success of any policy effort to make the procure-ment process faster and less costly.

Indeed, the structural constraints in the market for equity capital, and the inher-ently uncompetitive nature of the DBFO procurement process, imply that a change in, or expansion of, the regulatory regime may be required to drive investor returns down to the efficient level and thereby minimize the cost pres-sures generated by such contracts for public authorities. In sectors of the economy where competition is not plausible or not efficient (e.g. in network industries with significant economies of scale), government intervention in the form of economic regulation is widespread and the rationale for it in terms of correcting market fail-ures is widely accepted by economists and policy-makers.

Under many versions of price regulation, for example, regulators set the price a utility can charge so as to enable investors in that utility to earn only a specified maximum rate of return (Helm 2009). This 'fair' rate of return is set according to the regulator's assessment of the utility's WACC (with the cost of equity derived through the CAPM along with consideration of the company's effective cost of debt, taxation and gearing) (ibid.). It is evident from earlier sections of this chap-ter that a similar approach could be developed for SPVs undertaking DBFOs. Specifically, the application of capital budgeting methods developed in this chap-ter could be used to recalibrate unitary charges on future projects so as to generate cashflows sufficient to provide a 'fair', rather than an excess, return to investors of equity capital.

Interestingly, the UK government review of PFIs, being undertaken at the time of writing, specifically asks respondents to consider the role of regulating the equity return (HM Treasury 2011b). It acknowledges that 'in other markets, approaches are taken to limiting or regulating the economically efficient level of return that can be made by investors in infrastructure networks and services' (p.8) and asks interested parties to comment on whether regulation, capping or sharing of returns above a particular level 'would be more economically efficient' than market pricing (p. 9). Such measures also appear to have some support from prominent individuals within the PFI policy-making community. James Stewart, a former chief executive of Partnerships UK and Infrastructure UK and the current head of Infrastructure Advisory Services at KPMG, has suggested that by regulating the cashflows to equity the cost of capital could be reduced significantly (Stewart 2009). In a similar vein, Nick Prior, currently head of infrastructure at the financial consultancy group Deloitte (and a former head of PFI at the Ministry of Defence), has suggested that regulating the rate of return would reduce the level of political opposition to the PFI programme (Prior 2009).

Regulation of the equity return is likely to become a more important concern of policy as the proportion of equity to debt in the capital structure is increased. A less heavily geared structure is likely to have a number of advantages, for example in enhancing the flexibility of the project finance model, an important concern in areas of public service such as healthcare, in which changes in technology and clinical practice are rapid and changes in the specification of services agreed within long-term contracts are inevitable. In addition, the change in capital structure should serve to 'de-risk' DBFO contracts from the perspective of the debt-holder and enable a greater diversity of debt providers to enter the market. Given the structural problems of the banking sector, this is necessary. From the perspective of the equity return it is also be desirable since, as discussed in previous sections, the scale of excess profitability can partly be attributed to the extreme risk aversion of the major banks.

In addition, it is important to recognize that regulatory intervention may be required throughout the contract period, and not just at the point that contracts are signed and base case rates of return agreed. As noted elsewhere (Hellowell 2011), a private firm in charge of services over a 30-year contract is likely to find opportunities to reduce operational costs within the period. Of the services included within the DBFO structure, only support services such as catering and cleaning are routinely benchmarked or market-tested during the contract period. Typically (for example, under the current version of the UK *Standardisation of PFI Contracts Guidance* (HM Treasury 2009)), there is no mechanism under which the gains from efficiencies in maintenance or life-cycle management can be shared with authorities. As a result, any gains accrue to equity holders in their entirety and this may increase the return on equity substantially beyond the rate agreed at financial close. Along with the gains from refinancing and secondary market sales, it is likely that this is the source of the skewed distribution of returns around their expected value (i.e. the tendency of IRRs to overshoot the return forecast by investors in financial models) as discussed earlier in the section on efficiency of equity returns.

This is undesirable of itself, but may also lead to opportunistic behaviour. Currently, where 'soft' facilities management services are benchmarked/market-tested, there is an incentive for a bidder (working within the context of a strict public sector budget constraint) to under-price this element of the services at the point of financial close, while over-pricing the hard facilities management services (i.e. build in a margin above the market level). When, in subsequent years, the price of the soft facilities management services are benchmarked, this often leads to the price going up (NAO 2010). The public sector then pays a *current* market price for soft services and an *above*-market price for hard facilities management, and it will pay this latter price for the entirety of the contract term.[11]

One option would be to examine the potential for broadening the benchmarking/market-testing process to include all services. However, this is complex. For example, there would be a need to consider how the prices paid for maintenance services interact with the costs of life-cycle replacement and, in practice, this may not be possible. A simpler, and potentially more effective, method would be to ensure that any free cashflow to equity investors in excess of that required to provide equity investors with the rate of return projected at finan- cial close is *shared with the public sector*. This would ensure both that the private sector retains an incentive to invest in productivity gains in maintenance (since they would have a partial claim to the resources this generated) but that the bene- fits from this accrue across all project stakeholders. Just as regulation could be used to address efficiency problems that arise from fragmented demand and concentrated supply for new DBFOs, an attempt to co-ordinate the management of existing contracts may assist in managing the ongoing costs, to ensure that excess returns are not being made at the expense of public authorities, many of which are now operating in a context of severe budgetary pressure.

In a recent paper, Jensen and Blanc-Brude (2010) suggest a national regulator, modelled broadly on the lines of independent utility regulators, and employing a form of RPI-X incentive regulation and well-established techniques of compara- tive competition, would provide the best institutional structure for regulating DBFO contracts. However, where institutional structures are well developed, the need for a new regulatory agency is not clear. In particular, where standard contracts exist (such as the UK Treasury's *Standardisation of PFI Contracts*) these may well provide the most convenient, and possibly the most efficient, means of regulating primary equity returns. One of the functions of standard contracts is to spell out the government's favoured model of risk allocation. Currently, the standard contract specifies the transfer of construction and avail- ability risk to the private sector counter-party, as well as the general risks of assets ownership (HM Treasury 2009). For this standard model, an allowable range in the reasonable return could be specified. The standard contract could also, through relatively minor amendments to existing clauses, ensure that any free cashflow to equity in excess of that required to provide investors with the return projected at financial close is shared with the authority.

Of course, it is one thing for central government to announce changes to stan- dard contracts and a regulated return, it is quite another to persuade the private sector to accept this. Therefore, the consolidation of the public sector purchasing function is likely to be a prerequisite for any regulatory action to succeed. Making full use of the government's considerable market power in the construction, facil- ities management and project finance markets will be required. Examples of good practice in centralized procurement do exist. For example, there is a much greater degree of centralization in the Republic of Ireland, where the National Development Finance Agency is responsible for delivering all aspects of DBFO programmes undertaken by government departments. Within the UK, the Scottish Futures Trust, which is taking forward a pipeline of DBFOs worth £2.5 billion on behalf of the Scottish government, has also sought to reduce the fragmentation of the public sector's purchasing function, with the explicit aim of maximizing the amount of investment secured for a fixed proportion of its revenue budget allocated to paying for DBFO contracts (Scottish Government 2011). By consolidating the public purchasing function, standardizing initial rates of return on an appropriate CAPM basis, and ensuring that actual returns converge to the acceptable level throughout the contract, policy-makers can eliminate the problem of excess returns on the (increasingly prominent) equity element of a project's capital investment. This is likely to yield significant financial benefits for individual public authorities involved. It will then fall to them to put adequate monitoring mechanisms in place to ensure that the quality of construction and service delivery is in line with contracted standards.

Concluding remarks

The DBFO procurement process takes too long and costs too much. It represents a barrier to entry for investors such as pension funds and is thus a key source of market concentration. Consequently, it cannot be assumed that competition in the procurement of contracts is sufficient to ensure efficiency in rates of return to investors. In sectors of the economy where competition is similarly unachievable, the rationale for regulating the return to equity is widely accepted by economists and policy-makers. Therefore, the case for regulating returns in the DBFO market ought to command broad support – and there are indications that this is, indeed, the case. In the UK, standard contracts, mandated by central government, outline a particular approach to the allocation of risk between public and private sectors. There is no reason why these contracts cannot also stipulate a range of expected returns appropriate to that allocation. Because of its dominance in corporate finance practice, the CAPM provides the most acceptable method for doing this. And since there is a consistent pattern of actual returns overshooting those projected at financial close, there is also a need for sharing returns above the level stipulated in contracts. Equity investors are more likely to accept sharing returns above the CAPM-determined level rather than accept a regulated maximum, since this would significantly increase downside risk at the portfolio level. Again, adjustments to the standard contract are the most appropriate method for stipulating how such a sharing mechanism should operate. If the Treasury uses its current review to regulate equity returns, it may be able to lower the overall cost of capital for privately financed contracts while increasing the proportion of equity in the DBFO capital structure, which is likely to be a prerequisite to achieving the government's central infrastructure policy objective: getting pension funds and other institutional investors into the market, and to replace the banks that no longer lend at a cost-effective rate of interest.

Notes

1   At a recent evidence session of the Public Accounts Committee (at which one of the authors – MH – also gave evidence), Geoffrey Spence, the chief executive of Infrastructure UK, which leads Treasury policy on the PFI, said: 'Capital market issues... could be the cheapest form of long-term debt finance that is available going forward. Increasingly, they will have to be A-rated bond issues. If they're A-rated bond issues, it's necessary for the leverage of these [i.e. project companies] to be lower than it has been' (Q.159) (House of Commons 2012).

2   The Internal Rate of Return on a project is that rate which, when applied as a discount rate to a stream of projected cashflows, produces a Net Present Value (NPV) of zero. As an alternative, a firm may calculate the NPV with a discount rate set equal to its cost of capital. A positive NPV project increases the value of the firm.

3   Investors expect their return over the life of the project to be volatile. Large debt payments, high fixed costs, and the way that investors receive the residual cashflow value remaining in the project when it is complete, mean that small changes in the cashflows can have large effects on the equity return (National Audit Office 2012). Although equity investors transfer most cost-related risk to their contractors, they remain exposed to a range of risks. For example, early or late delivery of construction can lead to large changes in the equity return. This may imply that a significant proportion of the variance is the result of infrequent extreme deviations, as opposed to frequent modestly sized deviations.

4   In the UK at least, interest rate risk in DBFO contracts is substantially hedged through the use of interest rate swaps, which effectively provide the SPV with fixed-rate funding (HM Treasury 2007). The periodic payment to the private sector is also linked by some ratio to the rate of inflation, such that the potential for returns to be reduced by unexpected inflation is limited. Where contracts specify a high level of indexation (and a ratio of 100 per cent is not uncommon in the UK) (HM Treasury 2006), it is possible that the nominal value of investor returns will be lower than initially expected. However, in most cases this risk is hedged by investors through the use of inflation swaps, which provide greater certainty over cashflow (Yescombe 2008).

5   As a result of this report, the Treasury negotiated arrangements with investors to share refinancing gains, and increases in returns of this scale have not arisen in more recent contracts (National Audit Office 2012).

6   Equity betas were unleveraged through the use of the standard formula: *asset* beta = *equity* beta $\div$ *[1 + (1 – tax rate) $\times$ (amount of debt $\div$ amount of equity)]*.

7   In effect, reversing the process in which the sectoral asset *betas* were derived from the observable equity *betas*, thus: *equity* beta = *asset* beta $\times$ *[1 + (1 – tax rate) $\times$ (amount of debt $\div$ amount of equity)]*.

8   The effect of the Blume adjustment is to reduce the difference between the *beta* and the market average (i.e. 1). Blume (1971) found that adjusting estimated equity *betas* toward unity improved their ability to forecast subsequent period stock returns. He found that the tendency towards unity is well described by the following: (0.67) $\times$ βOLS + (0.33) $\times$ 1. This was the formula applied to the equity *beta* in the study.

9   This is the total yield to maturity of the asset, including the repayment of principal. Daily prices and yields are as reported by the UK Debt Management Office (http://www.dmo.gov.uk/index.aspx?page=Gilts/Daily_Prices).

10   This study is based on a data set which includes 2,639 project finance contracts (accounting for 45 per cent of project finance projects globally originated during a period from January 1983 to December 2008).

11   With thanks to Peter Reekie, Finance Director of the Scottish Futures Trust, for this important insight.

References

Arrow, K. and Lind, R. (1970) Uncertainty and the Evaluation of Public Investment Decisions. *American Economic Review,* June, pp. 364–78.

Blume, M. E. (1971) On the Assessment of Risk. *The Journal of Finance*, March, pp. 1–10.

Competition Commission (2010) *Market Investigation References: Competition Commission Guidelines.* London: Competition Commission.

Croce, R. D. (2011) Pension Funds Investment in Infrastructure: Policy Actions. *OECD Working Papers on Finance, Insurance and Private Pensions*, No. 13. Paris: OECD.

Dimson, E., Marsh, P. and Staunton, M. (2002) *Triumph of the Optimists: 101 Years of Global Investment Returns.* Princeton, NJ: Princeton University Press.

Dudkin, G. and Välilä, T. (2005) Transaction Costs in Public–Private Partnerships: A First Look at the Evidence. *EIB Economic and Financial Report 2005/03.* European Investment Bank, Luxemburg.

econ (2004) *Assessing the Impact of Public Sector Procurement on Competition.* London: Office of Fair Trading.

European Public–Private-Partnerships Expertise Centre (EPEC) (2011) *Risk Distribution and Balance Sheet Treatment: Practical Guide* (available at: http://www.eib.org/epec/, accessed 6 December 2011).

EPEC (2012) *Market Update: Review of the European PPP Market in 2012* (available at: http://www.eib.org/epec, accessed 1 April 2011).

Fama, E. and French, K. (1992) The Cross Section of Expected Stock Returns. *Journal of Finance*, 47: 427–65.

Graham, J. R. and Harvey, C. (2002) How Do CFOs Make Capital Budgeting and Capital Structure Decisions? *Journal of Applied Corporate Finance*, 15: 8–23

Gregory, A. and Michou, M. (2009) Industry Cost of Equity Capital: UK Evidence. *Journal of Business Finance and Accounting*, 36: 679–704

Hellowell, M. and Vecchi, V. (2012) An Evaluation of the Projected Returns to Investors on 10 PFI Projects Commissioned by the National Health Service. *Financial Accountability and Management,* 28(1): 77–100.

Hellowell, M. (2011) Box 3: Returns on PFI investment, in Treasury Select Committee *Private Finance Initiative.* London: The Stationery Office.

Helm, D. (2009) Infrastructure Investment, The Cost of Capital, and Regulation: An Assessment. *Oxford Review of Economic Policy*, 25(3): 307–26.

Hirshleifer, J. (1958) On the Theory of Optimal Investment Decision. *Journal of Political Economy*, 66: 329–52.

HM Treasury (2006) *Interest Rate and Inflation Risks in PFI Contracts* (available at: http://www.hm-treasury.gov.uk/d/pfi_hedging120506.pdf, accessed 1 April 2011).

HM Treasury (2007) *Quantitative Assessment User Guidance: User Guide* (available at: http://www.hm-treasury.gov.uk/ppp_vfm_index.htm. accessed 1 April 2011).

HM Treasury (2009) *Standardisation of PFI contracts. Version 4 (updated)* (available at: http://www.hm-treasury.gov.uk/ppp_standardised_contracts.htm, accessed 6 December 2011).

HM Treasury (2010) *HM Treasury Review of Competitive Dialogue* (available at: http://www.hm-treasury.gov.uk/d/ppp_competitive_dialogue.pdf, accessed 1 April 2011).

HM Treasury (2011a) *National Infrastructure Plan 2011* (available at: http://www.hm-treasury.gov.uk/national_infrastructure_plan2011.htm, accessed 6 December 2011).

HM Treasury (2011b) *Reform of the Private Finance Initiative* (available at: http://www.hm-treasury.gov.uk/d.conduc_pfi_call_for_evidence.pdf).

House of Commons (2012) *Uncorrected Evidence – HC-1846i* (available at: http://www.publications.parliament.uk/pa/cm201012/cmselect/cmpubacc/uc1846-i/uc184601.htm, accessed 15 March 2012).

Inderst, G. (2009) Pension Fund Investment in Infrastructure. *OECD Working Papers on Insurance and Private Pensions*, No. 32, Paris: OECD Publishing.

Jenkinson, T. (2003) Private Finance. Oxford Review of Economic Policy, 19(2): 323–34.

Jensen, M. and Meckling, W. (1976) Theory of the Firm: Managerial Behaviour, Agency Costs and Capital Structure. *Journal of Financial Economics*, 3: 305–60.

Jensen, O. and Blanc-Brude, F. J. (2010) *Why the PFI Needs a Regulator.* London: Infrastructure Economics.

Lintner, J. (1965) The Valuation of Risk Assets and the Selection of Risky Investments in Stock Portfolios and Capital Budgets. *Review of Economics and Statistics*, 47: 226–37.

Lonsdale, C. and Watson, G. (2007) Managing Contracts under the Private Finance Initiative. *Policy and Politics*, 35(4): 683–700.

Markowitz, H. (1952) Portfolio Selection. *The Journal of Finance,* 7(1): 77–91.

Mehra, R. and Prescott, E. (1985) The Equity Premium: A Puzzle. *Journal of Monetary Economics*, 15(2): 145–61.

Modigliani, F. and Miller, M. (1958) The Cost of Capital, Corporation Finance, and the Theory of Investment. *American Economic Review,* 48: 261–97.

Moody's (2010) *Default and Recovery Rates for Project Finance Bank Loans, 1983–2008.* London: Moody's Investors Services (available at: http://www.moodys.com/research documentcontentpage.aspx?docid=PBC_123903, accessed 1 April 2011).

National Audit Office (NAO) (2005) *The Refinancing of the Norfolk and Norwich PFI Hospital: How the Deal can be Viewed in the Light of the Refinancing.* London: The Stationery Office (available: www.nao.org.uk/publications, accessed 1 April 2011).

NAO (2007) *Improving the PFI Tendering Process.* London: The Stationery Office (available at: www.nao.org.uk/publications, accessed 1 April 2011).

NAO (2010) *The Performance and Management of Hospital PFI Projects.* London: The Stationery Office (available: www.nao.org.uk/publications, accessed 1 April 2011).

NAO (2012) *Equity Investment in Privately Financed Projects.* London: The Stationery Office (available: www.nao.org.uk/publications, accessed 15 March 2012).

PricewaterhouseCoopers and Franks, J. (2002) *Study into Rates of Return Bid on PFI Projects.* The Office of Government Commerce. London: The Stationery Office.

Prior, N. (2009) Tories be Bold. *Partnerships Bulletin*, 7 April. London: Rockliffe Publishing (available at: http://partnershipsbulletin.co.uk/features/view/891, accessed 10 July 2010).

Scottish Government (2011) *Spending Review and Draft Budget* (available at: http://www.scotland.gov.uk/Resource/Doc/358356/0121130.pdf, accessed 1 September 2011).

Sharpe, W. F. (1964) Capital Asset Prices: A Theory of Market Equilibrium under Conditions of Risk. *Journal of Finance*, 19: 4254–442.

Shleifer, A. and Vishny, R. (1997) A Survey of Corporate Governance. *The Journal of Finance*, 52(2): 737–61.

Spackman, M. (2001) *Risk and the Cost of Risk in the Comparison on Public and Private Financing of Public Services.* London: National Economic Research Associates.

Stewart, J. (2009) How New Procurement Approaches will Transform the Delivery of

Public Services. Speech to the Partnerships UK annual conference, 15 October. London: City and Financial.

Threlfall, R. (2011) PFI Review – Government Should Encourage UK Pensions Funds to Invest in Infrastructure. *The Telegraph*, 18 November, p. 12.

Vecchi, V. and Hellowell, M. (forthcoming) 'Securing a Better Deal from Investors in Public Infrastructure Projects: Insights from Capital Budgeting. *Public Management Review*.

Vecchi, V., Hellowell, M. and Gatti, S. (forthcoming) Do Private Sponsors Extract too Much Value from Public Private Partnerships? Evidence from the UK Health Sector. SDA Bocconi School of Management Working Paper.

Yescombe, E. R. (2008) *Public–Private Partnerships: Principles of Policy and Finance*. London: Elsevier Finance.

4 Mind the gap

Accountability and value for money in public–private partnerships in Ireland

Eoin Reeves

Introduction

Governments around the world face ongoing pressure to invest in physical infra-structure as they strive to encourage economic growth and improve competitiveness as well as rising to the challenges posed by factors such as tech-nological progress, ageing populations, urbanization and migration, security concerns, and environmental issues (Stevens and Schieb 2007). Given the public finance pressures faced by most countries (which have been heightened by the global financial crisis) there are constraints on the scope for public investment in infrastructure. As a consequence, the participation of the private sector in the provision of physical infrastructure and related services has become an attractive policy option. Such arrangements, which are commonly referred to as private sector participation (PSP) or public–private partnership (PPP), have seen increased private sector involvement in the delivery of public infrastructure and services in sectors such as health, education, transport, and environmental serv-ices such as water and waste management services.

Wettenhall (2010) describes how 'public–private mixing has existed since the beginnings of organized government...But it has flourished again in the recent period, as the evolution of governance systems has required governments to develop new roles as they share significant power and influence with market institutions and civil society (p. 17). In this sense the adoption of PPP in the form of long-term infrastructure contracts (LTICs)[1] can be viewed as one of the many initiatives adopted as part of the ongoing commercialization and privatization of public services, particularly over the last 30 years (Prasad 2006).

Among the many challenges arising from increased commercialization and privatization are those of accountability and transparency. The shift towards greater private sector involvement in public service delivery weakens the thread of accountability between citizens, parliament and those responsible for service delivery (executive government). As a consequence the rise in popularity of PPP has often been accompanied by reasonably well developed institutional frame-works that incorporate formal accountability mechanisms such as *ex ante* appraisal of procurement options (value for money (VfM) testing), detailed contract documents and formal auditing mechanisms, which provide the scope for *ex post* performance review. Despite the establishment of such frameworks, concerns about the quality of accountability remain widespread. Demirag and Khadaroo summarize these concerns in the context of the Private Finance Initiative (PFI) in the UK:

> Despite the many claimed advantages of PFI contracts relating to accountability and VfM, critics of PFI argue that the commercial confidentiality and secrecy of the contractual process hinder accountability and the assessment of VfM (Edwards, Shaoul, Stafford and Arblaster 2004). Ball, Heafey and King (2001), for example, indicate that there is a lack of objectivity, clarity and information on the methodology for preparing the Public Sector Comparator (PSC) and the basis of risk transfer remains unresolved (Broadbent, Gill and Laughlin 2003). Newberry and Pallot (2003) point out that PFI contracts provide governments with 'a means of escaping' from public and parliamentary scrutiny as the liabilities arising from PFI contracts are excluded from public sector liabilities and estimates.
>
> (Demirag and Khadaroo 2008: 456)

This chapter examines the question of accountability and transparency in the context of the PPP experience in the Republic of Ireland. Since 1999 the PPP model has been adopted for the procurement of over 100 infrastructure projects, making Ireland one of the world leaders in terms of PPP activity (measured in terms of national income and gross domestic capital formation). More specifically, this chapter examines the practice of PPP procurement in Ireland in terms of the extent to which they satisfy official guidelines designed to safeguard accountability. In particular it focuses on the question of value for money. Official documents articulating PPP policy in Ireland emphasize VfM as a key objective of the PPP model. Moreover, a detailed framework has been established to ensure the appraisal of potential PPP projects in terms of VfM. The practice of PPP assessment is therefore examined in addition to other aspects of accountability including contract management, auditing and accountability to Parliament.

PPP: economic objectives, accountability and transparency

Governments adopting PPP tend to offer similar economic justifications for adopting this model instead of more direct forms of public provision. One of the key justifications for PPPs is that they serve to control public expenditure. Eurostat rules dictate that under appropriate conditions (concerning risk transfer), PPP investments in the Eurozone do not count towards public borrowing; infrastructure is thereby provided through off-balance-sheet financing (Eurostat 2004). Second, where PPPs are structured on the basis of private finance, governments can avoid up-front capital costs. Spreading these costs over a longer period can assist in meeting fiscal targets. A third rationale for PPP is that they provide a model for delivering infrastructure and services at lower cost (VfM) resulting primarily from superior private sector scale efficiencies and technical efficiency

(Vining *et al.* 2005). A key driver of VfM is the scope for risk transfer under PPP. This scope for risk transfer provides a fourth argument in favour of PPP. If risks are appropriately allocated between public and private contractors, this provides an alignment of incentives that encourages greater efficiency. A fifth justification for PPPs is that they provide scope for better innovation and accrual of dynamic efficiencies as bids are tendered on the basis of an output specification instead of detailed input specifications that characterize traditional procurement.

Whether PPPs succeed or fail in the achievement of these objectives is open to question. Evaluations of PPP outcomes have only started to emerge in recent years. These tend to focus on the question of VfM, and while the findings tend to be mixed, the quality of evaluations is undermined by the fact that most PPP contracts are at early stages and there are no published studies based on statistical analysis of a reliable sample of PPP projects.

Accountability is an important issue in the PPP debate. As PPPs are institutions 'exercising public powers, using public resources and providing public services, they need to be accountable to those on whose behalf they act' (Jones and Stewart 2009: 59). Accountability is considered the obligation to account for activities to another person or body. Using the language of Behn (2001), the accountability *holder* is accountable to the accountability *holdee*. Behn acknowledges how the accountability holder may not be able to define what accountability means but the holdee knows that 'accountability means punishment' (2001: 3). In the context of PPP, the public sector client is both a holder and holdee. The client is responsible for making the contractor accountable for performance in accordance with a written contract. However, the client is ultimately accountable (to some degree) to Parliament and the wider citizenry for service delivery and its management of the PPP.

Transparency serves to improve accountability. The more accessible and assessable PPP arrangements are, the greater the degree of vertical accountability within the policy process and horizontal accountability among interested parties and stakeholders. The importance of accountability and transparency is recognized in most jurisdictions. Barrett (2003) notes that in the case of Australia, accountability and transparency rank with VfM as a core principle of procurement under PPP. Demirag and Khadaroo (2008) review government publications in the UK that emphasize the importance of transparency and accountability. PFI contracts are claimed to make improvements in this regard. For example, HM Treasury claims that

> the presentation of the conclusions and recommendations to decision makers and key stakeholders can be as important as the analysis itself. In all cases, transparency is vital. Presentations and reports should be clear, logical, well founded, and geared towards helping the decision at hand...
>
> (HM Treasury 2003a: 6)

> This [transparency] will not only lead to better management of programmes and projects in the future, but also increases the accountability and openness of the programme.
>
> (HM Treasury 2003b: 92)

Despite these claims, the international experience suggests that PPPs are characterized by shortcomings *vis-à-vis* expectations in this regard. In their review of the international experience with PPP, Hodge and Greve (2007) note that:

> PPPs also seem to have provided only limited levels of transparency or public participation. With limited transparency and complex adjustment formulae in PPPs, the clarity of partnership arrangements can also be difficult to fathom. This does not give citizens confidence in the arrangements, when despite the rhetoric of risk sharing with private financing, a significant financial role for the government is often the reality (p. 552).

It is, however, worth noting that deficiencies in relation to issues of transparency and accountability are not confined to the PPP model of procurement. Flyvbjerg *et al.* (2003), in their comprehensive analysis of the procurement of mega-projects (largely conventionally procured in the transport sector), attribute the serious problem of cost overruns[2] on conventionally procured projects to factors including, *inter alia*:

- the relegation of discussions of policy objectives to be achieved by projects and an over-emphasis on technical alternatives from the beginning;
- limited involvement of negatively affected stakeholder groups and the general public impact in terms of setting performance standards;
- the absence of risk analysis;
- the lack of definition of the regulatory regime that will apply to a project and the consequence of this for risks and costs and for the overall appraisal and decision-making process.

Whereas Flyvbjerg *et al.* did consider privatization and PPP models as an alternative to conventional procurement, they did not conclude that this provided a panacea for risk and accountability problems:

> [However], given an appropriate and properly implemented institutional framework, private involvement may be helpful in certain ways, although the experience of private sector involvement in transport infrastructure is still too limited to allow firm conclusions.
>
> (Flyvbjerg *et al.* 2003: 104)

The following section considers some of the elements of what Flyvbjerg *et al.* refer to as a 'properly implemented institutional framework', focusing in particular on mechanisms that improve accountability under PPP.

Mechanisms for accountability under PPP

As PPP arrangements become more and more popular, governments employ a number of mechanisms in order to achieve accountability. This section describes some of the basic mechanisms focusing in particular on accountability in the context of the VfM process at the *ex ante* and *ex post* stages of the contract life cycle.

Ex ante *accountability – value for money testing and competition for contracts*

Prior to awarding PPP contracts, important decisions must be made by the public sector client with regard to the financial case for PPP and the conduct of the tendering process. One of the key elements of mechanisms for making the public sector client accountable under PPP is the VfM assessment process. Ball *et al.* (2007: 295) define VfM in the context of the PFI as:

> related to the idea that the PFI scheme can produce a flow of services of at least equivalent quality to that which could be provided by the public sector, but at a lower overall cost (taking into account, particularly the allocation of risk).

The VfM test is consistent with a narrow 'agency' form of accountability which Demirag and Khadaroo (2008) explain

> is mostly concerned with the 'external' processes for defining and regulating the behaviour of the agent to foster congruence with the expectations of the principal(s) (Gray and Jenkins 1993; Broadbent, Dietrich and Laughlin 1996; and Gray, Dey, Owen, Evans and Zadek 1997). It does not deal with the changing needs of the different interest groups even though it explores how and what forms of accountability the agent is willing to acknowledge, prioritize and discharge (Gray *et al.* 1997: 333).
>
> (Demirag and Khadaroo 2008: 457)

The VfM test is designed to make the public sector client accountable for its decision to adopt PPP. It is consistent with Behn's (2001) perspective on public sector accountability insofar as it covers the question of finances, but its effectiveness in this regard depends on the rigour applied in conducting the test and the extent to which the VfM process is transparent.

Focusing on the conduct of the VfM test, a quantitative assessment of VfM generally involves a comparison of the cost of the PPP with a hypothetical scenario that estimates the net present value (NPV) of the expected life-cycle cost if the project were to be pursued by traditional procurement (Morallos and Amekudzi 2008). This hypothetical scenario, which is generally referred to as the public sector comparator (PSC), has been the subject of some critique in the PPP literature. A full discussion of such issues is beyond the scope of this chapter but it is important to emphasize that a number of authors have drawn attention to vagueness around the VfM concept and pitfalls associated with the implementation of VfM tests (Heald 2003; Hodge and Greve 2007; Boardman and Vining 2010). Specific concerns in this regard include the possibility of errors in estimating cost and revenue flows and associated probabilities. In addition, the identification and quantification of risks is an inexact exercise and there is evidence to suggest that this element of the VfM exercise can be used to swing decisions in favour of preferred outcomes (Ball *et al.* 2001). It has been argued that the PSC concentrates on aspects that can be easily quantified and expressed in monetary terms and that insufficient attention is paid to issues such as service quality (Kintoye *et al.* 2002). Moreover, the importance of transaction costs in the context of PPP procurement has been highlighted by a number of writers (Lonsdale 2005; Reeves 2008) and this aspect is rarely given adequate attention in VfM assessments. The Commission on PPPs in the UK (2001) has drawn attention to the questions of transparency and accountability in relation to VfM assessments. They recommend that, at the very least, a PSC should be constructed and that the PSC should be discussed regularly throughout the negotiation process and should be fully disclosed at the appropriate time. VfM decisions can therefore be 'assumed to be a function of accountability. More and better accountability is therefore expected to yield improved VfM decisions (assuming resources input (sic) remains the same) in PFI' (Demirag *et al.* 2004: 15).

Another mechanism for achieving accountability at the *ex ante* stage is competition for contracts. This is a key element of market-based reforms such as PPP (Demsetz 1968) and a well-managed tendering process can enhance overall accountability by creating competitive tensions that encourage the private sector to innovate and deliver VfM. Obstacles to competition, such as opportunistic behaviour, loss-leading or collusion, must however, be recognized (Sappington and Stiglitz 1987) and safeguarding against these dangers presents a significant challenge of accountability to partners in the public sector.

Ex post *accountability – the contract document and contract management*

Achieving accountability under PPP requires the recognition on the public sector side that its responsibility for contract management does not end once the contract has been awarded. PPPs require monitoring, supervision, performance measurement and relationship management following the execution of contractual agreements and over the life of the contract. The contract document is the principal instrument for regulating the relationship between the public agency and private contractor and therefore serves as an important tool of accountability. As the duration of PPP arrangements can run for decades, accountability depends heavily on factors including the procedures and decision rules included in the original agreement. These include mechanisms for enforcing risk transfer, rewarding success and punishing underperformance (e.g. penalty points, payments deductions). The role of the contract should not, however, be overstated. The long-time duration and (sometimes) complex nature of PPP arrangements increase the likelihood of relational contracting, and the literature on incomplete contracting and socio-legal theory illuminate a host of extra-contractual mechanisms, such as trust and reciprocity, that also serve to regulate the public–private relationship (Vincent-Jones 2006).

Effective contract management demands an adequate stock of public sector skills, which allows public sector clients to strike a balance between enforcing the agreement while maintaining co-operative relations. As Forrer *et al.* (2010) assert:

> PPPs need to be stewarded by the government in order to ensure that public interests are met throughout the arrangement. '[T]he public partner should seek a leadership role that defines the tenor of the partnership' (Ghere 2001: 448). Thus, while both partners develop interdependence in the partnership, ensuring public accountability requires government to play an upper hand. This requires public managers to be aware of various dimensions of public sector accountability (p. 479).

External oversight: auditing and accountability to Parliament

As the public and private sectors converge and the management environment becomes complex, concerns for public accountability intensify. Whereas the contract document serves to make the private contractor accountable, the question of accountability of public sector clients also arises. Oversight by independent auditors and Parliament takes on increased importance in this regard. According to Pat Barrett, former Auditor General for Australia, 'Auditors-General are an essential element of the accountability process by providing that unique blend of independence, objectivity and professionalism to the work they do' (2003: 21). However, the extent to which Auditors-General can effectively safeguard the public interest can be constrained in the context of PPP.

Among the challenges faced by Auditors-General is the need to fully understand the transactions being undertaken by agencies in order to conduct VfM reports, as well as examining the appropriateness of the methods of accounting for transactions. A team of experienced officers who understand the commercial nature of the transactions and the overlaying public accountability issues is therefore required.

Difficulties in accessing information about PPP contracts present another obstacle for independent auditors (as well as independent researchers). Increased private sector involvement, through contractual arrangements, in activities traditionally undertaken by the public sector can lead to a reduction in the flow of information available to assess performance and satisfy accountability. This can arise where performance data is held exclusively by the private sector or where the private sector makes claims in relation to commercial confidentiality that seek to limit or exclude the availability of information from the wider public or the oversight of Parliament. Most confidentiality claims regarding contracts are claims about the commercial sensitivity of the material. As PPPs are, essentially, long-term contractual arrangements, this issue is of considerable significance to the maintenance of accountability. Partnerships with government need to be open, well documented and conducted with integrity – not only because the public has a right to know how public funds are spent, but also because anything less may expose the state to litigation, thereby imposing costs and undermining public confidence.

Public agencies that are parties to PPP contracts also have obligations to be accountable to Parliament. The proliferation of long-term PPP contracts, however, raises concerns about the extent to which parties fulfil these obligations. Barrett (2003) draws attention to how these concerns have arisen in the Australian context as a result of difficulties that parliaments have experienced in gaining access to relevant documentation relating to PPP arrangements. He cites the example, in relation to the M2 motorway project in New South Wales, where the parliament was denied access to the contract deed between the public sector roads authority and the private sector counterpart. Similar situations have arisen in other jurisdictions. A number of issues arise therefore in relation to parliamentary oversight. These include the powers of Parliament (or parliamentary committees) to access information in relation to aspects such as tendering procedures, bid evaluation and contract documents. In addition, there are issues in relation to the extent to which information can be withheld from Parliament on the grounds of commercial confidentiality and the extent that Parliament will go to compel the attendance of witness and the production of relevant documentation.[3]

Overall, the essential characteristic of accountability is access to information. Virtually all accountability relies on transparency and the availability of reliable and timely information. Information is the lifeblood of accountability. The logical conclusion in this regard is well articulated by Flyvbjerg *et al.* (2003) who assert that:

> The role of government is, in principle, to protect the public interest (as defined by Parliament or legal precedent) and therefore it must at all times be possible for the public to verify whether this is indeed the case. The transparency requirement means, *inter alia*, that all documents and other information prepared by the government and its agencies should be made available to the public... it is hard to find legitimate reasons for not informing citizens fully about projects, and for not letting citizens have a say concerning what they think about them. Consequently, two-way communication with civil society, and with stakeholder groups and media, should be given high priority.
>
> (2003: 111)

Ensuring that the PPP model meets required standards of public accountability is a key challenge and central to the legitimacy of PPP as a form of governance. As PPP is a relatively recent phenomenon, the evidence in relation to this question is scarce. The remainder of this paper examines this issue in the context of the Republic of Ireland where PPPs have played an increasingly important role in the delivery of infrastructure and asset-backed public services over the last decade.

PPP activity in Ireland

Ireland has followed the global trend towards PPPs for the provision of infra-structure and asset-backed services. On the basis of available data, we estimate that there were 101 PPP projects at different stages of the procurement and project life cycle in December 2011. Table 4.1 shows that PPP is being adopted in areas including, *inter alia*, road and rail transport, waste management (including incineration), education (school and university buildings), health (a national radiotherapy network), social and affordable housing, and courts facilities. While the scale of PPP investment appears ambitious, it can be noted that progress to date has been slow with just 11 projects (outside the water and waste-water sector) at the stage where assets are in operation.

The planned scale and reach of Ireland's PPP programme has expanded significantly since the first PPP projects were announced in 1999. Although reliable comparable data is difficult to source, Deloitte (2007) and the Irish Business Employers Council (2009) have both published reports that claim that Ireland is a world leader in terms of PPP activity. Ireland therefore presents a useful case study for examining the extent to which the PPP model satisfies standards of public accountability.

Table 4.1 PPP projects in Ireland in December 2011

	Pre-tender[a]	Procurement	Construction	Operation	Total
Roads	0	0	0	9	9
Rail	3	1	0	0	4
Waste management	1	1	0	0	2
Courts	1	0	1	0	2
Education	4	0	1	4	9
Health	1	0	0	0	1
Arts	1	1	1	0	3
Prisons	2	0	0	0	2
Housing	0	0	0	1	1
Harbour redevelopment	1	0	1	0	2
Water	–	8	1	2	11
Wastewater	–	16	15	24	55
Total	14	27	20	40	101

a Pre-tender projects are at various stages of the appraisal procedures for investment under PPP.

Source: Data is derived from the PPP website housed by the Department of Finance and updated in March 2010. It is supplemented by information for water and wastewater projects provided by the Department of the Environment, Community and Local Government in November 2011 and information for roads projects provided by the National Roads Authority in April 2012

PPP and accountability in Ireland

It is important to note that our analysis is not based on a comparison of account-ability mechanisms under PPP with those that exist under traditional procurement. We do, however, explore the question of accountability under PPP in a context where the 'progressive contractualization of the state's services and activities has been accompanied by the general assumption of increased account-ability in all its forms' (Hodge 2007: 324). Focusing on public accountability, we examine the extent to which the mechanisms discussed above, namely VfM assessment, contract management and auditing, and parliamentary oversight, have served to provide the PPP model with legitimacy.

Ex ante *accountability: PPP and VfM assessment*

The *ex ante* VfM test provides one of the principal mechanisms of accountability for the PPP model. The Central PPP Policy Unit at the Department of Finance is the central point of access to the PPP process in Ireland. The unit describes its key functions as covering the development of the legislative framework, providing technical and policy guidance to support the PPP process and to disseminate best practice in PPPs. Its main guidelines for procurement under PPP place much emphasis on VfM, and according to Morallos and Amekudzi (2008) in their inter-national review of the practice of VfM analysis, Ireland is among the group of countries with the most comprehensive frameworks in this regard.

The most recent guidelines in relation to VfM assessment, issued in October 2007, describe four separate VfM tests, which take place at the following stages:

1   *VfM Test 1* takes place at the detailed appraisal stage, which applies to all capital projects that fall within the capital appraisal guidelines. When a proj-ect is under consideration for procurement under PPP, the detailed appraisal includes a *PPP Procurement Assessment*. The guidelines require that this VfM test be mainly qualitative in nature and that it covers questions such as whether the project is of sufficient scale and has a risk/operational profile that justifies a PPP approach; and whether the project has the potential to deliver value for money if procured as a PPP.
2   *VfM Test 2* involves a compilation of a detailed public sector benchmark[4] (PSB) prior to commencement of the procurement process.
3   *VfM Test 3* takes place when the PSB is compared to private sector bids as part of the tender evaluation process.
4   *VfM Test 4* takes place when the PSB is compared to the final bid after nego-tiations with the preferred bidder are complete and before awarding the contract.

In terms of public accountability, the key question is whether the conduct of VfM assessments is such that concerns are addressed in relation to accuracy, reliability and manipulation.

Evidence in relation to the conduct of VfM assessments in Ireland is not readily available. Although there is a need for the public sector to balance the requirement for transparency against the public interest in a vibrant competitive process, Siemiatycki (2007) suggests that in Ireland the balance has tipped in favour of confidentiality. The same writer states that the central Private–Public Partnership Unit within the Department of Finance reported that confidentiality in DBFO projects is specifically necessary to provide the private sector with incentives to deliver innovative technologies, limit costs, protect commercially sensitive information, and encourage flexibility to re-engineer business processes (Siemiatycki 2006: 145).

To examine the conduct of VfM assessment in the Irish case, this paper focuses on two sectors: schools and water services. In the case of schools, we examine the contract for the design, build, operation and finance of five secondary schools. To study the question of VfM in this case we utilize data available in the *Value for Money Report* on the grouped schools PPP, which was published by the Comptroller and Auditor General (C&AG) in 2004. In the case of water services, we analyse six separate VfM assessments that were conducted by individual local authorities at the pre-contracting stage. These documents were analysed in order to derive insights into the quality of VfM assessment and the extent to which it served to safeguard public accountability.

To examine the *ex post* management of PPP contracts we focus on the case of the grouped schools PPP. Information was collected from semi-structured interviews (which were conducted over the period January–March 2006) with the private contractor, the official in the Department of Education and Science with chief responsibility for the PPP and each of the five school principals. Interviews focused on the practice of contracting at the post-contractual stage of the PPP covering aspects that included the quality of client–contractor relations and aspects of performance management including monitoring, reporting and problem-solving.

Case 1 – VfM assessment for the grouped schools PPP

The contract for a group of five schools was announced as one of the original group of pilot projects in June 1999 and was the first to proceed through the stages of procurement and reach the stage where the assets were in operation. A private sector consortium was contracted to design, build, operate and finance the schools over a 25-year period and all five schools were opened in early 2003.

The C&AG estimated that the public sector obligations under the contract amount to €283 million (€150 million in NPV terms). It reported that the initial VfM exercise conducted by the Department of Education and Science (DES) estimated that PPP would yield cost savings of 6 per cent compared to traditional procurement. On the basis of their examination, however, the C&AG highlighted a number of significant errors in the original VfM exercise. Having corrected for these errors, the C&AG estimated that the PPP would be between 13 and 19 per cent more expensive. The C&AG also accounted for elements of the deal that changed after the VfM exercise (namely, changes in interest rates and treatment of VAT). Including these elements ultimately led the C&AG to conclude that the final PPP deal was in the range 8 to 13 per cent more expensive than under traditional procurement.

In addition to highlighting the unreliability of the original VfM estimates, the C&AG drew attention to other shortcomings. These included the failure to set an affordability cap, an exercise which is a standard component of the PPP procurement process. This involves making a reliable assessment of the maximum amount the state is willing to spend. In the case of the schools project, this exercise was not undertaken. According to the C&AG, this restricted the public sector's ability to 'form a view about the suitability of the PPP procurement route for the project and the value for money this approach was likely to deliver' (2004:32).

Another shortcoming highlighted by the C&AG concerned the timing of the calculation of a public sector benchmark (PSB). In this case the PSB was calculated following the appointment of the preferred bidder. An obvious inference in this case is that the procurement was going to proceed on the basis of the PPP model regardless of the findings from the VfM assessment. The latter therefore served little value as a mechanism for accountability in this case.

Case 2 – VfM assessment for water services PPPs

The water services sector accounts for a significant majority of PPP projects in Ireland with over 60 contracts at various stages of the PPP project life cycle. In all cases the private sector is contracted to design, build and operate (DBO) water infrastructure such as water and wastewater treatment facilities. For the purpose of this analysis, separate VfM assessments for six projects were reviewed. When the whole-life cost of providing water services was compared under both procurement models, PPP was estimated to provide better VfM in five of the six assessments examined. On average, the whole-life cost of PPP procurement was estimated to be 4.5 per cent lower compared to traditional procurement.

With regard to the question of reliability, the methodology adopted in deriving these estimates is worthy of attention. In each case, local authorities provided estimates of the cost of designing and building the water/wastewater plants under traditional procurement. These estimates were based on in-house experience in the construction and operation of such facilities and the specifications for the project in question. Estimates of capital costs under DBO were based on data sourced from other Irish local authorities that had recently adopted this form of procurement. However, the number of comparator plants used in the analyses varied considerably with just one benchmark plant used in one case and 19 in another. Furthermore, the majority of capital cost estimates were based on tendered costs rather than costs agreed in the final contracts.

The methodology adopted for estimating operating and maintenance (O&M) costs under traditional procurement was based on local authorities providing estimates based on past experience and the project specifications. For O&M costs under DBO, the estimates were based on data sourced from contractors with experience of DBO in the Irish water services sector. In all cases, O&M costs were estimated annually for the contract period (20 years) and a NPV was calculated. However, a number of specific issues concerning the cashflows used in these cases cast doubt over the reliability of estimates derived.

First, a critical issue that arises in decision-making in this context is the identification of incremental cashflows that are relevant to the procurement decision. The analysis of the cases examined in this study found that a common omission was the cost involved in redeploying labour within the local authority if DBO was the chosen procurement option. Where local authority labour is not transferred to the private contractor, the possibility of an incremental cost to the local authority arises. Although the precise accounting treatment of these costs may depend on issues such as whether labour is productively redeployed, it should be noted that the issue ought to be accounted for in the analysis as it may have an important bearing on the VfM assessment. Second, it is recommended practice when appraising projects to consider allocated overheads as non-incremental (or sunk costs) and therefore not to include them as a relevant cost in the assessment. However, the practice in all cases covered in this study was to allocate a central management charge (estimated as a percentage of all other O&M costs) to the traditional procurement option. Third, the choice of discount rate is a critical factor in any NPV analysis. In each of the cases covered in this study the practice was to discount cashflows that were not adjusted for inflation over the contract period. However, it is not clear whether the discount rate applied was 'real' or 'nominal'. Consequently, the possibility arises that 'real' cashflows were discounted at a nominal rate.[5]

An important factor in relation to the choice of procurement model is the question of transaction costs. Such costs are in addition to the costs normally included in VfM estimates and include 'the costs of negotiating, monitoring, and, if necessary, re-negotiating contracts with profit-maximizing firms' (Vining *et al.* 2005: 204). Although transaction costs can be difficult to measure, Klein *et al.* (1996) reviewed 33 projects across different countries and concluded that they are usually about 3 to 5 per cent (of total project costs) in well-developed policy environments, while they may be 10 to 12 per cent in pioneering projects. This is particularly relevant in the context of the studies reviewed in this paper where VfM was estimated to be 4.5 per cent (on average) of traditional procurement costs.

A final issue concerns the issue of sensitivity analysis. The PPP guidelines followed by Irish local authorities in the cases examined required detailed VfM assessments at a very early stage of the procurement process. As a consequence, the assessments are conducted in the context of significantly incomplete information, particularly with regard to expected private sector costs. In this respect, it is worth noting that sensitivity analysis was not conducted in any of the cases covered and this constitutes a notable shortcoming in the analyses underpinning procurement decisions in the Irish water services sector.

As VfM assessments are necessary to ensure that the PPP model meets basic standards of accountability, an important question is whether the assessments are complete, reliable and robust. A second question is whether appropriate arrangements are in place to ensure that the VfM assessments lend to responsible decision-making that serves the public interest. The cases from the Irish water services sector reviewed in this chapter suggest a qualified 'no'. Another issue of relevance in this regard concerns the official policy of the Department of Environment, Heritage and Local Government (DOEHLG), which oversees PPP procurement in the water services sector. The DOEHLG explicitly states that DBO is its 'preferred model' of procurement and this preference is clearly communicated to local authorities. In reviewing the cases included for this paper we found that some local authorities operated on the basis that VfM assessments should favour the DBO model of procurement. DBO was viewed as the only game in town (Reeves 2011). If local authorities made recommendations in favour of traditional procurement there was a danger that project approval would be delayed or not forthcoming. Official DOEHLG policy therefore had the potential to undermine the objectivity and usefulness of the VfM assessment exercise and effectively eliminated any prospect that VfM assessment could serve as a useful instrument of accountability.

Ex post *contractual accountability: managing and monitoring PPP contracts*

Although the numbers of PPP projects in Ireland that are built and in operation has gathered momentum, little is known about the management of contracts. To gather information regarding the management of PPP contracts we focus on the five schools PPP. On the basis of data collected from semi-structured interviews with key stakeholders we found a number of problems that impeded the operation of the PPP project as well as issues that undermined the extent to which effective contract management could enhance accountability under the PPP.

Among the issues highlighted by school principals was concern in relation to the level of skills and experience of the public sector client (Department of Education and Science) as well as the commitment to enforce the terms of the contract. Despite instances of contractor under-performance, no penalties (e.g. reduced payments) had been imposed, thereby raising doubts about the willingness or capacity of the public sector client to effectively manage the contract.

Significant problems arose in terms of communication between the public sector client and the ultimate users of the contracted service, i.e. the schools. Particular concern was expressed by schools due to a lack of transparency regarding the rights and responsibilities of parties to the contract. As a result, this PPP has been characterized by marked dissatisfaction on behalf of most schools.

The conclusion of this analysis is that if PPPs in the education sector are to be characterized by accountability, this requires accurate quantification of the costs and benefits of PPP at the *ex ante* stage. In addition, a sufficient flow of information to all key stakeholders is necessary. Transparency can secure a level of 'buy in', which can underpin the development of long-term co-operation and mutual benefit.

Access to information and parliamentary oversight

A number of concerns arise in relation to the availability of information regarding PPP to citizens and statutory bodies charged with duties of oversight in the public interest. The most rigorous analysis of PPP procurement to date has been conducted by the C&AG in relation to the first schools project. Since the publication of the VfM report on this project in 2004, there has been no further published detailed analysis of PPP projects from the C&AG. This is a matter of some concern as the scale of PPP activity has expanded in the interim.

Reports by the C&AG provide the principal source of information for the Public Accounts Committee (PAC) of Dáil Éireann (Irish parliament). Although the PAC can compel the accounting officers of government departments to come before its enquiries, these powers do not extend to the private sector. As a consequence, the PAC has expressed frustration in relation to the level of transparency. For example, in 2007 the PAC expressed the view that:

> The PAC in recent years has held several plenary sessions relating to significant PPP projects. These meetings of the committee were informed by particular chapters of the annual reports of the Comptroller and Auditor General, as well as a number of Value For Money reports that also emanated from his office... While the circumstances applying to each of these projects vary widely, and the history of each differs, some common threads have appeared. The largest common factor has been the frustration expressed at the Committee of either not having appropriate access to information relating to these projects, or being publicly unable to refer to information deemed to be commercially sensitive. This committee believes that this obstacle needs to be overcome. Public accountability and value for money are very important issues.
>
> (Dáil Éireann, Public Accounts Committee 2007: 7–8).

External oversight of PPP arrangements is effectively confined to the office of the C&AG. With just a single published VfM report covering procurement under PPP, the dearth of detailed analysis of PPP has serious consequences for public accountability in this regard.

Conclusions

A key challenge that arises in the case of procurement models such as PPP relates to the question of accountability. The Commission on PPPs in the UK asserts that:

> Public accountability is a pre-condition for the legitimate use of public authority. It is the basis on which citizens are willing to delegate power to others to act on their behalf. It underpins government based on consent. Without proper accountability mechanisms, organisations delivering services are not subject to democratic oversight and control, the rights of citizens are

uncertain and services are unlikely to reflect the needs of service users. Accountability is therefore an end as well as a means.

(2001: 231)

The PPP literature that has emerged in the last two decades demonstrates widespread concerns about the performance of the PPP model in terms of meeting the accountability challenge. The tenor of such concerns is neatly captured by Hodge (2007) who suggests that in the Australian case, new partnership arrangements lack legitimacy and 'We might even posit that PPPs as they currently operate in Australia have become very much an illegitimate child of the partnership family' (p. 324). Similar concerns have been voiced in the context of the UK (Ball *et al.* 2007; Commission on PPPs 2001), the USA (Forrer *et al.* 2010) and Canada (Siemiatycki 2007).

Policy-makers have commonly sought to address the accountability challenge under PPP through a combination of market-oriented mechanisms such as contracts and competition, and public sector instruments such as rules of transparency and public control that apply to the public sector. Ireland, which is considered by some to be a world leader in PPP procurement, has applied a mix of such mechanisms in the implementation of its significant PPP programme. However, the evidence presented in this paper draws attention to a number of concerns that still exist in terms of the extent to which the accountability challenge has been met in the Irish case.

If concerns in relation to accountability are to be addressed, a number of the mechanisms that are intended to serve in this regard require attention. The Irish experience highlights how parties to PPP contracts are not always subject to adequate levels of oversight by auditors and Parliament. If concerns in this regard are to be addressed, it is necessary to adequately resource auditors-general and ensure that more and more PPP projects are subjected to detailed scrutiny and VfM audits. The oversight powers of parliamentary committees can also be strengthened by conferring the powers necessary to compel witnesses from the public and private sector sides of PPP contracts.

It is necessary to recognize that more complex forms of procurement such as PPP place significant demands on public sector skills and resources. These demands are relevant at all stages of the project life cycle starting at the initial stages of appraisal and continuing throughout the life of the contract. This has been addressed to some degree in the Irish case where the National Development Finance Agency (NDFA) has taken responsibility for most elements of the *ex ante* procurement stage. By centralizing these tasks in the NDFA, the burden of procurement is removed from government departments and scope is provided for a single body to specialize in PPP procurement. However, the NDFA does not take responsibility for the management and monitoring of PPP. One of the lessons from international experience and the cases examined in this paper is that challenges in relation to governance of PPP arrangements do not stop once contracts are signed. Skilled and well-resourced management of PPP over the life of the contracts is necessary if the public interest is to be served.

A perennial issue that arises in most countries adopting PPP concerns the need to strike a balance between demands for an appropriate level of accountability and the need to reap the benefits of private sector participation in the context of competitive tendering. The Irish experience has been similar to that in the UK where critics (Monbiot 2004; Shaoul 2005) argue that the protection of private sector interests takes precedence over the wider public interest. There are clear challenges in terms of improving transparency and the extent of information concerning individual contracts that is released to the public, and the timing of any such releases. When considering the need for confidentiality on commercial grounds, however, policy-makers must recognize that large amounts of public funds are committed to PPPs. Moreover, the reach of PPP is extending more and more into sectors that are sensitive in terms of the nature of services involved (e.g. education, health, water and environmental services). These sectors are of such importance to the public interest that the case for tipping the balance in favour of the public interest is compelling. One possibility in this context is to place the onus on public agencies to justify why the withholding of information is warranted. The reverse-onus principle has been adopted to varying degrees in a number of Australian states (Barrett 2003). In general, contracts or contract summaries are made available on the internet. On the question of non-disclosure, the case of New South Wales is illustrative of the general approach where governments are accountable for agreeing to any non-disclosure and must be prepared to justify such decisions.

The global trend towards engaging the private sector in the delivery of public services looks set to continue. Procurement models such as PPP, however, pose considerable questions for accountability. The evidence presented in this paper illuminates the scope for devising and improving accountability mechanisms, even in countries with reasonably developed institutional frameworks. The challenges in this regard are likely to be ongoing. Whereas concerns about aspects such as value for money are usually given high priority, it is important that policy-makers give at least equal consideration to the accountability challenge under PPP. This is essential if the PPP model is to serve as a legitimate form of governance and public services are delivered to meet citizens' needs.

Notes

1   Hodge *et al.* (2010) describe LTICs in terms of their emphasis on tight specification of outputs in long-term legal contracts (as exemplified in UK Private Finance Initiative projects). However, LTICs are themselves a large group.

2   Flyvbjerg *et al.* (2003) provide details of a study led by Aalborg University in Denmark. In their study of 258 projects worth approximate $258 billion (1995 prices) they found that project costs were underestimated in nine out of 10 transport projects. For all project types the average cost overrun was 28 per cent.

3   Barrett (2003) notes that in Australia the power to issue a summons for a witness to appear or to make an order to produce documents is rarely used.

4   The public sector benchmark is the equivalent of the public sector comparator conducted in other countries including the UK.

5   If an unduly high discount rate is applied, this can potentially favour the PPP option

as future finance repayments spread over the life of the contract are discounted at a higher rate than ought to be the case, and therefore appear to be smaller than they are in reality.

References

Ball, R., Heafey, M. and King, D. (2001) Private Finance Initiative – A Good Deal for the Public or a Drain on Future Generations? *Policy and Politics*, 29(1): 95–108.

Ball, R., Heafey, M. and King, D. (2007) The Private Finance Initiative in the UK – A Value for Money Analysis. *Public Management Review*, 9(2): 289–310.

Barrett, P. (2003) Public Private Partnerships: Are there Gaps in Accountability? Paper presented to Australasian Council of Public Accounts Committees 7th Biennial Conference, Melbourne.

Behn, R. D. (2001) *Rethinking Democratic Accountability*. Washington, DC: Brookings Institution Press.

Boardman, A. E. and Vining, A. R. (2010) Assessing the Economic Worth of Public–Private Partnerships, in G.A. Hodge, C. Greve and A.E. Boardman (eds) *International Handbook on Public–Private Partnerships*. Cheltenham: Edward Elgar.

Broadbent, J., Gill, J. and Laughlin, R. (2003) Evaluating the Private Finance Initiative in the National Health Service in the UK. *Accounting, Auditing & Accountability Journal*, 16(3): 422–45.

Commission on Public Private Partnerships (2001) *Building Better Partnerships*. London: Institute for Public Policy Research.

Comptroller and Auditor General (2004) *The Grouped Schools Pilot Partnership Project*. Dublin: Stationery Office.

Dáil Éireann Committee of Public Accounts (2007) *First Interim Report: Access to the Private Element of Public Private Partnerships – An International Comparison*. Dublin: Stationery Office.

Deloitte (2007) *Closing the Infrastructure Gap: The Role of Public Private Partnerships*. London: Deloitte Research.

Demirag, I. and Khadaroo, M. I. (2008) Accountability and Value for Money in Private Finance Initiative Contracts, *Financial Accountability and Management*, 24(4): 455–78.

Demirag, I., Dubnick, M. and Khadaroo, M. I. (2004) A Framework for Examining Accountability and Value for Money in the UK's Private Finance Initiative. *Journal of Corporate Citizenship*, 15(3): 64–76.

Demsetz, H. (1968) Why Regulate Utilities? *Journal of Law and Economics*, 11: 55–66.

Edwards, P., Shaoul, J., Stafford, A. and Arblaster, L. (2004), *Evaluating the Operations of PFI in Roads and Hospitals*. ACCA Research Report. London: Certified Accountants Educational Trust.

Eurostat (2004) New Decision of Eurostat on Deficit and Debt Treatment of Public–Private Partnerships. *Eurostat News Release*, Luxembourg.

Flyvbjerg, B., Bruzelius, N. and Rothengetter, W. (2003) *Megaprojects and Risk – The Anatomy of Ambition*, Cambridge: Cambridge University Press.

Forrer, J, Kee, J. E., Newcomer, K .E. and Boyer, E. (2010) Public Private Partnership and the Public Accountability Question, *Public Administration Review*, May/June: 475–84.

Ghere, R. K. (2001) Probing the Strategic Intricacies of Public–Private Partnership: The Patent as a Comparative Reference. *Public Administration Review*, 61(4): 441–51.

Gray, A. G. and Jenkins, W. I. (1993) Codes of Accountability in the New Public Sector. *Accounting, Auditing & Accountability Journal*, 6(3): 52–67.

Gray, R., Dey, C., Owen, D., Evans, R. and Zadek, S. (1997) Struggling with the Praxis of Social Accounting: Stakeholders, Accountability, Audits and Procedures. *Accounting, Auditing and Accountability Journal*, 10(3): 325–64.

Heald, D. (2003) Value for Money Tests and Accounting Treatment in PFI Schemes. *Accounting, Auditing and Accountability Journal*, 16(3): 342–71.

HM Treasury (2003a), *The Green Book: Appraisal and Evaluation in Central Government.* London: HMSO.

HM Treasury (2003b) *PFI: Meeting the Investment Challenge.* London: HMSO.

Hodge, G. A. (2007) Public Private Partnerships and Legitimacy. *University of New South Wales Law Journal*, 29(3): 318–27.

Hodge, G. A. and Greve, C. (2007) Public Private Partnerships – An International Performance Review. *Public Administration Review*, May/June: 545–58.

Hodge, G. A., Greve, C. and Boardman, A. E. (2010) Introduction: The PPP Phenomenon and its Evaluation, in G.A. Hodge, C. Greve and A.E. Boardman *International Handbook on Public Private Partnerships*. Cheltenham: Edward Elgar.

Irish Business Employers Council (2009) *Delivering During Recession.* Dublin: IBEC.

Jones, G. and Stewart, J. (2009) Accountability in Public Partnerships – The Case of Local Strategic Partnerships. *Public Money and Management*, 29(1): 59–64.

Kintoye, A., Beck. M. and Hardcastle, C. (2002) *Framework for Risk Management and Management of PFI Projects.* Final Report, EPSRC/DTI. Glasgow: Glasgow Caledonian University.

Klein, M., So, J. S. and Shin, B. (1996) Transaction Costs in Private Infrastructure Projects – Are they too High? *Public Policy for the Private Sector.* Note No. 95. The World Bank.

Lonsdale, C. (2005) Post-contractual Lock-in and the UK Private Finance Initiative (PFI): The Cases of the National Savings and Investments and the Lord Chancellor's Department. *Public Administration*, 83(1): 67–88.

Monbiot, G. (2004) A Scandal of Secrecy and Collusion. *The Guardian*, 28 December.

Morallos, D. and Amekudzi, A. (2008) The State of the Practice of Value for Money Analysis in Comparing Public Private Partnerships and Traditional Procurements. *Public Works Management Policy*, 13(2): 114–25.

Newberry, S. and Pallot, J. (2003) Fiscal (Ir)responsibility: Privileging PPPs in New Zealand. *Accounting, Auditing & Accountability Journal*, 16(3): 467–92.

Prasad, N. (2006) Privatization Results: Private Sector Participation in Water Services After Fifteen Years. *Development Policy Review*, 24(6): 669–92.

Reeves, E. (2008) The Practice of Contracting in Public Private Partnerships: Transaction Costs and Relational Contracting in the Irish Schools Sector. *Public Administration*, 86(4): 969–86.

Reeves, E. (2011) The Only Game in Town – Public Private Partnerships in the Irish Water Services Sector. *Economic and Social Review*, 42(1): 95–111.

Sappington, D. E. M. and Stiglitz, J. E. (1987) Privatisation, Information and Incentives. *Journal of Policy Analysis and Management*, 6(4): 567–82.

Shaoul, J. (2005) The Private Finance Initiative or Public Funding of Private Profit, in C. Greve and G. Hodge (eds) *The Challenge of Private–Public Partnerships – Lessons from International Experience.* Cheltenham, Edward Elgar.

Siemiatycki, M. (2007) What's the Secret? Confidentiality in Planning Infrastructure Using Public/Private Partnerships. *Journal of the American Planning Association*, Autumn, 73(4): 388–403.

Siemiatycki, M. (2006) Implications of Private–Public Partnerships on the Development of Urban Public Transit Infrastructure: The Case of Vancouver Canada. *Journal of Planning Education and Research*, 26: 137–51.

Stevens, B. and Schieb, P. (2007) Infrastructure – Mind the Gap. *OECD Observer*, April.

Vincent-Jones, P. (2006) *The New Public Contracting – Regulation, Responsiveness, Relationality.* Oxford: Oxford University Press.

Vining, A. R., Boardman, A. E. and Poschmann, F. (2005) Public–Private Partnerships in the US and Canada: There are no Free Lunches. *Journal of Comparative Policy Analysis*, 7(3): 199–220.

Wettenhall, R. (2010) Mixes and Partnerships through Time, in G. A. Hodge, C. Greve and A. E. Boardman (eds) *International Handbook on Public–Private Partnerships.* Cheltenham: Edward Elgar.

5 Enhancing innovation in public organizations through public–private partnerships

The role of public managers[1]

Tamyko Ysa, Marc Esteve and Francisco Longo

Introduction

Innovation is no stranger to public organizations. In fact, it has been defined as pretty much imperative for them (Osborne 1998). For example, several scholars have highlighted the global importance of innovation in public organizations over the last decade. The public management literature has identified inter-organizational relations as an innovation in the governance of a public organization (see Mandell and Steelman 2003). From this perspective, public organizations engaging in inter-organizational collaboration interact with other organizations in a network-based relationship, instead of the classic principal-agent position of the traditional public organization with a hierarchical culture.

In the last decade, inter-organizational relations have become very popular in the public sector (see, for a review, Hodge and Greve 2009). For that reason, this chapter considers innovation not only as the creation of an inter-organizational relationship but also as the new ideas, objects or practices created through inter-organizational relations. The underlying thesis is that inter-organizational collaborations between public, private, or non-profit organizations allow them to work together toward a shared objective and, as a result, offer a perfect scenario for innovation to emerge. Two research questions are explored in this chapter: how can innovation in public organizations be enhanced; and what is the role of public–private partnerships (PPPs) in the development of innovations? We believe that these enquiries are timely and significant for both improving practice and developing theory in the public administration field.

Next, we define the concept of innovation and pull together the different perspectives on innovation observed in public management. We go on to present a case study of the Catalan Blood and Tissue Bank, and the methodology used to gather data. The subsequent discussion assesses the findings of the case study and presents several propositions that will help practitioners and academics to better understand the role played by organizational arrangements and public managers in the creation of innovation. The argument in this chapter is that whilst PPP can be a good vehicle to enhance innovation, it can also lead to increased costs and significant uncertainty, depending on the role played by public managers. We end with concluding remarks.

Innovation – a broad concept

As Damanpour and Schneider (2009: 496) state, 'innovation is a complex construct and is studied from multiple perspectives at different levels of analysis by scholars from a variety of academic disciplines'. Because of this, before we can understand how innovation occurs and can be enhanced in PPPs, it is important to clarify how innovation is conceptualized.

Walker (2006) provides a broad definition of innovation that embraces most of the definitions that have been suggested in the public management literature. According to him, innovation is 'a process through which new ideas, objects and practices are created, developed or reinvented and which are new and novel to the unit of adoption'. A classic view of innovation points towards the development of new products and services. In governments, this is exemplified by recognizing new citizens' needs that have to be satisfied by a public organization (Walker 2008). After the recognition of the need, public organizations have to deliver a new service oriented towards citizens' demands. Arguably, there are three types of innovation in new products and services in public organizations, depending on the relationship between the public organization and the user-citizens (Osborne 1998). The first occurs when new products or services are provided to new users. Walker and Jeanes (2001) exemplify this with the provision of private rented housing by English housing associations. In this example, the product is new (private renting), and the users of the service can be also considered new, since they are economically better off than those on whom public housing organizations typically focus.

A second type of innovation in products and services is known as expansionary innovation. In this case, public organizations decide to provide an existing service to a new group of users. The service is not new, but the users who receive it have not previously benefited from it. An example would be the financial help that some governments give young people to help them rent accommodation. Governments have generally helped some specific groups to rent properties, but in this case a new group of users (young people) has been identified as new target users who would benefit from a public service.

The third innovation type is evolutionary innovation, when a public organization improves an existing service to satisfy the needs of its users. For example, some local governments have developed a network of public bikes to allow users to cycle around the city. Before this initiative, local governments were already facilitating user mobility through public transport systems (bus, tram, metro), but here they have developed a new product (the public bike network) to improve users' mobility.

However, innovation does not only refer to the development of new products and services. For example, Young *et al.* (2001) also consider the adoption of a new managerial practice as an organizational innovation. In their study of how the characteristics of top managers influence the adoption of innovation, they measure innovation as the implementation of the managerial practice known as total quality management (TQM). According to the above authors, an innovation does not merely refer to the creation of a new concept or practice, but to a concept or practice that has not been adopted yet. This idea acknowledges that innovations occur within organizations and can be aimed at changing organizational features, not just the outputs that the organization offers its users.

Moore and Hartley (2008) identify another innovation concept: governance innovations, which differ in two major ways from classic innovations:

> On the one hand, the innovations are conceived and implemented above the organizational level: they involve networks of organizations, or the transformation of complex social production systems rather than changes solely within a particular organization. On the other hand, these innovations focus not only on concrete changes in what particular things are produced through what particular production processes, but also on the ways in which productive activity is financed (or, more broadly, resourced), the processes that are used to decide what will be produced, and the normative standards used to evaluate the performance of the social production system.

Moore and Hartley's perspective of innovation goes beyond the organizational level towards the understanding of the role public organizations play within society. Their perspective is embedded in a broader conceptualization of how the development of public services can be developed through collaborations with other organizations or citizens (see Alford 2002). Mandell and Steelman (2003) also refer to the concept of inter-organizational innovations to explain the complex arrangements some public organizations operate to deliver public goods. It is from this perspective that PPPs have been related to innovation. Partnerships have been seen as a new governance arrangement for providing public services or developing public goods. Arguably, the innovation is the development of the partnership. From this perspective, partnerships are a structural innovation towards markets or pure hierarchies in Powell's (1987) well-known differentiation.

Figure 5.1 is an attempt to clarify the many and various conceptualizations of innovation in relation to public organizations. As the summary shows, we have divided innovations according to whether they are oriented towards the development of a new product or service, or whether they are focused on changing an organizational feature. Innovation can then take the form of new patents, products or services, structures, managerial practices or resources. In each of the cases, the organization aims at a specific benefit. For example, by developing new patents, the organization earns financial resources and prestige; whereas by developing new services or new products, the organization can provide its users with better services or more offerings. Finally, successful innovations in organizational features result in an optimization of resources, both financial and non-financial (i.e. the employees needed to perform a specific task).

Methods

Our evidence is drawn from an exploratory case study of the Catalan Blood and Tissue Bank, a public organization that leads the vanguard for its sector in Spain

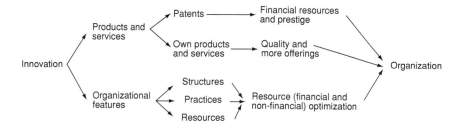

Figure 5.1 Innovation types in public organizations

and is noted for its ability to interact with other organizations. In the last decade, the Blood and Tissue Bank has grown from a very small organization to monopolize the supply of blood components to all the public and private hospitals and clinics in Catalonia, and become the leading blood components supplier in Spain. In 2009, the Blood and Tissue Bank was given an award in company competitiveness by the Catalan Ministry of Innovation, Universities and Enterprise.

Exploratory case studies have been used extensively in the public administration field (see, for example, de Graaf and Huberts 2008; Saz-Carranza and Serra 2009) and case studies elucidating best practices have been acknowledged as a reliable support to assess performance in general as well as how innovation occurs in public organizations (Borins 2001). Our case study approach uses qualitative methods, which have been recommended for research that aims to understand the dynamics present in a single setting (Eisenhardt 1989). In this case, the dynamics we assess are innovation, and the setting is inter-organizational collaborations.

Case selection

Single case studies are arguably a valid methodology for theory building in the fields of public administration and management (Eisenhardt 1989; Barzelay 1993). However, the validity of the method is sometimes criticized because of the implications of case selection (see Borins 2001). The case study of the Catalan Blood and Tissue Bank was not selected randomly, but because of its performance in collaborative activities and innovation. As Siggelkow (2007) points out, case studies are not randomly selected, because they do not aim for generalization and representativeness, but to explain a specific phenomenon. Siggelkow argues that some case studies are chosen because they allow researchers to find characteristic insights that help a better understanding of the object of study.

We choose the Catalan Blood and Tissue Bank for three main reasons. First, collaboration and innovation are two of its major objectives, reflected in its strategic plans. Second, it has a large portfolio of innovation; while its main objective is to provide blood and tissue, unlike most public organizations, it has research laboratories and creates patents. This means it has innovations in products, services and organizational features. Third, the Bank represents a successful public organization, outstanding in the way its managers promote innovation and for the leadership of its general director. These criteria are in line with previous studies on best practices cases (see, for instance, Barzelay 1992; Overman and Boyd 1994).

Case study: the Catalan Blood and Tissue Bank

The Catalan Blood and Tissue Bank (BST) is a public enterprise of the government of Catalonia and was created in 1995 to ensure the provision and proper use of blood and tissue, conduct immunology diagnostics and develop advanced haemotherapies. Over the next 10 years, BST unified all 12 existing blood banks in Catalonia, and since 2006 has been responsible for meeting the need for blood components in all the public and private health centres in the region. In order to provide these services, BST has a budget of €73.8 million (2010) and a staff of 640. Its main activities focus on blood, tissues, advanced haemotherapies, congenital coagulopathies and diagnostics. In terms of its organizational structure, BST's corporate areas are quality, management control, projects and innovation (oriented towards the development of scientific knowledge as well as new products and services), marketing, human resources, communication and public services.

BST is a highly knowledge-based, innovative organization, committed to serving the public interest. Its 2010 annual report highlights values like coherence, excellence, commitment to people, innovation and research, service to society, transparency and expertise. It has a quality policy to ensure innovation and advancement towards a sustainable model of excellence. Its mission and vision are focused on innovation and international reach.[2] It is also worth noting that BST's Strategic Plan 2010–15 defines five focal areas: meeting society's demands while ensuring sufficiency, safety and quality; promoting research and innovation; expanding markets (partly through the formulation and deployment of strategic alliances); developing a people-based management model; and ensuring economic and financial sustainability. Consequently, BST has obtained major quality accreditations and certifications such as ISO 9001:2008, Applus, CAT, CCA-OCATT, NETCORD-FACT, EFI and IQUA.

BST also stands out for its significant management autonomy, which has facilitated rapid adaptation in a dynamic environment, and for its professionalized model of corporate governance and executive leadership, which has protected BST from political interference and provided the necessary stability to achieve its goals.

The BST management model is based on sustainability (monitoring the environment, use and transfusion safety, maximizing customer orientation), excellent management systems and strengthening Research and Development (R&D). The goal of sustainability is to focus on customers' high degree of exigency in terms of service quality, security and information. This is benefiting the society as it means a reduction in blood donations needs and ensures product availability. In parallel, there is, as well, the mission to ensure that the products delivered accomplish the highest rates of quality, security and information for traceability purposes. Management excellence is borne out by BST's receipt of the Excellence Award (400+) in 2010. The EFQM evaluators highlighted four key strengths of BST's management: the juridical formula of public enterprise (balanced with self-sustained economy and financial control); the integral management of blood from 'vein to vein'; the best for scientific innovation and the generation of new products and services; and the dynamism and high degree of implication of the professionals. Finally, for BST, R&D is a strategic activity to provide high-quality services and to incorporate the improvements generated in the field while developing new diagnostic and therapeutic tools. BST has international recognition in terms of published material. In 2010, 43 articles were published in scientific magazines with an aggregated impact factor of 95.53.

BST's strategic alliances

BST considers strategic alliances with both public and private organizations, as well as NGOs, essential for the success and the sustainability of their projects. Hence, it promotes agreements with suppliers, laboratories, universities, companies, hospitals, foundations and associations, and transfusion centres with the objective of taking advantage of synergies, shared costs and knowledge. Research and innovation is a major objective for BST's established alliances with other public or private actors.

One of the most relevant BST alliances is the one that is being established by the advanced therapies division through XCelia, which is focused on promoting health through stem cell therapy. XCelia is expected to become the first BST private spin-off; however, XCelia's administrative board consists of BST executives.

In partnership with Grifols chemical company and a network of public and private hospitals, they aim to research, develop, register and commercialize advanced therapy medicinal products. XCelia and BST also participate in an alliance called RedOnTap, which brings together researchers from the University of Leipzig, Applikon Biotechnology and XCelia and is co-ordinated by the University of Liverpool. This research project aims to discover the conditions required for rapid and continuous creation of red blood cells from adult stem cells. The alliance of public and private companies with a 15-year projection, assuming a share of risk-taking, in addition to the intention of obtaining a gain on the outcome, defines this project as a public–private joint venture.

BST is one of the European R&D leaders in umbilical cord blood. There are two relevant alliances in this area: Concordia Program and NetCord. The first, led by BST, aims to make possible the allogenic use of umbilical cord blood with the collaboration of five health departments from Spanish autonomous communities and Andorra. From the BST point of view, this programme will make it easier to start up donor programmes efficiently, it will respond to the growing demand for high blood quality levels, it will facilitate transplants, promote co-operative clinical and biological research on the umbilical cord, and enable technical protocols to be shared. In short, the programme will share knowledge and risks, reduce costs and take advantage of synergies. Meanwhile, NetCord's aim is to take advantage of the synergies between 15 leading public and private umbilical cord blood banks worldwide and to create a register of umbilical cord blood units available for hospitals wanting them for transplants. Apart from the 15 leading banks, which are mainly from the EU but also from the USA, Australia, South Korea and Japan, there are 16 more banks (both public and private) registered as provisional members of the network. Finally, the high involvement of BST was demonstrated by the appointment of the director of the advanced therapies division, as network president in the period 2008–10.

BST also collaborates with technological companies in the validation phase and for the tuning of new technologies that will be applied in the elaboration of different products. An example is the Automation of Blood Components Elaboration unit (ABCE). In order to enhance the blood treatment that is required to process it, BST and Caridian jointly defined an automation process to substitute the manual process that BST was using. This partnership was settled with the intention of acquiring the desired objectives, and presupposes substantial financial, technical and operational risks. Caridian is an international company from the USA that aims to improve lives through innovation, quality and services as well as through the development of products and processes in blood component technologies. It should be noted that ABCE has successfully implemented a coded inlet/outlet system with blood storage bags, improving traceability while controlling the weight and temperature of the product, and has also increased productivity, reducing labelling and validation resources.

As we have shown, BST operates within a large subset of relations with other actors, formalized through a variety of organizational arrangements. Table 5.1 presents examples of cases where the BST operates alone, via contract with private providers, in contractual partnerships and also in public–private joint ventures.

Table 5.1 Examples of BST's institutional arrangements

	BST	*Contract*	*CPPP*	*JV*
Example	Integrated management of blood	Caridian (critical supplier)	RedOnTap Concordia NetCord	XCelia

Data collection

This research has been conducted using some of the qualitative data-collection methods proposed by Marshall and Rossman (1999): in-depth interviews, document analysis and questionnaires. By using these three methods, we aim to triangulate the information gathered with each technique (Eden and Huxham 2002). This triangulation can also be facilitated by multiple sources, theories and investigations (Janesick 1994; Miller and Crabtree 1994; Richardson 1994). These help us to shed light on the issue from different angles (Fine *et al.* 1994) and reduce the likelihood of misinterpretation arising from data redundancy through the concurrent use of multiple perspectives (Stake 1994).

Data were collected through on-site visits to the organization. During the visits, face-to-face in-depth interviews were conducted with the whole managerial team. The interviews were conducted by two of the authors, and 14 were carried out. The interviews consisted of 10 principal questions about collaboration and innovation issues. The questions were used as a guide for each interview but were modified as necessary, to meet the specificities of each interviewee. All interviews were recorded and transcribed to enable their coding.[3] Table 5.2 describes the people interviewed and their job titles.

To ensure the reliability of our findings and to avoid observer bias, two of the authors individually coded each interview following a grounded strategy (Strauss and Corbin 1994). The interviews were read without any preliminary code in mind; instead, the researchers let the data emerge by looking at which management strategies were used by the interviewees to enhance innovation in collaboration. After several coding waves, the researchers pooled their codes and discussed each of their coded sentences to elaborate a final coding.

Internal documentation from the organization was also collected, especially that concerning interactions between the two organizations and other documents referring to company strategy, mission and statutes. These data were consulted to ensure the appropriateness of the final codes and to understand better some of the situations described in the interviews.

Table 5.2 BST managers interviewed

Name	Charge
Ramon Pau Pla Illa	General Director
Isabel López Asión	Assistant to General Director
Gabriela Marín Cobo	Economics and Finance Director
Esther Solà Saplana	People and Values Director
Albert Herrero Espinet	Information and Communications Technologies Director
Joan Ovejo	General Services Director
Lluís Puig Rovira	Blood Division Director
Aurora Navarro	Tissue Division Director
Joan Garcia López	Advanced Therapeutics Division (XCelia) Director
Eduardo Muñiz Díaz	Immunohematology Division Director
Ricard Pujol Borrell	Immunobiology Division Director
Rafael Parra López	Congenital Coagulopathies Division Director
Eva Villamayor	Responsible for the Customer Service Unit
Pilar Ortiz Murillo	Blood Division Technical Director

Findings and discussion

The analysis of the interviews developed in the case study reveals that innovation in partnerships can be enhanced by two major factors. The first is institutional – the type of relationship between the partners. The second is leadership style. In this section we interpret the words of interviewees to explain which institutional and leadership factors smooth the progress of innovation.

Institutional factors

BST is in charge of a large number of projects that are developed through different organizational arrangements, including various types of alliance with private and public actors. This is of special interest because during the interviews the managerial team recognized that the type of institutional arrangement chosen to undertake a project has a substantial influence on the level of innovation within the project. More specifically, projects developed via joint ventures see one or more partners facilitate the interaction with other actors and, as a result, benefit from more innovative solutions. Thus, different types of alliance enhance the development of innovations when compared to production and service provision from BST alone.

Drawing on the interview material, Figure 5.2 proposes a relation between organizational arrangement and the degree of innovation that takes place. As the figure shows, in order to innovate, one must allow other organizations to come closer and interact actively with them. We propose that the organizational arrangements in which projects are developed will have a strong effect on the degree of innovation in each project.

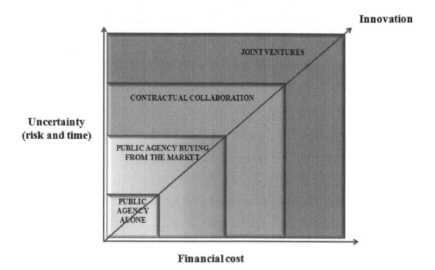

Figure 5.2 Institutional arrangements facilitating innovation

However, innovation comes at a cost, as BST's managers warn. Each institutional arrangement is accompanied by a certain degree of uncertainty and presumed financial costs. For instance, in the XCelia case there were many potential innovation outputs, but at the same time, BST had to devote high financial resources to their relationship with private partners. And since the whole XCelia project relied on other actors, the degree of uncertainty was also very high.

Over the last few years, several researchers have focused on diverse aspects of alliances between organizations. Alliances are commonly defined as short- or long-term voluntary relationships between organizations in one or more areas of activity in which both parties regulate their future conduct *ex ante* by means of mutual forbearance and more or less formally-specified contractual mechanisms (Buckley and Casson 1988; Gulati 1998; Dacin *et al.* 2007). These studies have concluded that alliances have important advantages for organizations. Das and Teng (2000) explain some of the benefits that organizations can achieve by bringing together their resources, including entry into new markets for alliance partners (García-Canal *et al.* 2002), access to unique resources and capabilities (Gulati 1999), increase in market power (Eisenhardt and Schoonhoven 1996), the transmission, acquisition and exchange of information (Kogut 1991; Mowery *et al.* 1996; Davis and Greve 1997), reductions in liabilities of foreignness, and also in government or trade barriers (Hagedoorn 1993; Zaheer 1995; Mezias 2002).

The main impression the interviews give is that in order to innovate it is necessary to work closely with another partner. This is clearly illustrated by one of the interviewees who stated that the collaboration with a private partner allowed them to see that they could improve their products by implementing innovations. As she said:

> When someone from outside comes to your house and sees that you are toasting the bread in a frying pan he thinks that you are very pedestrian. Finally he shows you the electric toaster and even if the end result seems the same, since in the end you always get toast, the process has improved a lot, because you can control the time and regularize each step.

This interviewee was referring to BST's collaboration with Caridian, a private company that helps BST with the automation of the process of separating blood components through to storage.

As a result of its interaction with Caridian, BST was able to develop an innovative organizational feature. This would not have been possible if BST had tried to develop the machinery to process the blood by itself, nor if it had tried to buy it from the market, since it was specifically designed for BST. Following the success of BST's experience, several blood and tissue banks are now using this machinery.

One of the interviewees explained that in joint ventures BST is able to operate under private rules and receive direct economic donations to support research and innovation. Also, with this kind of organizational arrangement, the political influence perceived by members of BST is less strong than when they operate alone as a public agency. BST is a shining example of how to develop an institutional framework to collaborate with another partner and achieve innovation. This is the case of XCelia, a joint venture with a major private partner, devoted to the creation of advanced therapies. For example, the human resources director said: 'We decided to develop [XCelia] as an spin-off of BST to have more room for manoeuvre, not only in human resources issues, but in everything.'

The interviewees explained that developing a product with a private provider leads to very satisfying results, but of course it is much more expensive than buying an existing product from the market. As one of them concluded: 'Being innovative in several projects implies high economic costs, since it is not as simple as buying an existing product.' It is highly difficult to predict in advance the final price of a product that has to be developed in collaboration with one or more private partners. During the interviews, the managers explained that many projects fail to achieve the desired results. As we show in Figure 5.2, it seems that organizational arrangements can help innovation to happen, but it is important to recognize that this has financial costs and corresponding risks due to the uncertainty that is always present in collaborations.

Leadership factors

The opinions reflected in the BST case suggest that public managers play an important role in innovation. Defined as 'a process whereby an individual influences a group of individuals to achieve a common goal' (Northouse 2001), leadership has long been related to inter-organizational collaborations. Thomson and Perry (2006), for instance, appraise the main drivers behind collaboration and draw a fundamental conclusion from their analysis: 'Don't collaborate unless you are willing to thoughtfully consider and educate yourself about the nature of the process involved.' Their advice clearly indicates that the public manager is essential for the development of collaboration.

In the same vein, Agranoff (2006) supports the role of the public manager by proposing several lessons that collaborative managers must consider when managing their networks. McGuire and Silvia (2009) analyse the leadership styles of public managers involved in policy networks and find that organization-related behaviours are positively correlated with network performance. Thus, the more successfully the public manager interacts with the network environment, the more successful the network will become.

Following this stream of research, the findings of the BST case study emphasize the importance of leadership in achieving innovation in collaborations. This is characterized by a statement from the technical director of the blood division: 'I had to impose a lot of order, because there were several small projects that had minimal impact.' After our analysis of the interviews, we came up with three distinct drivers: proactive personality, managers' networking, and entrepreneurial spirit.

Proactive personality

Innovation must be actively achieved by looking for partners. Proactive personality, also known as proactive behaviour, has been defined as 'taking initiative in improving current circumstances or creating new ones' (Crant 2000). This concept acknowledges the power that personality traits have over the development of organizations. This is not consistent with the idea that organizations are the result of their environment; instead, it indicates that they are the result of individual and collective decisions based on a host of personnel and environmental factors (Fuller Jr *et al.* 2010).

In public network studies, proactive personality has been related to network success. Goerdel (2006) focuses on two specific dimensions of proactive behaviour: framing and synthesizing. By framing, the author means giving form to a project, while synthesizing refers to a strategic approach to the development of network activities that uses reductions in the cost of network interactions. In this case, proactive management was measured by the number of interactions with network nodes (business leaders or relevant state legislators, among others) controlling for when those interactions were initiated by the public manager.

A clear example of how proactive personality influences innovation is provided by the general director of BST, Dr Ramon Pau Pla Illa, who describes how he decided to build new facilities to host BST's central offices:

> One day sitting on a plane, I was reading the national press and saw that a local consortium...had a project for financing bespoke buildings in the new 22@ district. When we landed I took my phone and rang the president and told him this could be the solution. Because one of the dramas we had was that at that time the public debt was limited.

Managers' networking

Managers' networking refers to those informal and formal contacts that public managers have with other organizations. Meier and O'Toole (2007) state that 'managers cannot engage in network-like behaviour with other actors in the environment without coming into contact with them'. Moreover, Fernandez and Pitts (2007) found that the more public managers interact with other actors from their environment, the more likely they are to develop organizational change.

BST's information and communication technologies (IT) director explained that several projects in the information systems department were developed thanks to BST's relationship with other blood and tissue banks around the world. He states: 'As an IT department, we decided to join an international group of IT departments of blood banks...and we meet every six months to analyse how we operate and improve our processes.'

Entrepreneurial spirit

Schumpeter (1939) describes entrepreneurs as individuals who have the ability to convince others to develop a change in a specific domain and are thus able to change organizations. Schumpeter's concept of the entrepreneur has been widely extended in the public management literature and has been adapted to many different situations (see, among others, Ramamurti 1986; Lambright 1994; Borins 2000; Lonti and Verma 2003; Page 2003).

In public management, Mack *et al.* (2008) assess the question of what the attributes of public entrepreneurships are by testing a model formed by personnel attributes (innovation, leadership, team-building, innate qualities, demographics) and situational attributes (networks of contacts, professional and community organizational membership, affinity for local community). Overall, they find significant support for their model, stressing the importance of personnel attributes such as leadership and demographics along with other situational variables such as connection to the local community and managers' networks. In the BST case, this is reflected by the tissue division director, who clearly states, 'Every time I recognize an opportunity I do not let it go. I will have time after to evaluate if it is adequate or not. But I always take it.'

Conclusions

There are two main conclusions of our case study of the Catalan Blood and Tissue Bank. First, more attention needs to be paid to the role of public managers in the development of strategic decisions; and second, it is equally important to allow public managers to manage, and by doing so enhance their capacity to collaborate and innovate.

Innovation in inter-organizational collaborations is no longer only the result of organizational arrangements. While our case study shows that organizational arrangements can be vehicles to enhance innovation, it also proves that they can lead to increased costs and significant uncertainty. We have found evidence that the role played by public managers has a significant effect on innovation in cross-sector collaborations.

The present research inevitably presents several limitations. The major and most obvious one is that our findings rely on data collected from a single case study. Because of this, the extrapolation of our findings to other public organizations should be made with extreme care. Future research would have to acknowledge the applicability of our frameworks in other types of public organization operating in other countries. While our findings shed some light on the relationship between partnerships and innovation, additional research is needed for a more developed understanding of this complex topic.

Notes

1   This chapter reports work undertaken by the authors as part of MICINN Research Award CSO2009/11351, and AGAUR Research Award SGR1483. We would like to thank the Catalan Blood and Tissue Bank for their access to the organization. We also thank the research assistance of Adrià Albareda.
2   Banc de Sang i Teixits; Informe 2010: Memoria EFQM de Solicitud del Sello de Excelencia Europea.
3   The interviews lasted an average of 48 minutes (32 minutes for the shortest, 63 minutes for the longest). The total recorded interview time is 667 minutes. On some occasions the interviewees asked the researchers to stop recording when explaining sensitive issues. The total interview time does not take these stoppages into consideration.

References

Agranoff, R. (2006) Inside Collaborative Networks: Ten Lessons for Public Managers. *Public Administration Review*, 66(1): 56–65.

Alford, J. (2002) Why Do Public Sector Clients Co-Produce?: Towards a Contingency Theory. *Administration and Society*, 34(1): 32–56.

Barzelay, M. (1992) *Breaking through Bureaucracy: A New Vision for Managing in Government*. Berkeley, CA: University of California Press.

Barzelay, M. (1993) The Single Case Study as Intellectually Ambitious Inquiry. *Journal of Public Administration Research and Theory*, 3(3): 305–18.

Borins, S. (2000) Loose Cannons and Rule Breakers, or Enterprising Leaders? Some Evidence about Innovative Public Managers. *Public Administration Review*, 60(6): 498–507.

Borins, S. (2001) Innovation, Success and Failure in Public Management Research: Some Methodological Reflections. *Public Management Review*, 3(1): 3–17.

Buckley, P. J. and Casson, M. (1988) A Theory of Co-operation in International Business. *Management International Review (MIR)*, 28(4): 19–38.

Crant, J. M. (2000) Proactive Behavior in Organizations. *Journal of Management* 26(3): 435–62.

Dacin, M. T., Oliver, C. and Roy, J. (2007) The Legitimacy of Strategic Alliances: An Institutional Perspective. *Strategic Management Journal*, 28(2): 169–87.

Damanpour, F. and Schneider, M. (2009) Characteristics of Innovation and Innovation Adoption in Public Organizations: Assessing the Role of Managers. *Journal of Public Administration Research & Theory*, 19(3), 495–522.

Das, T. K. and Teng, B.-S. (2000) A Resource-based Theory of Strategic Alliances. *Journal of Management*, 26(1): 31–6.

Davis, G. and Greve, H. (1997) Corporate Elite Networks and Governance Changes in the 1980s. *American Journal of Sociology*, 103(1): 1–37.

de Graaf, G. and Huberts, L. W. J. C. (2008) Portraying the Nature of Corruption Using an Explorative Case Study Design. *Public Administration Review*, 68(4): 640–53.

Eden, C. and Huxham, C. (2002) Action Research, in *Essential Skills for Management Research*, edited by D. Partington. London: Sage Publications.

Eisenhardt, K. M. (1989) Building Theories from Case Study Research. *Academy of Management Review*, 14(4): 532–50.

Eisenhardt, K. M. and Schoonhoven, C. B. (1996) Resource-based View of Strategic Alliance Formation: Strategic and Social Effects in Entrepreneurial Firms.

Organization Science, 7(2): 136–50.

Fernandez, S. and Pitts, D. W. (2007) Under What Conditions Do Public Managers Favor and Pursue Organizational Change? *American Review of Public Administration*, 37(3): 324–41.

Fine, M., Weis, L., Weseen, S. and Wong, L. (1994) For Whom? Qualitative Research, Representations, and Social Responsibilities, in *Handbook of Qualitative Research*, edited by N. K. Denzin and Y. S. Lincoln. Thousand Oaks, CA: Sage: 209–35.

Fuller Jr, J. B., Kester, K. and Cox, S. (2010) Proactive Personality and Job Performance: Exploring Job Autonomy as a Moderator. *Journal of Managerial Issues*, 22(1): 35–51.

García-Canal, E., López Duarte, C., Rialp, J. and Llaneza, A. V. (2002) Accelerating International Expansion through Global Alliances: A Typology of Cooperative Strategies. *Journal of World Business*, 37: 91–107.

Goerdel, H. T. (2006) Taking Initiative: Proactive Management and Organizational Performance in Networked Environments. *Journal of Public Administration Research & Theory*, 16(3): 351–367.

Gulati, R. (1998) Alliances and Networks. *Strategic Management Journal*, 19(4): 293.

Gulati, R. (1999) Network Location and Learning: The Influence of Network Resources and Firms Capabilities on Alliance Formation. *Strategic Management Journal*, 20(5): 397–420.

Hagedoorn, J. (1993) Understanding the Rationale of Strategic Technology Partnering: Interorganizational Modes of Cooperation and Sectoral Differences. *Strategic Management Journal*, 14(5): 371–85.

Hodge, G. A. and Greve, C. (2009) PPPs: The Passage of Time Permits a Sober Reflection. *Economic Affairs*, 29(1): 33–9.

Janesick, V. J. (1994) The Dance of Qualitative Research Design: Metaphor, Methodolatry, and Meaning, in *Handbook of Qualitative Research*, edited by N. K. Denzin and Y. S. Lincoln. Thousand Oaks, CA: Sage: 209–35.

Kogut, B. (1991) Joint-venture Formation and the Option to Expand and Acquire. *Management Science*, 37: 19–33.

Lambright, W. H. (1994) Administrative Entrepreneurship and Space Technology: The Ups and Downs of 'Mission to Planet Earth'. *Public Administration Review*, 54(2): 97.

Lonti, Z. and Verma, A. (2003) The Determinants of Flexibility and Innovation in the Government Workplace: Recent Evidence from Canada. *Journal of Public Administration Research & Theory*, 13(3): 283.

Mack, W. R., Green, D. and Vedlitz, A.(2008) Innovation and Implementation in the Public Sector: An Examination of Public Entrepreneurship. *Review of Policy Research*, 25(3): 233–52.

Mandell, M. P. and Steelman, T. A. (2003) Understanding What Can be Accomplished through Interorganizational Innovations. *Public Management Review*, 5(2): 197–224.

Marshall, C. and Rossman, G. (1999) *Designing Qualitative Research*, 3rd edn. Newbury Park, CA: Sage Publications, Inc.

McGuire, M. and Silvia, C. (2009) How Good? The Impact of Leadership on Network Effectiveness. *Public Management Research Association Conference*. Columbus, OH.

Meier, K. J. and O'Toole, L. J. (2007) Modeling Public Management. *Public Management Review*, 9(4): 503–27.

Mezias, J. M. (2002) Identifying Liabilities of Foreignness and Strategies to Minimize their Effects: The Case of Labor Lawsuit Judgments in the United States. *Strategic Management Journal*, 23(3): 229–44.

Miller, W. and Crabtree, B. (1994) Clinical Research, in *Handbook of Qualitative*

Research, edited by N. K. Denzin and Y. S. Lincoln. Thousand Oaks, CA: Sage: 340–52.

Moore, M. and Hartley, J. (2008) Innovations in Governance. *Public Management Review*, 10(1): 3–20.

Mowery, D. C., Oxley, J. E. and Silverman, B. (1996) Strategic Alliances and Interfirm Knowledge Transfer. *Strategic Management Journal*, 17: 77–91.

Northouse, G. (2001) *Leadership Theory and Practice*. Thousand Oaks, CA: Sage.

Osborne, R. N. (1998) Naming the Beast: Defining and Classifying Service Innovations in Social Policy. *Human Relations*, 51(9): 1133–54.

Overman, E. S. and Boyd, K. (1994) Best Practice Research and Postbureaucratic Reform. *Journal of Public Administration Research & Theory*, 4(1): 67–83.

Page, S. (2003) Entrepreneurial Strategies for Managing Interagency Collaboration. *Journal of Public Administration Research & Theory*, 13(3): 311.

Powell, W. W. (1987) Hybrid Organizational Arrangements: New Form or Transitional Development? *California Management Review*, 30(1): 67–87.

Ramamurti, R. (1986) Public Entrepreneurs: Who They Are and How They Operate. *California Management Review*, 28(3): 142–58.

Richardson, L. (1994) Writing: A Method of Inquiry, in *Handbook of Qualitative Research*, edited by N. K. Denzin and Y. S. Lincoln. Thousand Oaks, CA: Sage: 516–29.

Saz-Carranza, A. and Serra, A. (2009) Institutional Sources of Distrust in Government Contracting: A Comparison between Home-based and Residential Social Services in Spain. *Public Management Review*, 11(3): 263–79.

Schumpeter, J. (1939) *Business Cycles*. New York: Harper & Row.

Siggelkow, N. (2007) Persuasion with Case Studies. *Academy of Management Journal*, 50(1): 20–4.

Stake, R. E. (1994) Case Studies, in *Handbook of Qualitative Research*, edited by N. K. Denzin and Y. S. Lincoln. Thousand Oaks, CA: Sage.

Strauss, A. and Corbin, J. (1994) Grounded Theory Methodology: An Overview, in *Handbook of Qualitative Research*, edited by N. K. Denzil and Y. S. Lincoln. New York: Sage Publications.

Thomson, A. M. and Perry, J. L. (2006) Collaboration Processes: Inside the Black Box. *Public Administration Review*, 66: 20–32.

Walker, R. M. (2006) Innovation Type and Diffusion: An Empirical Analysis of Local Government. *Public Administration*, 84(2): 311–35.

Walker, R. M. (2008) An Empirical Evaluation of Innovation Types and Organizational and Environmental Characteristics: Towards a Configuration Framework. *Journal of Public Administration Research & Theory*, 18(4): 591–615.

Walker, R. M. and Jeanes, E. (2001) Innovation in a Regulated Service: The Case of English Housing Associations. *Public Management Review*, 3(4): 525–50.

Young., G. J., Charns, M. P. and Shortell, S. M. (2001) Top Manager and Network Effects on the Adoption of Innovative Management Practices: A Study of TQM in a Public Hospital System. *Strategic Management Journal*, 22(10): 935–51.

Zaheer, S. (1995) Overcoming the Liability of Foreignness. *Academy of Management Journal*, 38(2): 341–63.

6 Incorporating non-profit sector perspectives in the study of public–private partnerships

Anna A. Amirkhanyan and Sarah Pettijohn

Introduction

The introductory chapter of this volume begins with the discussion of the nature, diversity and success of public–private partnerships. With contracting out well-established as a service-implementation tool used by federal, state and local governments in the United States and in other countries (Brudney *et al.* 2005; Hodge 2000), evidence presented by Hodge, Greve and other authors warrants further research to better understand and explain the formation, functioning and performance of a wider variety of partnerships between government agencies and private organizations around the world. Conceptualizing governments' success in public–private partnerships cannot be done in isolation from the success of their non-profit and for-profit partners as well as from the success of the partnership as a whole. The first reason for this is the important role organizational constituencies play in the assessment of performance. In the traditional public administration literature, even while focusing on individual public organizations, assessing the attainment of internal goals provides only a limited view of organizational success (Etzioni 1964; Miles 1981; Price 1972). A broader perspective suggests also examining the extent to which an organization satisfies its multiple internal and external constituencies (Connolly *et al.* 1980; Miles 1981). Similarly, in the case of PPPs, a comprehensive understanding of their performance should go beyond the ability of a government agency to attain its goals, but it should also incorporate the ability of partners to achieve *their* organizational goals and to satisfy *their* constituencies. As Hodge and Greve note 'PPPs are established because they can benefit both the public and private sectors' (Hodge and Greve 2007). In addition, our view of PPPs' performance should incorporate *partnership-level* outcomes, such as the attainment of long-term capacities, greater efficiency and identifying additional partners for future projects. It should include the various *community-level* benefits – political, economic, technical and other – such as greater goal congruence between organizations, awareness of industry-wide problems, reduction of service overlap and more efficient use of resources, service innovations due to information sharing, new forms of democratic decision-making and greater social inclusion, and opening public services to wider constituency influences (Bovaird 2010; McQuaid 2000; Hodge *et al.*

2010). Furthermore, the performance of PPPs may influence the *success of implementation of broad national policies* by making them more responsive and flexible, by bringing together the resources that make certain policy outcomes possible, or by raising the legitimacy of a policy within a jurisdiction through the involvement of local participants (McQuaid 2000; Osborne 2000).

Public management research generally accepts that organizational performance in the public sector is a multidimensional construct, and that government agencies pursue a range of goals related to costs, quality, democratic accountability, regulatory and legal compliance, political gains, innovation, and others (Andrews *et al.* 2006; Selden and Sowa 2004). As the next section details, governments' private partners may pursue goals that are not entirely concordant with those of the government agencies. For non-profit organizations, serving some client groups and not others, reducing red tape and maintaining financial independence through marketing or increased private giving may be more important than fair distribution of resources or regulatory compliance. For-profit organizations, on the other hand, may be more concerned with the financial dimensions of performance. While some joint goals may be clearly articulated and some overlap between organizational goals may exist, partnering organizations may conceptualize these joint goals differently. Their assessments of performance may vary as well, and thus partnerships may fail to produce synergistic benefits (Hodge *et al.* 2010). Thus, a comprehensive assessment of PPPs' performance should encompass multiple entities, perspectives and performance dimensions.

Along with the broader conceptualization of PPPs' success, a broader conceptualization of its determinants may be needed. The emphasis on the selection of private partners as one of the key *policy choices* in the privatization process (Brown and Potoski 2003) directed the early privatization literature to focus on the capacities of private organizations. Indeed, for-profit and non-profit partners' management, personnel, financial, collaborative, and technological capacities are central to the success of PPPs, particularly because government delegates the important task of service implementation to the private partners. More recently, our understanding on private partners' capacities was broadened to include their stewardship abilities (Van Slyke 2007). However, just as the benefits of private partners have often been omitted from the discussion of PPPs' outcomes, the question of public sector capacities was initially less relevant for the *hollow-state* model. The more recent privatization research, however, supports the idea that government capacity to make 'make-or-buy decisions', develop and maintain competitive markets, as well as co-produce, fund, monitor and evaluate their partners are at least as important in determining the success of PPPs (Brown *et al.* 2006; Johnston and Girth, 2012). Thus, keeping environmental factors constant, the unique capacities of *both* public and private organizations, as well as the *synergy* between the two sectors, must be considered among the determinants of the many dimensions of PPPs' performance. This synergy within PPPs may refer to their structure, i.e. configuration of organizations within a network, power imbalances or organizational roles in the network. It may also refer to the more

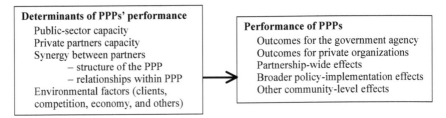

Figure 6.1 Performance of PPPs: towards a broader framework

informal relationships between organizations reflecting goal alignment, trust, open-mindedness, shared philosophy and exchange of values, all of which may minimize opportunistic behaviour of organizations and hence affect the outcomes (McQuaid 2000; Klijn and Teisman 2000).

The framework shown in Figure 6.1 reflects a broader understanding of PPPs' determinants and outcomes proposed here. Its breadth, however, presents numerous challenges for operationalization and testing. Operationalizing the outcomes for numerous partners – one of such challenges – represents a fruitful direction for the future research, as we discuss in the conclusion of this essay. Dealing with the recursive relationships may present another challenge. For instance, different outcomes may influence each other *and* positively or negatively affect the synergy of public–private relationships, as well as enhance or undermine public and private organizational capacities. The objective of this chapter is to look more carefully at some parts of this framework. In particular, we attempt to better understand the capacities and the objectives of the government's non-profit partners. We will also discuss the questions of designing and structuring public–private relationships in PPPs, and will elaborate on some of the influences PPPs may have on non-profit organizations. This chapter will conclude by proposing a set of research questions for the future research.

As a point of clarification, historically, the concept of PPPs referred to many kinds of collaborative arrangements (Hodge and Greve 2007). Some consider privatization conceptually different from public–private partnerships because, according to these authors, contracting implies ability to specify service outcomes (which is mostly done by the government agency), while public–private partnerships assume joint decision-making and more ambiguity (Klijn and Teisman 2000). This chapter views contracts and other privatization initiatives as a subset of public–private partnerships. This position is based on the contracting literature suggesting that privatization initiatives may vary greatly in terms of decision-making: from more unilateral to more collaborative (Amirkhanyan 2009; DeHoog 1990), and in terms of service measurability, from more to less measurable (Brown and Potoski 2006). In addition, the term 'private' in PPPs refers to any non-governmental (non-public) organizations. While this chapter is relevant to both public non-profit and public for-profit partnerships, its focus is primarily on the non-profit partners operating in the context of health and human services.

Synergies and conflicts between public and non-profit sectors

Theoretical frameworks on the role of the non-profit sector

Numerous authors point out the lack of studies examining the private side of PPPs: the capacities, the expectations and the motives of non-governmental partners that may affect the synergy and outcomes of public–private relationships (Carroll and Steane 2000; Hodge *et al.* 2010; Skelcher 2010: 301).[1] With approximately 1.8 million non-profit organizations nationally (Boris 2006; Salamon 2002), many of which are actively engaged in a variety of cross-sector partnerships, theoretical and empirical evidence on non-profit organizations may provide interesting insights on their role in PPPs.

Most of the theoretical frameworks explaining the existence and the role of non-profit organizations in the contemporary societies reflect the long-standing historical connection and an 'implicit partnership' between public and non-profit sectors (Gronbjerg and Salamon 2002: 447). The *government failure theory* suggests that non-profit organizations form as a result of government's inability to satisfy citizens' needs in terms of quality, type, level or accessibility of services (Weisbrod 1977; 1989; 1997). In response to this, citizens pursue a range of options, including that of creating non-profit organizations to address the expectations of diverse groups (Lipsky and Smith 1989–90; Salamon 1987). In addition, the *market failure theory* suggests that significant informational asymmetries of private markets result in service under-provision or the possibility of private firms' opportunistic behaviour at the expense of client welfare (Steinberg 2006; Hansmann 1980). Due to the high transaction costs associated with the prompt market entry for government agencies (Wellford and Gallagher 1988), the most feasible solution to these problems involves non-profit organizations entering and providing these services. Both of these fundamental theories highlight the inherent interdependence between the attributes and scope of public, for-profit and non-profit sectors. They also emphasize the important and legitimate roles played by each of the three sectors in a civilized society in satisfying the unmet social needs. Commenting on this interdependence from the perspective of the non-profit sector, Boris (2006: 3) notes: 'The interaction between government and non-profit organizations in civil society is complex and dynamic, ebbing and flowing with shifts in social and economic policy, political administrations, and social norms.' In the United States, where the direct provision of public social welfare services and healthcare is relatively more limited compared to other countries, non-profit organizations have been particularly visible as providers of these services[2] (Moulton and Anheier 2000; Carroll and Steane 2000; Gronbjerg and Salamon 2002).

Non-profit management theories identify many diverse and constantly chang-ing qualities of non-profit organizations. Some of these qualities make them similar to and compatible with public organizations, while others place them at odds with their public partners (Boris 2006; Weisbrod 1997: 549). The following two sections identify the theories and the practical implications pertaining to various non-profit qualities that make them more or less compatible with the government sector.

Public–non-profit synergies

Among the attributes that enhance the synergies between public and non-profit sectors, the most important is undoubtedly their mission-oriented and socially conscious character (Amirkhanyan 2010). Non-profit organizations pursue goals that reflect non-monetary, moral, ideological and other values of their leaders and members (Carroll and Steane 2000). In accordance with the market failure theory, many non-profits have missions that involve providing uncompensated goods and services that improve the welfare of vulnerable groups – missions compatible with those of many public social welfare policies (Ferris and Graddy 1986, 1991; Weisbrod 1997). For-profit organizations may also share these values and do extensive charity work; however, their existence is dependent on the profitability of their core operations. If these core operations involve services to vulnerable populations – often contracted by government agencies – these operations are pursued with the primary goal of generating profits for the company. This explains why public and non-profit organizations are often perceived as 'co-producers' (Alford and Hughes 2008; Smith and Lipsky 1993; Weisbrod 1997).

In addition, non-profit structures presume a set of safeguards critical in the markets with a limited number of providers and with significant informational asymmetry between producers and consumers. In such markets, for-profit providers may behave opportunistically and exploit consumer ignorance by charging higher prices and cutting costs at the expense of client welfare (Eggleston and Zeckhauser 2002; Hansmann 1980, 1986, 1996). Non-profits are legally prohibited from distributing profits and excessively compensating their leaders (Steinberg 2006), and are therefore less likely to behave opportunistically at the expense of service quality, as a general rule (Cohen 2001; Heinrich and Fournier 2004; Weisbrod 1989). Availability of volunteers, tax exemptions and deductions, private donations and other benefits further minimize moral hazard and ensure some level of financial stability for these organizations (Ferris and Graddy 1986; Smith and Smyth 1996). These structural safeguards may further improve the degree of goal compatibility between public and non-profit organi-zations.

Finally, accountability pressures from the various constituencies – donors, volunteers, boards, or professional associations – ensure additional oversight for non-profit service providers and lower the transaction costs associated with government monitoring (Brody 2002; Ferris and Graddy 1986, 1991: 545; Romzek and Johnston 1999; O'Regan and Oster 2002). Thus, non-profit organizations are expected to 'help build the networks of trust and reciprocity, the social capital that allows democratic societies to function effectively' (Boris 2006: 2). These qualities are hypothesized to further improve the synergy between public and private partners in PPPs.

Sources of conflict

Other qualities and incentives, however, may undermine their relationships with the public partners. Lester Salamon, whose seminal work underscores the ties between public and non-profit sectors, uses the term 'paradigm of conflict' to characterize this historic connection (Salamon 2006: 401). The tensions between sectors occur not only because the non-profit sector is often portrayed in political debates as an alternative or a replacement for the government growth (Gronbjerg and Salamon 2002), but also because of the many unique motives and goals of non-profit organizations, which may destabilize PPPs (Skelcher 2010).

Non-profit organizations are unique in that their motives and activities are based on several key interrelated ideas. The first is the value of pluralism (Boris 2006; Grobman 2007) – the idea that the unique needs of American communities should encourage their residents to satisfy their own needs in diverse and specific ways, while avoiding the 'generalist' approaches of the national government. The second is the idea of philanthropic particularism reflecting non-profits' propensity to define their own issues and problems and focus on specific ideological, moral or other groups rather than the general population (Steinberg 2006). In accordance with the theory of commons, non-profits tend to satisfy the needs of individuals within a certain social space, and often do so autonomously and irrespective of cost-effectiveness or efficiency considerations (Lohman 1992). The final closely-related principle is that of individualism, which, among other things, presumes that the citizens will act independently from the government in order to improve their welfare (Salamon 2002).

While defining the spirit and the priorities of the third sector, these principles and ideas may complicate the relationship between public and non-profit organizations. Government agencies are likely to partner with non-profit organizations with the intention of spending public funds in a universally accessible and financially fair, equitable and consistent manner across all racial, religious and jurisdictional boundaries. Meanwhile, non-profit organizations may pursue their advocacy and service delivery work with a specific community group rather than a 'median voter' in mind (Young 2006). In some healthcare markets, non-profit providers have been shown to minimize their service to the poor and focus on providing high-quality services to the more affluent community residents (Amirkhanyan *et al.* 2008). Furthermore, reliance on clients and volunteers who belong to a limited 'social space' may result in amateurism; and excessive mission-centeredness at the expense of cost-effectiveness may result in inefficient spending of resources (Steinberg 2006). For-profit organizations, on the other hand, may use more generous compensation packages to attract more experienced and skilled management and professional staff capable of achieving excellence and cost-effectiveness.

The government failure and transaction cost theories both suggest that non-profit organizations are typically able to respond quickly to various social problems. Salamon (2002) notes that non-profit organizations should be recognized as success- ful pioneers and first responders to the many recent social issues, such as HIV/AIDS prevention and others. While making a real impact on the prevalence and severity of these social problems, this flexibility and innovativeness may be at odds with the longer-term institutional environment of the public sector. Government agencies operate within the constitutional framework that involves extensive legislative and judicial oversight in programme development, implementation and evaluation; due process for collecting citizens' feedback or resolving programmatic issues; and expectations of transparency and responsiveness to public inquiries. These factors may be seen as red tape by non-profit organizations involved in PPPs. Thus, some non-profits may be forced to comply with these regulations, which may result in mission distortion and internal organizational problems. Others may actively resent these institutional pressures, which, in turn, may undermine their role in PPPs. The latter may become a potential source of conflict across sectors. Thus, prior research suggests that tensions between sectors may not only negatively influence the direc- tion and the scope of non-profit activities but also affect their funding sources and force commercialization (Moulton and Anheier 2000).

During recent decades, non-profit organizations have experienced growing levels of competition within its own sector as well as with the for-profit compa- nies that have entered traditionally non-profit markets (Gronbjerg and Salamon 2002; Salamon 1999). Coupled with the most recent economic recession in the United States and around the world, these environmental pressures affect both public and private sources of non-profit funding and encourage successful non- profits to be more professionalized and, eventually, more commercialized (Moulton and Anheier 2000). Today, non-profits are increasingly investing in better financial management, fundraising and marketing strategies, and are inter- ested in attracting new clients, members and donors. They are also increasingly pressured to demonstrate high levels of performance to their stakeholders (Salamon 2002). These trends produce growing concerns about business motives replacing the 'do-gooder' motives in the non-profit sector, motives that create the so-called 'for-profits in disguise' – non-profit organizations that may behave opportunistically in their interactions with their constituencies (Carroll and Steane 2000; Steinberg 2006). Thus while the early non-profit management liter- ature stressed that for-profit firms are more likely than non-profit organizations to use their political influence to avoid government oversight (Smith and Smyth 1996[3]), the more recent government contracting literature finds that non-profit organizations may also use political strategies, for instance, for the purposes of advocating for higher service rates with their public partners (Romzek and Johnston 2005). The more extreme instances of non-profit opportunism include cases of financial abuse at the most well-known charities worldwide such as The United Ways, American Red Cross or The Smithsonian (Arenson 1995; Grimaldi and Trescott 2008; Reaves 2001). These trends may further reinforce the percep- tion of governments and non-profits growing apart in their motives and strategies.

The final consideration that may reinforce the idea of the paradigm of conflict is determined, more objectively, by the nature of services produced by non-profit organizations. Most non-profit organizations in the US operate in the fields of health, education, and social services, where performance measurement is particularly challenging. Unlike the more easily measurable services typically produced by for-profit providers, such as trash collection, construction or equipment maintenance, the outcomes of social welfare- and education-related services are highly complex and less tangible, which affects the nature of accountability relationships (Amirkhanyan 2010). These service fields require more elaborate relational structures in public–non-profit partnerships.

Unanswered questions

This section reviews the many synergies and the potential philosophical and practical conflicts that may have serious implications for the design of public–private partnerships. With these considerations in mind, it is hard to advocate for a greater use of public–non-profit partnerships: each of the two sectors – non-profit and for-profit – plays its unique role in various markets and is affected by its fundamental attributes that define the outcomes of PPPs and the motives of the actors. Clearly, empirical evidence is needed to advance this discussion. First, more evidence is needed on the performance of non-profit organizations in comparison to their public and private counterparts in multi-sector industries (e.g. hospitals), as well as on the public–non-profit comparisons of performance in one- or two-sector industries (such as homeless services). Empirical studies conducted to date, mostly in the context of privatization, suggest that while for-profit service provision may be associated with lower operating costs, findings are generally mixed on the quality and client welfare aspects of services (Dias and Maynard-Moody 2006; Donahue 1989; Herzlinger and Krasker 1987; Hodge 2000; Rainey and Chun 2005; Savas 2000, 2005). Specifically, little evidence of non-profit superiority has been found in the studies focusing on services to vulnerable populations (Amirkhanyan *et al.* 2008; Gronbjerg 1990; Heinrich 2000; Herzlinger and Krasker 1987). In the nursing home care industry, for example, non-profit nursing homes have been found to deliver superior quality of care while restricting the number of clients funded by the Medicaid programme (Amirkhanyan *et al.* 2008). Meanwhile, for-profit nursing homes, often chain-affiliated, may use the economies of scale and other cost-cutting strategies and serve a higher share of Medicaid-eligible clients, while generally having lower levels of care quality (ibid.). This situation may require different regulatory and service-monitoring strategies by the partnering and regulating government agencies. More evidence of such industry-specific trends would help inform the public managers' decisions regarding PPPs within those fields.

Secondly, it is important to understand how the above-mentioned synergies and conflicts are perceived and experienced by non-profit and public partners at the national and local levels of government: Do they observe any evidence supporting the theoretical propositions presented above? What practical implications do these theoretical considerations have on government agencies' actions in PPPs? What effect do these partnerships have on the internal organizational management realities of non-profit actors in PPPs? The next section attempts to explore these questions by reviewing some of the recent empirical work as well as the findings of a brief survey conducted for the purposes of this study.

Public and private sectors' perspectives on ownership and PPPs

Partners' ownership and public–private relationships

As suggested earlier, the role of non-profit organizations is widely discussed by policy-makers in the political debates on the scope of public programmes (Young 2006). Nonetheless, the views and the experiences of civil servants – the actual partners of private organizations – have not received much attention. It is often assumed that government agencies need to recognize and manage the tensions between sectors (Osborne and Murray 2000). Governance of PPPs is a complex process where, as a part of designing governance mechanisms, public agencies are expected to lay out the rules constraining and controlling private actors as well as allowing some degree of flexibility (Skelcher 2010). With the possibility of cross-sector tensions discussed in the previous section, government agencies may be expected to utilize this knowledge in the design of PPPs' governance structures. Like the general population, government managers are exposed to the evidence of performance problems in private organizations (Brody 2002) and may be pondering the question of non-profit trustworthiness (Young 2006).

A recent study on the effects of ownership in a diverse sample of state and local government contracts with non-profit and for-profit organizations suggests that government managers question the commonly ascribed virtues of non-profit organizations and tend to reject the proposition that ownership plays a role in the decision to partner with private organizations as well as in the process of contract implementation (Amirkhanyan 2010).[4] Thus, government managers attempt to act as 'smart-buyers' (Kettl 1993) by avoiding sector-related stereotypes and searching for objective bases for their decisions (Amirkhanyan 2010). While reporting no 'biases' towards any sector, the empirical comparison of contract-monitoring practices in fact suggests some important differences in the way relationships are designed and private partners' performance is monitored. Specifically, public managers working with non-profit partners use less outcome-based, more informal and descriptive monitoring tools; they also allow a higher degree of flexibility and discretion for their non-profit partners (Carman 2008; Romzek and Johnston 1999, 2005; Smith and Smyth 1996). These partnerships are also more likely than the public for-profit ones to rely on qualitative performance data and focus on such outcomes as equitable access to services, contractors' reputation and regulatory compliance (Amirkhanyan 2010). The latter trend may be determined by the way governments conceptualize performance of each sector: the use of qualitative information and assessment of regulatory and legal compliance may suggest that public agencies realize the lack of clear-cut, short-term quantitative milestones in their partnerships with non-profit partners, and, instead, focus on constituency-satisfaction-related measures (Amirkhanyan 2010).

Partnerships with non-profit organizations are also more likely to involve self-reporting – data on outcomes supplied directly by the partners – and less likely to involve direct service monitoring (Amirkhanyan 2010). This is perhaps due to the government's strategy to minimize the transaction costs and let the contractors report on services with virtually unobservable or delayed outcomes where direct monitoring is less feasible (Amirkhanyan 2010). Finally, research suggests that non-profit organizations are more likely to initiate negotiations with their public partners on performance measurement and the overall programme implementation by providing feedback, supplying additional performance information, and clarifying the performance data (Amirkhanyan 2009). The latter may be explained by the fact that while for-profit organizations prioritize their financial bottom lines and comply with the government's monitoring requirements, 'measurement strategies used by non-profit organizations can be similar to those enforced by the government, and hence they will be more likely to integrate the internal and external evaluation systems to avoid administrative burden and redundancy' (Amirkhanyan 2009: 544). These findings suggest that while government agencies do not report utilizing different strategies with each sector, governance structures found in PPPs may, in fact, be different across sectors, involving different procedures, degree of transparency and level of private partners' contributions to the overall synergy of the relationship.

Evidence on the experiences of non-profit partners

As mentioned earlier, numerous authors note the lack of data on the way PPPs are perceived by non-profit organizations and what organizational effects they observe as a result of partnering with the public sector (Carroll and Steane 2000). While some positive effects have been suggested, such as additional financial support or ability to influence policy implementation (ibid.), the tensions prevalent in PPPs may also negatively affect the scope and direction of non-profit organizations and reduce non-public funding (Moulton and Anheier 2000). To inform this discussion, this section presents some preliminary findings of an exploratory study we conducted to examine the impact of government contracts on non-profit organizations operating in the field of health and human services.[5] The study is based on a stratified random sample[6] of 30 contracts awarded by the Health and Human Services (HHS) departments in five local jurisdictions. The study involved unstructured interviews covering organizational performance, the extent of public funding, organizational and managerial priorities, leadership style, personnel management, board governance, organizational political context, and prevalence of external pressures. While fully exploring the richness of the obtained data is beyond the scope of this section of our chapter, we will present some key findings relevant to this discussion.

First, most of our respondents – managers of non-profit organizations implementing health and human service contracts with county governments – indicated that their organizational priorities have changed considerably upon being awarded government contracts. Rather than focusing on their core missions, a significant portion of managers' attention was diverted to complying with contract stipulations, which did not always mirror the broader organizational priorities. Respondents reported 'becoming more like the government' and paying more attention to 'the contract' and 'public funding' rather than their organizational missions. The changes mentioned by non-profit managers involved creating the structures and processes for modified record-keeping, accounting practices, procedures to track employees' performance across contracted and non-contracted programmes, and other financial management changes necessary to ensure that public funds remain designated to specific programmes.

Performance-related reporting played a central role in public–private relationships and presented some additional challenges. For example, respondents argued that reporting requirements did not adequately capture their organizational success and provided a limited picture of their activities. Some non-profit managers were required to use standardized reporting forms, which constrained their ability to present a holistic picture of their accomplishments. In the cases when such opportunities were provided through optional narrative questions, managers regarded those optional features as 'a waste of [their] time'. Furthermore, some contractors were required to continuously provide the evidence of need for their services, for instance by showing an increase in the number of clients they served. The latter was perceived as misleading and done at the expense of programmatic activities. Notably, while one would expect that the leaders of non-profit organizations would be accustomed to being held accountable for the financial aspects of their performance, some respondents were frustrated that financial compliance appeared to be prioritized by their public partners over fulfilling the programmatic goals. Overall, these reporting expectations were perceived as excessive and constraining: respondents felt they were caught in the 'red tape of the government', which prevented their organization from using discretion and striving to find innovative solutions to the problems at hand. This finding is consistent with prior research on non-profits losing autonomy and becoming 'agents of government' (Smith and Lipsky 1993). These issues were especially prevalent in organizations that received a substantial percentage of their budgets from a government contract, particularly because their performance would have implications for the likelihood of receiving public funding in the future and, essentially, keeping their programmes alive.

Finally, in addition to the administrative changes, non-profit managers reported that their own leadership style and the way their employees perceived them had changed since receiving the contract. Several managers argued that their work relationships suffered to some degree, and a few respondents even felt ostracized from the programme staff. Thus the employees saw non-profit managers as key enforcers of the contract, and expected them to apply pressure to accomplish the goals of the contracted programmes. As one non-profit manager notes, '[she is] no longer a motivator. Now, [she is] just a nagger. All [she] do[es] is walk around and ask employees if they are filling out their forms.'

The preliminary evidence of this exploratory survey provides a snapshot of the many effects a PPP may have on the management, leadership, personnel and, perhaps, operational matters within private organizations. These concerns may have a noticeable influence on the perceived benefits (and costs) of the partnership for each private organization. Are these concerns going to impact the quality of the programmes and the benefits, as they are perceived by the public partners and other involved constituencies? Do they negatively affect inter-organizational relationships? How do public managers perceive and respond to these concerns? These questions may present important directions for the future research on PPPs. In the next section we offer some concluding remarks and point out some additional questions that may be answered in the future studies.

Conclusion and some additional unanswered questions

The intellectual history of public administration, in a way, represents a search for alternatives to the traditional 'bureaucratic' delivery of government programmes, a search for alternatives that can save costs and improve performance. Commonly, this search reflects some degree of dissatisfaction with the practice and the discipline of public administration: dissatisfaction with the Weberian orthodox 'machines'; with the responsive and democratically accountable government advanced during the New Public Administration era; and, more recently, with the private markets and the complex nature of the 'networked' government. The common aspect of these popular 'alternatives' is that for each of them, capable *public* management that guides the administration of policies through these arrangements still seems to be the key element in their success. Furthermore, in the search for the best approaches to PPPs, we are likely to come to the usual 'it depends' conclusion: different institutional contexts, contingencies and service areas introduce complexities that need to be accounted for in the analysis and understood by the practitioners. Without achieving this task, it may be reasonable to ask whether generalizations in the field of PPP research will have any value (Carroll and Steane 2000).

In addition to several research questions mentioned above, one promising direction for the future research on PPPs may involve understanding their diversity and creating typologies that facilitate the future theory-building efforts. Specifically, while much attention has been paid to various *service delivery* partnerships, some cross-sector partnerships may be focused on *advocacy* or *regulation*. Currently, a large number of non-profit organizations are involved in advocacy and some form of 'shared governance' (Smith and Gronbjerg 2006). They pressure public agencies to satisfy urgent social needs or create collaborative alliances to address those needs (Salamon 1999). Therefore, formal and informal public–private arrangements involving various kinds of advocacy need to be better understood. In addition, as governments increasingly delegate the task of service delivery to private markets, they often maintain or enhance their regulatory roles to make sure that the public interests are protected (Hodge *et al.* 2010). Gronbjerg and Salamon (2002) point out that regulation is already an important form of public–non-profit relationships. Furthermore, Steinberg (2006) and others have noted some important differences in government regulation of non-profit and for-profit organizations. The latter may be determined by the roles these organizations play in the regulatory process itself.

Finally, another area for future research may deal with the gargantuan task of conceptualizing and measuring the performance of PPPs. The impressive scope of performance-measurement research conducted to date has identified several major problems associated with this task in the context of public and privatized services. They include: (a) broad, ambiguous and complex missions that are hard to translate into manageable performance systems; (2) limited capacity to collect comprehensive and long-term performance data; (3) existence of perverse incentives for major stakeholders involved in the performance-monitoring process; (4) political trade-offs between numerous aspects of performance for different constituencies; (5) use of generic approaches that are not tailored to the unique organizational, environmental, professional, and policy contexts at hand; and (6) failure to account for the hidden costs of performance management (Amirkhanyan *et al.* 2008; Blasi 2002; Bouckaert *et al.* 2002; Callahan and Kloby 2007; Courty and Marschke 2007; Frederickson and Frederickson 2006; Gianakis 2002; Kravchuk and Schack 1996; Nicholson-Crotty *et al.* 2006; Radin 2000, 2006). These issues may be exacerbated by the multi-organizational nature of PPPs and need to be systematically examined. One point worth remembering is that PPPs are often established for political and ideological reasons (McQuaid 2000), and thus it is important to understand the political dimensions of PPPs' performance. In addition, the existence of multiple constituencies, whose performance contributes to the overall success of PPPs, motivates the study of the effect of structural, political, regulatory and other determinants on the outcomes for each participant within a partnership, as well as on the relationship between them. Thus, like non-profit managers surveyed in our study cited the many influences that public contracts have on their internal operation, it may be worthwhile to explore the question of how governments change as a result of these partnerships in terms of their structure, leadership capacity and other characteristics.

Notes

1   Work by Carroll and Steane (2000) is among notable exceptions, focusing on many of the issues discussed in this chapter.
2   Nonetheless these services are often financially supported by public funds.
3   Similar problems may occur in the case of public for-profit partnerships.
4   This is consistent with earlier empirical research suggesting low levels of awareness about sector-related differences (Steinberg 2006; James and Rose-Ackerman 1986).
5   The study was conducted in five local jurisdictions: Montgomery, Fairfax, Price Williams, Arlington Counties and the District of Columbia. These counties are more affluent than other areas in the United States. According to the US Census Bureau, in

these five areas the median household income (in 2009 inflation-adjusted dollars) ranges from 67,006 to 104,259, while the US median household income is $51,425.

6 The study focused on the contracts awarded in 2008. To qualify for the study, participating organizations had to receive the contract within the last three years. If the organization had received other contracts from HHS, the contract examined in this study had to be outside the scope of prior contracts. Interviewed contract managers had to work for the organizations before, during and after the contract was awarded. Samples were stratified by size of the award and size of the organization. Contract award sizes were grouped into three categories: small (less than $100,000), medium ($100,000 to $1 million) and large (over $1 million). Organizational size is measured by the organization's expenses for 2008. This variable was collapsed into three groups: small (less than $1 million) medium ($1 million to $5 million), and large (more than $5 million).

References

Alford, J., and Hughes, O. (2008) Public Value Pragmatism as the Next Phase of Public Management. *The American Review of Public Administration,* 28(2): 130–48.

Amirkhanyan, A. (2009) Collaborative Performance Measurement: Examining and Explaining the Prevalence of Collaboration in State and Local Government Performance Monitoring. *Journal of Public Administration Research and Theory (JPART),* 19 (3): 523–54.

Amirkhanyan, A. (2010) Monitoring across Sectors: Examining the Effect of Non-profit and For-profit Contractor Ownership on Performance Monitoring in State and Local Government Contracts. *Public Administration Review,* 70(5): 742–55.

Amirkhanyan, A., Kim, H. Y. and Lambright, K. T. (2008) Does the Public Sector Outperform the Non-profit and For-profit Sectors? Evidence from a National Panel Study on Nursing Home Quality and Access. *Journal of Policy Analysis and Management,* 27(2): 326–53.

Andrews, R., Boyne, G. A. and Walker, R. M. (2006) Subjective and Objective Measures of Organizational Performance: An Empirical Exploration, in Boyne, G. A., Meier, K. J., O'Toole, L. J. and Walker, R. M. (eds) *Public Service Performance: Perspectives on Measurement and Management.* New York: Cambridge University Press, pp. 14–34.

Arenson, K. W. (1995) Ex-united Way Leader Gets Seven Years for Embezzlement. *New York Times,* 23 June.

Blasi, G. J. (2002) Government Contracting and Performance Measurement in Human Services. *International Journal of Public Admin,* 25(4): 519–38.

Boris, E. T. (2006) Introduction: Non-profit Organizations in a Democracy: Roles and Responsibilities, in Boris, E. and Steuerle C. E. (eds) Non-profits and Government: Collaboration and Conflict. Washington, DC: The Urban Institute Press, pp. 1–35.

Bouckaert, G. and Peters, B. G. (2002) Performance Measurement and Management: The Achilles Heel in Administrative Modernization. *Public Performance & Management Review,* 25(4): 359–62.

Bovaird, T. (2010) A Brief Intellectual History of the Public–Private Partnership Movement, in Hodge, G., Greve, C. and Boardman, A. (eds) *International Handbook on Public–Private Partnerships.* Cheltenham: Edward Elgar, pp. 43–67.

Brody, E. (2002) Accountability and Public Trust, in Salamon, L. (ed.) *The State of Non-profit America.* Washington, DC: Brookings Institution Press, pp. 471–98.

Brown, T. L. and Potoski, M. (2003) Contract-Management Capacity in Municipal and County Governments. *Public Administration Review,* 63 (2): 153–64.

Brown, T. L. and Potoski, M. (2006) Contracting for Management: Assessing Management Capacity under Alternative Service Delivery Arrangements. *Journal of Policy Analysis and Management*, 25: 323–46.

Brown, T. L., Potoski, M. and Van Slyke, D. M. (2006) Managing Public Service Contracts: Aligning Values, Institutions, and Markets. *Public Administration Review*, 66(3): 323–31.

Brudney, J., Fernandez, S., Ryu, J. and Wright, D. (2005) Exploring and Explaining Contracting Out: Patterns among the American States. JPART 15: 393–419.

Callahan, K. and Kloby, K. (2007) Collaboration Meets the Performance Measurement Challenge. *Public Manager*, 36 (2): 9–24.

Carman, J. G. (2008) Non-profits, Funders, and Evaluation: Accountability in Action. *American Review of Public Administration*, 39(4): 376–90.

Carroll, P. and Steane, P. (2000) Public–Private Partnerships: Sectorial perspectives, in *Public–Private Partnerships. Theory and Practice in International Perspective*, edited by S. Osborne. London and New York: Routledge, pp. 36–56.

Cohen, S. (2001) A Strategic Framework for Devolving Responsibility and Functions from Government to the Private Sector. *Public Administration Review*, 61(4): 432–40.

Connolly, T., Conlon, E. J. and Deutsch, S. J. (1980) Organizational Effectiveness: A Multiple Constituency Approach. *Academy of Management Review*, 5: 211–17.

Courty, P. and Marschke, G. (2007) Making Government Accountable: Lessons from a Federal Job Training Program. *Public Administration Review*, 67(5): 904–16.

DeHoog, R. (1990) Competition, Negotiation, or Cooperation: Three Models for Service Contracting. *Administration and Society*, 22: 317–40.

Dias, J. J. and Maynard-Moody, S. (2006) For-profit Welfare: Contracts, Conflicts, and the Performance Paradox. *Journal of Public Administration Research and Theory*, 17(2): 189–211.

Donahue, J. D. (1989) *The Privatization Decision: Public Ends, Private Means.* New York: Basic Books.

Eggleston, K. and Zeckhauser, R. (2002) Government Contracting for Health Care, in *Market-Based Governance: Supply Side, Demand Side, Upside, Downside*, edited by Donahue, J. D. and Nye Jr, J. S., Washington, DC: Brookings Institution Press, pp. 29–65.

Etzioni, A. (1964) *Modern Organizations.* Englewood Cliffs, NJ: Prentice-Hill, Inc.

Ferris, J. and Graddy, E. (1986) Contracting Out: For What? With Whom? *Public Administration Review*, 46(4): 332–44.

Ferris, J, and Graddy, E. (1991) Production Costs, Transaction Costs, and Local Government Contractor Choice. *Economic Inquiry*, 29(3): 541–54.

Frederickson, D. G. and Frederickson, G. (2006) *Measuring the Performance of the Hollow State.* Washington, DC: Georgetown University Press.

Gianakis, G. A. (2002) The Promise of Public Sector Performance Measurement: Anodyne or Placebo? *Public Administration Quarterly*, 26(1/2): 35–64.

Grimaldi, J. V. and Trescott, J. (2008) Smithsonian Official Resigned in Wake of Ethics Probe: Internal Report Cited Latino Center Leader for Multiple Violations. *Washington Post*, 15 April.

Grobman, G. (2007) Introduction to the Nonprofit Sector: A Practical Approach for the 21st Century. Harrisburg, PA: White Hat Communications.

Gronbjerg, K. A. (1990) Poverty and Non-profit Organizational Behavior. *Social Service Review*, 64(2): 208–41.

Gronbjerg, K. A. and Salamon, L. (2002) Devolution, Marketization, and the Changing

Shape of Government-Nonprofit Relations, in Salamon, L. (ed.) *The State of Nonprofit America*. Washington, DC: Brookings Institution Press, pp. 445–70.

Hansmann, H. B. (1980) The Role of Nonprofit Enterprise. *Yale Law Journal*, 89(3): 835–901.

Hansmann, H. B. (1986) The Role of Nonprofit Enterprise, in *The Economics of Nonprofit Institutions: Studies in Structure and Policy*, edited by Rose-Ackerman, S. New York: Oxford University Press, pp. 57–86.

Hansmann, H. B. (1996) *The Ownership of Enterprise*. Cambridge, MA: Belknap Press.

Heinrich, C. J. (2000) Organizational Form and Performance: An Empirical Investigation of Nonprofit and For-profit Job-training Service Providers. *Journal of Policy Analysis and Management*, 19(2): 233–61.

Heinrich, C. J. and Fournier, E. (2004) Dimensions of Publicness and Performance in Substance Abuse Treatment Organizations. *Journal of Policy Analysis and Management*, 23(1): 49–70.

Herzlinger, R. E. and Krasker, W.S. (1987) Who Profits from Nonprofits? *Harvard Business Review*, 65(1): 93–106.

Hodge, G. A. (2000) *Privatization: An International Review of Performance*. Boulder, CO: Westview Press.

Hodge, G. and Greve, C. (2007) Public–Private Partnerships: An International Performance Review. *Public Administration Review*, May-June, 545–58.

Hodge G., Greve, C. and Boardman, A. (2010) Conclusions: Public–Private Partnership – International Experiences and Future Challenges, in Hodge, G., Greve, C. and Boardman, A. (eds). *International Handbook on Public–Private Partnerships*. Cheltenham: Edward Elgar, 594–610.

James, E. and Rose-Ackerman, S. (1986) *The Nonprofit Enterprise in Market Economics*. New York: Harwood Academic.

Johnston, J. and Girth, A. (2012) Government Contracts and 'Managing the Market': The Implications of Strategic Management Responses to Weak Vendor Competition. *Administration & Society*, 44(1): 3–29.

Kettl, D. F. (1993) *Sharing Power: Public Governance and Private Markets*. Washington, DC: Brookings Institution.

Klijn, E.-H. and Teisman, G. (2000) Governing Public–Private Partnerships, in *Public–Private Partnerships. Theory and Practice in International Perspective*, edited by S. Osborne. London and New York: Routledge, pp. 84–102.

Kravchuk, R. S. and Schack, R. W. (1996) Designing Effective Performance-measurement Systems under the Government Performance and Results Act of 1993. *Public Administration Review*, 56(4): 348–58.

Lipsky, M. and Smith, S. (1989–90) Nonprofit Organizations, Government and the Welfare State. *Political Science Quarterly*, 104(4): 625–48.

Lohman, R. (1992) The Theory of the Commons, in Ott, J. S. (ed.). *The Nation of the Non-profit Sector*. Boulder, CO: Westview Press, pp. 89–95. Cited in Grobman, G. (2007). *Introduction to the Nonprofit Sector: A Practical Approach for the 21st Century*. Harrisburg, PA: White Hat Communications.

McQuaid, R. W. (2000) The Theory of Partnership, in *Public–Private Partnerships. Theory and Practice in International Perspective*, edited by S. Osborne. London and New York: Routledge, pp. 6–35.

Miles, R. H. (1981) *Macro Organizational Behavior*. Glenville, IL: Scott, Foresman and Company.

Moulton, L. and Anheier, H. K. (2000) Public–Private Partnerships in the United States, in

Public–Private Partnerships. Theory and Practice in International Perspective, edited by S. Osborne. London and New York: Routledge, pp. 106–19.

Nicholson-Crotty, S., Theobald, N. A. and Nicholson-Crotty, J. (2006) Disparate Measures: Public Managers and Performance-Measurement Strategies. *Public Administration Review*, 66(1): 101–13.

O'Regan, K, and Oster, S. (2002) Does Government Funding Alter Nonprofit Governance? Evidence from New York City Nonprofit Contractors. *Journal of Policy Analysis and Management*, 21(3): 359–79.

Osborne, S. P. (2000) Introduction: Understanding Public–Private Partnerships in International Perspective: Globally Convergent or Nationally Divergent Phenomena?, in *Public–Private Partnerships. Theory and Practice in International Perspective*, edited by S. Osborne. London and New York: Routledge, pp. 1–5.

Osborne, S. and Murray, V. (2000) Understanding the Process of Public–Private Partnerships: Sectorial Perspectives, in *Public–Private Partnerships: Theory and Practice in International Perspective*, edited by S. Osborne. London and New York: Routledge, pp. 70–83.

Price, J. L. (1972) The Study of Organizational Effectiveness. *Sociological Quarterly*, 13(1): 3–13.

Radin, B. A. (2000) The Government Performance and Results Act and the Tradition of Federal Management Reform: Square Pegs in Round Holes? *Journal of Public Administration Research and Theory*, 10(1): 111–35.

Radin, B. A. (2006) 'One Size Fits All', in *Challenging the Performance Movement: Accountability, Complexity, and Democratic Values*. Washington, DC: Georgetown University Press, pp. 33–52.

Rainey, H. G. and Chun, Y. H. (2005) Public and Private Management Compared, in *The Oxford and book of Public Management*, edited by Ferlie, E., Lynn Jr, L. E. and Pollitt, C. Oxford: Oxford University Press, pp. 72–101.

Reaves, J. (2001) Red Faces at the Red Cross. *Time*, 14 November.

Romzek, B. S. and Johnston, J. M. (1999) Reforming Medicaid through Contracting: The Nexus of Implementation and Organizational Culture. *Journal of Public Administration Research and Theory*, 9(1): 107–39.

Romzek, B. S. and Johnston, J. M. (2005) State Social Services Contracting: Exploring the Determinants of Effective Contract Accountability. *Public Administration Review*, 65(4): 436–49.

Salamon, L. M. (1987) Partners in Public Service: The Scope and Theory of Government–non-profit relations, in Power, W. W. (ed.) *The Non-profit Sector: A Research Handbook*. New Haven, CT: Yale University Press.

Salamon, L. M. (1999) *American's Nonprofit Sector: A Primer*. The Foundation Center.

Salamon, L. M. (2002) The Resilient Sector: The State of Nonprofit America, in Salamon, L. (ed.) *The State of Nonprofit America*. Washington, DC: Brookings Institution Press, pp. 3–64.

Salamon, L. (2006) Government–non-profit Relations from an International Perspective in Boris, E. and Steuerle, C. E. (eds) *Non-profits and Government: Collaboration and Conflict*. Washington, DC: The Urban Institute Press, pp. 399–435.

Savas, E. S. (2000) *Privatization and Public–Private Partnerships*. New York: Chatham House.

Savas, E. S. (2005) *Privatization in the City: Successes, Failures, Lessons*. Washington, DC: CQ Press.

Selden, S. C. and Sowa, J. E. (2004) Testing a Multi-dimensional Model of Organizational

Performance: Prospects and Problems. *Journal of Public Administration Research and Theory*, 14: 395–416.

Skelcher, C. (2010) Governing Partnerships, in Hodge, G., Greve, C. and Boardman, A. (eds) *International Handbook on Public–Private Partnerships*. Cheltenham: Edward Elgar, pp. 292–304

Smith, S. and Gronbjerg, K. (2006) Scope and Theory of Government–Non-profit Relations, in Powell, W. and Steinberg, R. (eds) *The Non-profit Sector: A Research Handbook*, 2nd edn. New Haven, CT and London: Yale University Press, pp. 221–42.

Smith, S. R. and Lipsky, M. (1993) *Non-profits For Hire: The Welfare State in the Age of Contracting*. Cambridge, MA: Harvard University Press.

Smith, S. R. and Smyth, J. (1996) Contracting for Services in a Decentralized System. *Journal of Public Administration Research and Theory*, 6(2): 277–96.

Steinberg, R. (2006) Economic Theories of Non-profit Organizations, in Powell, W. and Steinberg, R. (eds) *The Non-profit Sector: A Research Handbook*, 2nd edn. New Havel, CT and London: Yale University Press, pp. 117–39.

Van Slyke, D. (2007) Agents or Stewards: Using Theory to Understand the Government–non-profit Social Service Contracting Relationship. *Journal of Public Administration Research and Theory*, 17: 157–87.

Weisbrod, B. A. (1977) *The Voluntary Non-profit Sector*. Lexington, MA: D. C. Heath.

Weisbrod, B. A. (1989) Rewarding Performance that is Hard to Measure: The Private Nonprofit Sector. *Science*, 244(4904): 541–46.

Weisbrod, B. A. (1997) The Future of the Nonprofit Sector: Its Entwining with Private Enterprise and Government. *Journal of Policy Analysis and Management*, 16(4): 541–555.

Wellford, W. and Gallagher, J. (1988) Unfair Competition? The Challenge to Charitable Tax Exemption. Washington, DC: The National Assembly of Voluntary Health and Social Welfare Organizations.

Young, D. R. (2006) Complementary, Supplementary, or Adversarial? Non-profit–government Relations, in Boris, E. and Steuerle C. E. (eds) *Non-profits and Government: Collaboration and Conflict*. Washington, DC: The Urban Institute Press, pp. 37–79.

7 A Foucault perspective on public–private partnership mega-projects

Sophie Sturup

Introduction

Long-term contracts are increasingly being used by governments to procure mega urban transport projects (tunnels, bridges, roads and rail lines) that are designed to ameliorate the problem of urban congestion. Mega urban transport projects are increasing in size, number and complexity across the world (Capka 2004a; Ekenger 1987; Kumaraswamy and Morris 2002). At the same time Flyvbjerg (2005) notes that in nine out of ten such projects, cost overruns of 50 per cent are common, and 100 per cent cost overrun is not uncommon. The estimated positive economic and development benefits of mega urban transport projects are mostly 'non-existent, marginal or even negative' (ibid.: 20). Similar results have been found by other authors (Allport 2005; Boyce 1990). Additional problems faced by mega urban transport projects are that they are often poorly integrated into the transport networks they inhabit and lack public acceptance (De Bruijn and Leijten 2008).

Public–private partnerships have been touted as a solution to the issue of cost overruns in mega urban transport projects; the introduction of private sector expertise and competitive business practices being seen as a way to: overcome public sector incompetence and overspending; create a focus on risk management; incentivize innovation and promote tighter construction times; and access private sector funds. A plethora of research has been undertaken with increasingly elegant solutions generated to improve the outcome of these partnerships. This has included research into better aligning the purposes of the partners (Koppenjan 2008; Samset 2008; Siemiatycki 2006), bringing private sector focus on profitability into cost–benefit analysis (Sturup 2006), and the appropriate level and method of risk allocation (Arndt 2000). Despite these improvements to the technology of PPPs, the issues faced by mega-projects have shown significant intractability. The statistics noted in the previous paragraph have not significantly varied over the last 70 years (Flyvbjerg *et al.* 2003). This suggests that the 'problem' faced by mega-projects is not one of a lack of understanding of the technology of PPP and its application to mega-projects; rather, something distorts the application of the technology. It is suggested here that this distorting influence is the art of the government of mega-projects.

This chapter therefore examines the art of government of mega-projects (specifically mega urban transport projects) and its relationship to PPPs. The work is based on findings from research that examined the art of government in play in three mega urban transport projects in Australia (Sturup 2010). The theories around governmentality, which were inspired by Michel Foucault, were used to investigate how the amalgam of rationality, technology and knowledge used in the mega-projects generates the specific art of government of mega urban transport projects. Key features of the art of government of mega-projects common to all three projects were identified. These key features of the art of government can be used to explain how the actors involved in mega-projects behave. It offers new insights into the role PPPs play in enrolling us in the awe of mega-projects.

The art of government

Central to this work are the theories inspired by Foucault in his discussion of governmentality. In particular the concern is with the concept of the art of government (Dean 1999; Foucault 1977, 1991, 2003). An art of government involves the development and employment of particular *technologies*, which are built from and act to reinforce particular *rationalities*, which leverage and create a particular set of *knowledge*, and thus right behaviour in the world. Arts of government are about creating the conditions for governing, but they do not do this through overt domination; rather they create the conditions from which right behaviour is generated by the individuals themselves. That is, an art of government creates a particular occurrence of the world, from which 'right' behaviour is a logical and natural outcome. Thus they can be understood as related to or analogous to a particular interpretative framework that gives 'being' to the people within the organization, project or situation, and thus what is possible. The art of government of PPP mega-projects creates a certain mode of being, which in turn has ramifications for effective management of PPP mega-projects. This is because the mode of being defines what it is possible to hear and what can be said, and it determines what occurs as rational action. In other words, an art of government is a particular form of Heideggerian episteme; a way of being that determines what we see and therefore what it is logical to do (Braun and Castree 1998). In effect, the interpretation of the world creates the conditions from which management decisions within the project are generated, and how those management decisions are interpreted by the staff implementing them.

The following explains further the relationship between being and action. It is understood that a person is not a singular being. People have access to multiple interpretations of the world, and thus multiple modes of being. People are called into these modes of being in particular circumstances. For example, when confronted by an angry teenager, what is brought forward in a parent is whatever mode of being they have developed for 'parenting'. This will occur whether they are that particular teenager's parent or not. In a mega-project, what is called forward is the mode of being of a mega-project. It is possible for an individual to counter the mode of being called for in a particular situation; for example, in a work situation a person called to be 'parent' by a younger co-worker might instead take on something like 'work colleague'. However most people do not manage this shift of being most of the time (there are a number of possible explanations for this that are outside the scope of this chapter). In any case, people will act from the mode of being in which they find themselves. Their actions will be in perfect accord with the way the world occurs for them. Seemingly contradictory action occurs from contradictions in the world view, or from sudden shifts from one world view to another. From a management point of view, this suggests that managing the interpretation of the world, and thus the mode of being that is generated by particular technologies and their rationales as used by the organization, could dramatically improve outcomes across a wide variety of businesses and activities.

Features of the art of government for any particular situation can be identified through a detailed review of the technologies, rationalities and knowledge used by actors in that process. What is required is detailed observation of what is said, what technologies are used and how, and which knowledge is used. The types of actions taken and the explanations people have of their actions make it possible to describe the modes of being exhibited in such processes. Cross-referencing the two sets of data allows us to compose a picture of how the world must look, or the features of interpretations of the world a person acting in this way must have. From this, an analysis of the likely interpretive framework or world view that generated that mode of being can be drawn. This art of government is complex and a challenge to define, but by cross-referencing across a group of similar projects it is possible to draw conclusions about key features of the art of government that might be driving actions.

The research on which this chapter is based undertook this type of analysis using three case studies of mega urban transport projects in Australia (Sturup 2010). The projects were Melbourne CityLink, the Perth to Mandurah Railway, and the Cross City Tunnel (CCT) in Sydney. All three of the projects used the private sector in some capacity in conjunction with government capacity. Melbourne and Sydney were funded, built and managed by the private sector, and ownership will be transferred to the state government in the future. Perth was entirely funded by government and built under more typical construction contracts, although the underground contract (Package F) has a three-year maintenance contract for the underground stations. A brief description of the delivery structure of each project and findings on why that structure was selected is given below.

Melbourne

Melbourne CityLink is a 22-km toll road connecting three freeways around the central business district of Melbourne. The road includes upgraded sections of already existing freeway, an elevated section of roadway, a bridge and two tunnels. CityLink was built under a Concession Deed granted to a consortium of Transfield/Obayashi to design, build, finance, operate, levy tolls and maintain it for 34 years until 14 June 2034.[1] Ownership will then transfer to the government of Victoria (Infrastructure Partnerships Australia 2006). The project cost A$2.6 billion.

The introduction of the private sector through the public–private partnership resolved several issues for the state government, in particular their 'inability' to fund the project. It also provided construction jobs and private sector investment at a time when the government of Victoria was dealing with a slowdown in the economy and a downgrading of the state's credit rating (from AAA to AA). The private sector engineers provided expertise in tunnelling in the difficult ground conditions, and innovation in dealing with the preservation of heritage bridges over the Monash Freeway. The introduction of another party to the project provided the possibility to shift risk away from the government, and for a less risk-averse organization to plan the project on the basis of a series of unproven technologies (for example electronic tolling). The introduction of the profit motive through the inclusion of the private sector is thought by interviewees to have led to a shorter build time, due to the fact that the project could not earn revenue until completed. It also led to the development of free-flow electronic tolling (a technology that has allowed the subsequent development of a number of toll roads in places with space restrictions.)[2]

Perth

The Perth to Mandurah Railway (also known as the Southern Suburbs Railway or South West Metropolitan Railway) is owned and operated by the state of Western Australia. It stretches 70.1 km from central Perth to Mandurah in the south. The line includes two major river crossings, two sets of tunnels, construction of two underground stations as well as numerous above-ground stations. Much of the line passes along the central median of the south-bound freeway. The operation of the railway is undertaken by Transperth, a part of the Western Australian government's Public Transport Authority. Construction commenced in January 2004 and the line opened on 23 December 2007. The cost of the project is esti-mated at A$1.184 billion (Longhurst 2008: 5).

The South West Metropolitan Railway line was fully financed by the Western Australian state budget in the years in which it was built. No additional state debt was accrued to the project, and thus Transperth does not have any debt-servicing obligations relating to the project. The rail line was built by the Public Transport Authority, through eight design-and-build contracts between the state and the private sector. These contracts, known as 'packages', were tendered in separate processes to maximize competition and enable some smaller players to participate in the project. The delivery of the underground stations, tunnel and track through the centre of Perth was via Package F, which included a three-year maintenance contract.

The Western Australian state government conducted a review of the relative benefits of private and public funding of the project prior to seeking tenders, and concluded that private finance would not represent value for money in this instance. In choosing not to undertake the project as a single BOOT (build, own, operate, transfer) project, a number of considerations were brought into play. Firstly, there was recognition that it is difficult to get private parties interested in public transport initiatives, especially in areas where there is no established public transport usage. Secondly, there was a concern with the cost of borrowing, especially the increased cost of private sector loans over state government ones (Department of Transport 2000). One consequence of the choice to fund the project with government revenue was that negotiations between the building contractors and the state were much less complicated, in part because financiers did not need to be convinced of the project's viability in the way that was done in CityLink (Interviewee 052). The question of the value for money in the investment, which is a much broader question with a longer time-frame than the question of financial viability, was the concern of Treasury officials not outside financiers. This is not to say that there is no concern for a proper return on investment, as exemplified in the following quote:

> Treasury of course, they want a sort of financial review, and they do have the financial reviewing involvement at the front end and in the middle and at the back end of projects. They're very concerned that we can demonstrate over time that there has been a proper return on the investment.
>
> (Interviewee 044)

Sydney

The Sydney Cross City Tunnel project was built under a public–private partnership between the government of NSW and CrossCity Motorway Company. The contract included three stages: design, finance and build twin tunnels (2.1 km in length following roughly the line of William St); design, finance and build changes to the surface streets (to ensure the decongested streets did not induce further traffic); maintain and operate surface street changes and the tunnel for a concession period of 30 years and 2 months (Catalyst Communications 2003).

Ownership of the project will revert to government on 18 December 2035. The final cost for development, design, construction, fit out and commissioning was reported as A$680 million in 2005. The surface road and property works are also to be maintained by the consortium (Roads and Traffic Authority NSW 2005). The estimated total cost including financing costs of the project is just over A$1 billion (Sendt 2006). Construction of the tunnel commenced in January 2003 and it was completed and opened to traffic in August 2005. The surface works (both the initial changes and the subsequent reversals of changes) were completed by the end of 2006 (AAP 2007).

The decision to undertake the project as a PPP was motivated by the NSW Government's commitment to reduce debt, and an associated directive that new projects could only proceed on the basis of 'no cost to government'. There is some evidence to suggest that the objectives of the project were compromised because of this:

it is clear that when determining the value for money for the CCT, the government focused on a policy of 'no cost to government'. The value for money to those paying for the project, that is, the tunnel users, was not adequately considered.

(Joint Select Committee on the Cross City Tunnel 2006: xiii).

The NSW Road Traffic Authority placed considerable weight on the objective to undertake the project at no cost to government. This led to acceptance of the bid, which contained the maximum business consideration fee, and to a number of amendments to the contract to ensure the Road Traffic Authority incurred no cost in other parts of its yearly budget.

Key features of the art of government of mega urban transport projects

Before they are anything else, mega urban transport projects are projects. They are therefore dominated by the logic of project, which is essentially to produce object X by time Y. According to the Project Management Body of Knowledge (PMBoK) a project is 'a temporary endeavor undertaken to create a unique product or service' (Project Management Institute 2000: 4).[3] Projects are therefore a unique product with a defined timeline. This distinguishes them from business as usual. Project management uses a variety of technologies designed to ensure that: project elements are integrated; scope, time, costs and quality are controlled; and risks, human resources and communications are managed. For example, Gantt charts are used in project integration management and project time management, and assist with ensuring that all project elements that must follow each other are properly scheduled. Project managers use scope definition, up-front establishment of objectives, and risk-management identification technologies to manage scope creep and construction timelines, and thereby control costs and quality. The project documentation establishes what is to be done and by whom, and the governance of the project, including when changes can be considered and who will approve works as they progress. These technologies work to support the tight definition of the project prior to its commencement, and to set parameters that reduce outside interference once the project is up and running.

In Australian mega-projects, projects become projects when they are, as a former government minister put it, 'a defined task which is not incapable of delivery'. Thus, although it is not necessary to have a project plan, budget etc. for a mega-project to become a project, it does require a realistic prospect of being delivered. That prospect necessarily includes some sort of commitment that the project will proceed assuming the parameters can be worked out and met in a reasonable fashion. It also necessarily means that something can only be declared a project by someone who has the resources to deliver it. Mega-projects thus include the process of planning them, but they are clearly distinguished from a whim or an idea by a commitment to develop the above-mentioned project plans and budgets and a commitment to provide the resources to deliver the project once these items are developed. In this sense the art of government of mega-projects follows a logic of power that is strongly sovereign or pharaonic (Boyce 1990).

The sovereign nature of power in mega-projects is based on the logic that 'my will be done, I am the king'. Project management technology works to support this. The PMBoK states that the process of project initiation is simply 'authorizing the project or phase' (Project Management Institute 2000: 32); nothing is said about who should do this authorizing nor how they should be legitimated. The legitimacy of the decision is presumed and placed outside the project. In best practice project management, the first task is to establish who has authority to make required decisions. The second task is to create the documentation on which decisions must be taken (ILX Group PLC 2009). A plan is developed that, at least in theory, bounds the activity of those working in the project. As noted above, the commencement of a project occurs when someone with capacity to deliver states it will occur. The authorizer of the project is thus the source of authority on which all subsequent work proceeds. Following that decision the project plan is developed, which authorizes the action of those working in the project. The originating authority is made remote from the process of pursuing the project. Decision-making in this logic is defined by the parameters of the project, and is seen to be simply following the logic of the project. The question of power is largely avoided, the legitimacy of project actors being intertwined with the original decision that was taken. A consequence of this logic is that the original decision must be made by an authority whose ability to do so is inviolate. The integrity of the entire project that follows rests on that assumption. In this logic, the decision is the basis for all future action on the project, and thus people's ability to act requires that they do not question whether the project should be going ahead. In this way mega-project decisions are rendered apolitical.

A further key finding from governmentality studies concerns the relationship between problem design and solution. Problems are generated to fit the solutions that are at hand (Li 2007). In each of the projects studied, the problem and the solution to it were articulated and re-articulated until the solution was to build a piece of infrastructure. The generation of the problem and the solution produce the rationality for the project. The rationality given for the problem is therefore bounded by, but also bounds, the rationality of the solution and subsequently the design of the project. Once this process is complete, the solution proposed (the mega-project) occurs as the only rational solution. By the time the project reaches what Miller and Lessard (2008) call the 'ramp up phase', the logic of the problem and solution are embedded in the project. Given that in all cases studied the solution is a piece of built infrastructure, one outcome of this activity is to re-articulate what can be intense political struggles as a technical problem solvable by construction.

Private sector involvement: how the technology of PPPs interacts with the art of government of mega-projects

There is significant overlap between the processes of contracting and the processes of project management, possibly because these technologies have, to some degree, developed together. Both successful project design and successful contracting requires that the objectives of the activity be clearly stated, along with the standards the work is to meet. In both processes, the risks are to be fully identified and handed to those who have incentives to manage them properly. In all three projects studied in this research, the involvement of the private sector (whether through PPP or standard design/build contracts) required this specification of the technical requirements of the project. Since the public service in Australia no longer retains the experience or manpower to undertake construction work in-house, the use of the private sector in some form is now impossible to avoid. Therefore the extra discipline that is imposed by the requirement to build a contract with the private sector is imposed on virtually all projects. Indeed, in both CityLink and the Perth to Mandurah Railway, contracts were used in this fashion. For example, the CityLink contract includes the full technical specifications for every element of the roadway. These specifications were negotiated during the contracting process, which ran concurrent to the process of determining the exact nature of the project.

Because of the way project is defined, effective project planning necessitates that the project be a unique deliverable. It must be distinguished from business as usual and tightly bound to avoid outside interference once the project commences. The process of negotiating contracts between parties in PPPs is a logical extension of this process. In both CityLink and the Perth to Mandurah Railway this process of tightly bounding the project was enabled by the passage of specific legislation authorizing the projects and isolating them from independent planning scrutiny. Administration of the projects was undertaken by specifically created agencies. Interestingly, in the case of the Cross City Tunnel, the relationship between the contracting process and finalization of the project was never a simple matter of reaching agreement between the two parties. Approval for the project was subject to independent planning permission, wherein the Minister for Planning added 292 conditions to the project after the initial contract was agreed. Many interviewees were of the view that it was the expectation of these additional conditions (which would necessarily impose additional costs that could not be passed to the contractor) that led to the imposition of an A\$100 million business consideration fee on the project. At 15 per cent of the total cost of the project, this business consideration fee, at least partially, contributed to the financial instability of the project.

Thus we can see the discipline imposed by the inclusion of the private sector in projects reinforces key elements of project technology, especially the identification and allocation of risk and clear articulation of the project specifications. Both of these activities support the art of government of mega urban transport projects. Inclusion of the private sector in the project also helps justify keeping the project away from political interference. This is important because in Australia it is common wisdom that if this is not done, the cost of any adjustment to the contract is likely to be unreasonable because it will occur in an uncompetitive process. The private sector party that holds the contract can effectively 'name their price'. Inclusion of the private sector also increases the complexity of the project, and its relations, again providing justification for the uniqueness of the project and its separation from normal business. In this sense the technology of private sector involvement supports the role of governance arrangements in mega urban transport projects.

Private sector involvement: how the art of government disrupts the intended effect of PPPs

Unfortunately, the inevitable focus of the art of government of mega urban transport projects on a specific unique deliverable, acts contrary to efforts to incentivize the private sector to focus on building projects that are 'fit for purpose' by including operations segments in traditional build projects (the movement of projects from government-design, contractor-build, government-run arrangements to contractor design, finance, build, operate (DFBO) arrangement (Siemiatycki 2006)). A consequence of the logic of project is that it focuses attention on the project deliverable. This deliverable must be bound in terms of time. In mega urban transport projects this focus translates into a focus on the infrastructure build process. This element of the project is the most easily translated into a specific deliverable. The operations phase of the project inevitably looks like business as usual. Indeed, successful management of the operation of the project requires a very different state of being than that of project management. This was clearly exemplified in the CityLink project where a fundamental shift in the focus of management occurred part way through the construction phase and a deliberate decision was taken to shift focus to how the company would operate long term.

> We made some really fundamental decisions about a year and a half out. We sacked the operator. We brought the tolling system in-house, albeit with the same subcontractors and whatever, but we massively changed it. At that point we started to realize that we had to become, as a utility, a very customer-focused and community-focused entity. And that was a big changing point for the company. It sounds obvious, but it was like a flash.
>
> (Interviewee)

Similarly, the art of government of mega-projects interferes with the logic behind the introduction of private sector financial discipline. Proponents of private sector financial commitment in the project argue that finance by the private sector focuses attention on the internal rate of return of the project and imposes an additional layer of scrutiny of the project through the introduction of private banks. Of course, in publicly funded projects it is the role of the Treasury to act as financier and attend to ensuring a rate of return. The real difference seems to be in terms of time-frame in which the return is expected, and the fact that the private sector requires the return to be in monetary form. The private sector is focused on rapid returns so that investment funds can be regained for use in other projects, and the return must be in a form that allows for that reinvestment. Maximizing internal rate of return focuses a project manager's attention on ensuring that the minimum is spent on build, and that the project can commence earning as soon as possible. In this respect it can operate to bring on the benefits of the project sooner and decrease the costs at the scale of the project build. Of course, this cost-cutting can also be achieved at the expense of quality and longevity. The tendency of the art of government of mega-projects to focus attention on the construction element of projects acts to reinforce a tendency to cost-cutting. Again, the fact that CityLink was seen to have managed to impose careful financial control and also produce a project that was fit for purpose may well have more to do with the transformation in management focus to long-term operations discussed above than the fact that the private sector was involved in the contract. The Sydney project demonstrates that the private sector is by no means infallible when it comes to forecasting and understanding project profitability. This is perhaps a function of the sublime associated with mega-projects, which is discussed below.

In the interviews conducted for this research, the general response to concerns raised about the failure of PPPs to meet expected rates of return for private investors is that the success of PPPs lies in the fact that the risk of poor financial return is transferred to the private sector and therefore is not of significant concern to the public sector. The problem with this stance is that political risk is difficult to transfer, and it is the government that must maintain the public's trust in its ability to provide infrastructure projects, lest it lose the ability to implement projects at all (Capka 2004b). As several interviewees from the Sydney project pointed out, the financial failure of the tunnel operators was a direct result of fewer people using the tunnel than expected. The question was thus raised whether this private sector money could have been invested in a project that was more needed or wanted by the people of Sydney. Waste in any sector of the economy reduces the opportunities for other projects in that economy.

One claim of proponents of PPPs is that private sector innovation is critical to the success of the projects, and that incentives for innovation stem from the need to build fit-for-purpose projects because of the 'operate' part of the contract. However, all three projects studied included significant innovation in engineering, even though not all the projects included significant operations phases for the contract. This suggests that the source of innovation in engineering is not actually dependent on incentives produced by a private company's financial stake in the operation of the project. It may be that the prevalence of engineering innovation in mega urban transport projects is more related to the space allowed for within the requirements of providing a unique project under specific time-frames, such space providing the opportunity for engineers to express an otherwise latent willingness to invent solutions to difficult or unique engineering problems.

The sovereign nature of power in the art of government of mega-project also interferes with creating partnership in PPPs. The contract is the ultimate articulation of sovereign power. It stymies efforts to operate in partnership. In all of the mega-projects studied, the government granted the private sector permission to build and/or operate a piece of infrastructure. The process of signing the contract therefore reinforced the sovereign nature of the mega-project. Having established this relationship of permission and delivery, it is small wonder that the PPP mega-projects have little of the character of partnership. Indeed, partnership, in fact, requires a very different set of capabilities than those needed for successful project delivery.

Finally, we return to the question of budgets and projects. As stated above, 'on budget' is not a part of the core definition of a project in the PMBoK. A project is simply a unique product delivered in a specified time. The critical success factor built into the definition of a project is to deliver the project (X) by a set time (Y). The budget is set as part of the technology of managing the project. Meeting the budget is not part of the definition of a project. It is small wonder then that projects generally fall short of budget before they fall short of delivery time. It is built into the definition of project that success can be obtained even if excess costs are incurred, assuming it allows the project to be delivered on time. Under these circumstances it is not surprising that project managers commonly choose to incur excess costs in order to complete the project on time.

Technical, political and projects sublime: how the art of government of mega-projects reduces critical distance from the project

Trapenberg Frick (2008) articulates the idea of sublime as 'the repeated experience of awe and wonder associated, often tinged with an element of terror, which people experience when confronted with particular natural sites, architectural forms and technological achievements' (Nye 1994 in Trapenberg Frick 2008: 239). Without doubt, mega-projects often have this sense of the sublime. It can be observed in the enthusiasm engendered in those who work on these projects, and those who observe them. Two elements in the sublime of mega-projects, technical and political, have been identified in previous research. The technical (or design) element is the one that Trapenberg Frick describes; it includes the attraction of the engineering, the 'fit' of the project with its environment, the beauty and seduction of something whose form perfectly matches its function. This is the sublime that affects engineers and designers. From the thrill of big machines that move masses of materials, through the graceful lines built of tonnes of steel and concrete, to the delivery of new options and the conquering of obstacles.

The political element can be seen in the opening of these projects, in the 'rock star' appeal of politicians who can produce a result, open a bridge, solve a problem. The political sublime pulls the project from 'something that could be done' to 'something that must be done'. Once they make this transformation, those who deliver them are our heroes, their mark left on the landscape in enduring legacy.

The study of the activity of agents in this research has identified a third element in the sublime of mega urban transport projects. It is the seduction of project itself, the project management element. Projects make things manageable; they render the intention do-able. They break the seemingly impossible into fragments, deliverable within a budget, inside a time-frame. The vast, chaotic co-ordination effort is bracketed, contained, managed. 'The possible' is brought under control.

The sublime of mega-projects is a merging of these elements. The attraction of these projects is the sheer size, the edge-of-the-seat management required, the sense of opening your veins, giving everything to something bigger than yourself. As George Bernard Shaw put it so well:

> This is the true joy in life, the being used for a purpose recognized by yourself as a mighty one; the being a force of nature instead of a feverish, selfish little clod of ailments and grievances complaining that the world will not devote itself to making you happy...
>
> I want to be thoroughly used up when I die, for the harder I work the more I live. I rejoice in life for its own sake. Life is no 'brief candle' for me. It is a sort of splendid torch which I have got hold of for the moment, and I want to make it burn as brightly as possible before handing it on to future generations.
>
> (Shaw 1973: 84)

In the two 'successful' projects (Melbourne and Perth), the instigators of the project, who were part of forming its key rationality and the rationality of the solution, remained part of the project. In the Sydney project, which was a failure according to the public press (see also Pretorius 2007), this didn't happen. Thus, actors are agents for the stickiness of the rationalities of the project and if they are absent it is possible for the project to become derailed; to lose its purpose. The role of actors is to be passionate about the project, to demonstrate the being that is generated by the sublime of mega-projects. This is critical to maintaining the art of government of mega-projects because it staves off questioning of the project, especially if intelligent, known, respected figures are willing to put themselves on the line. People who are willing to sell themselves to these projects generate a level of respect, even if it is grudging respect, from observers. Concurrently, having sold oneself into a project, the personal investment is extreme. It is painful enough just to hand over some of the control of the project let alone to actively question whether the project was worth the investment. Once people have committed themselves to the project they become the project. The longer they act from the art of government of mega urban transport projects, the more times they have to choose between the mode of being generated in mega-projects and an alternative. Each choice leads to actions that must be justified. Whether consciously or unconsciously, the person builds a rationality for their own participation. Through this process, questioning the project becomes a questioning of all those choices, leaving the person with an unjustified existence. Most people simply do not have this capacity, it would destroy them. Possibly this is why mega-projects don't really fail, their failures rather get reinterpreted into justified outcomes. Certainly, it goes some way to explaining why projects that perhaps should be re-evaluated and abandoned are not.

The movement from political to technical described in the first section of this chapter is necessary not just to make the project manageable but also to allow the sublime to seem rational. The problem must be solved, and the siren song of the mega-project is that it will solve it. In the theory of governmentality, freedom is not a product of avoiding the domination of a structure, but rather it is the capacity to choose from a multiplicity of ways to be bound (Rose *et al.* 2009). The art of government of mega urban transport projects provides a particular form of being and a particular way of being bound. It lives and breathes through the people who operate from it. People create the technology, rationality and knowledge of the art of government of mega urban transport projects even as they are given being through it. The mega-project sublime provides an explanation for why people choose to bind themselves in this way.

Conclusion

The relationship between the art of government of mega-projects and the technology of PPPs is complex. PPPs have been touted as the solution to the problems of mega-projects, especially the ability to deliver them on time and budget, without risk to government. However, the technology consistently fails to deliver as expected. This chapter has proposed that this is not a function of the technology of PPPs being misunderstood or insufficiently understood. Rather the problems of mega-projects are a logical outcome of the state of that generated within them, a state of being which determines what can be seen, known and acted upon. This state of being is generated in the amalgam of technology, knowledge and rationality, or art of government, used in mega-projects.

The art of government of mega urban transport projects is based on the logic of power commonly described as sovereignty. The action of this sovereign power is to legitimate the project on the basis that the sovereign has said it would happen. The art of government of mega-projects is dominated by the generalized art of government of project, and the definitions of project that have been built into the project-management body of knowledge. This definition acts to focus attention on the 'build' element of the project. Finally, mega-projects occur inside a set of rationalities about the problem and the solution that are built to support the project. In the case of mega urban transport projects this means that, generally, difficult political problems are rendered soluble by the imposition of some piece of infrastructure. This art of government of mega-projects is both reinforced by PPPs and also interferes with the uptake of specific logics that PPPs are theoretically supposed to impose.

The technology of PPPs reinforces the logic of sovereignty in the project through the contract. The power of the contracting party to determine that the project will go ahead is built into the contract process. A consequence of this is that the idea of partnership in PPPs is rendered meaningless. Authority to act is clearly granted by the sovereign. The equality required to make the concept of partnership relevant will be very difficult to establish because it will always be built on this foundation.

The technology of PPP supports and reinforces the technology of project. Specifically, the process of negotiating and writing the contract can act to support proper identification, allocation and costing of risks as well as creating clarity about the exact parameters of the project. The contract therefore supports placing boundaries around the project and keeping it free of political interference. However, this also tends to exacerbate the tendency of projects to focus on the deliverable – the construction phase – rather than the business phase (operations), which in mega urban transport projects is often considerably longer and, arguably, more important.

In reinforcing the art of government of mega urban transport projects, PPPs fundamentally reinforce the sublime of mega-projects, a sublime that is not only technical and political but also managerial. In so doing, PPPs may reduce our capacity to resist the siren song of projects. In some cases this means that what should be contested political questions are rendered technical, to the detriment of the project and the society in which they are built.

Notes

1   The Concession Deed can be extended to 54 years in some circumstances.
2   The profit motive is thought to be related to the development of electronic tolling because without a profit motive there would have been no need to toll the road and thus the issue of toll plazas and the need to find a way to collect tolls without them would not have arisen.
3   Note that the concept of the budget (which might be expressed as 'for cost Z' in the project logic) is not included in the PMBoK definition of a project. The ramifications of this omission are significant and discussed below.

References

AAP. (2007) Leighton Leads $700m Buyout of Cross City Tunnel. *Sydney Morning Herald*, 20 June.

Allport, R. (2005) Operating Risk: the Achilles' Heel of Major Infrastructure Projects. *Civil Engineering: Magazine of the South African Institution of Civil Engineering*, 13(10): 16.

Arndt, R. H. (2000) *Getting a Fair Deal: Efficient Risk Allocation in the Private Provision of Infrastructure*. Melbourne: University of Melbourne.

Boyce, J. K. (1990) Birth of a Megaproject – Political-economy of Flood-control in Bangladesh. *Environmental Management*, 14(4): 419–28.

Braun, B. and Castree, N. (1998) *Remaking Reality: Nature at the Millennium*. London and New York: Routledge.

Capka, J. R. (2004a) Megaprojects: Managing a Public Journey (guest editorial). *Public Roads*, 68(1): 1.

Capka, J. R. (2004b) A Well-conceived Plan will Pull it all Together: A Successful Billion-dollar Journey Starts and Finishes with a Roadmap. *Public Roads*, 68(1), 65(10).

Catalyst Communications (2003) Cross-City Tunnel: Summary of Contracts (available at: http://library.sl.nsw.gov.au/search~S2?/aCatalyst+Communications/acatalyst+communications/-3%2C-1%2C0%2CB/frameset&FF=acatalyst+communications&1%2C%2C2).

De Bruijn, H. and Leijten, M. (2008) Management Characteristics of Mega-projects, in B. Flyvbjerg, B. van Wee and H. Priemus (eds) *Decision-making on Mega-projects.* Cheltenham: Edward Elgar Publishing Limited, pp. 23–40.

Dean, M. (1999) *Governmentality: Power and Rule in Modern Society.* London, New Delhi and California: Sage.

Department of Transport (2000) *South West Railway Metropolitan Railway Master Plan and Appendices* (report to cabinet for decision). Perth: Department of Transport.

Ekenger, P. (1987) Large-scale Infrastructure Projects in Europe. *Technology in Society*, 9: 87–95.

Flyvbjerg, B. (2005) Machiavellian Megaprojects. *Antipode*, 37(1): 18.

Flyvbjerg, B., Bruzelius, N. and Rothengatter, W. (2003) *Megaprojects and Risk: An Anatomy of Ambition.* Cambridge: Cambridge University Press.

Foucault, M. (1977) *Discipline and Punish: The Birth of the Prison* (trans. A. Sheridan). New York: Vintage Books.

Foucault, M. (1991) Governmentality, in G. Burchell, C. Gordon and P. Miller (eds) *The Foucault Effect Studies in Governmentality with Two Lectures by and an Interview with Michel Foucault.* Hertfordshire: Harvester Wheatsheaf, pp. 87–104.

Foucault, M. (2003) Society Must Be Defended. Lectures at the Collège De France 1975–1976 (trans. D. Macey). Vol. 1. New York: Picador.

ILX Group PLC (2009) What is Prince2? Retrieved 30 August 2009 from: http://www.prince2.com/what-is-prince2.asp

Infrastructure Partnerships Australia (2006) *Case Studies – CityLink Melbourne.* Melbourne.

Joint Select Committee on the Cross City Tunnel (2006) *Inquiry into the Cross City Tunnel First Report – Media Release.* Retrieved 12 February 2009 from: www.parliament.nsw.gov.au/crosscitytunnel

Koppenjan, J. (2008) Public–Private Partnership and Mega-projects, in H. Priemus, B. Flyvbjerg and B. van Wee (eds) *Decision-making on Mega-projects: Cost–benefit Analysis, Planning and Innovation.* Cheltenham: Edward Elgar Publishing Limited, pp. 189–212.

Kumaraswamy, M. M. and Morris, D. A. (2002) Build-Operate-Transfer Type Procurement in Asian Megaprojects. *Journal of Construction Engineering and Management – ASCE*, 128(2): 93–102.

Li, T. M. (2007) *The Will to Improve: Governmentality, Development and the Practice of Politics.* Durham and London: Duke University Press.

Longhurst, D. (2008) *48 Months, 48 Minutes: Building the Perth to Mandurah Railway.* Perth: Rawlhouse Publishing Pty Ltd.

Miller, R. and Lessard, D. R. (2008) Evolving Strategy: Risk Management and the Shaping of Mega-projects, in H. Priemus, B. Flyvbjerg and B. van Wee (eds) *Decision-making on Mega-projects: Cost–benefit Analysis, Planning and Innovation.* Cheltenham: Edward Elgar Publishing Limited, pp. 145–72.

Pretorius, F. (2007) Infrastructure Finance: The Sydney Cross City Tunnel, in M. Ho (ed.) *Hong Kong: The Asia Case.* Research Centre, University of Hong Kong, p. 38.

Project Management Institute (2000) *A Guide to the Project Management Body of Knowledge (PMBoK Guide).* Newtown Square, PA: Project Management Institute Inc.

Roads and Traffic Authority, NSW (2005) *Cross City Tunnel: Summary of First Amending Deed*, 4 November.

Rose, N., O'Malley, P. and Valverde, M. (2009) Governmentality. Legal Studies Research Paper. Sydney: Sydney Law School.

Samset, K. (2008) How to Overcome Major Weaknesses in Mega-projects: The Norwegian Approach, in H. Priemus, B. Flyvbjerg and B. van Wee (eds) *Decision-making on Mega-projects: Cost–benefit Analysis, Planning and Innovation*. Cheltenham: Edward Elgar, pp. 173–88.

Sendt, R. J. (2006) *Performance Audit: The Cross City Tunnel Project* (No. 07347 21900). Sydney: Audit Office of New South Wales.

Shaw, G. B. (1973) *Man and Superman*. Baltimore, MD: Penguin.

Siemiatycki, M. (2006) Implications of Private–public Partnerships on the Development of Urban Public Transit Infrastructure – The Case of Vancouver, Canada. *Journal of Planning Education and Research*, 26(2): 137–51.

Sturup, S. (2006) *Contracting/Outsourcing in the UK: A Question of Transparency and Accountability*. Unpublished Masters thesis, University of Oxford.

Sturup, S. (2010) *Managing Mentalities of Mega Projects: The Art of Government of Mega Urban Transport Projects*. Unpublished PhD thesis, University of Melbourne.

Trapenberg Frick, K. (2008) The Cost of the Technological Sublime: Daring Ingenuity and the New San Francisco–Oakland Bay Bridge, in H. Priemus, B. Flyvbjerg and B. van Wee (eds) *Decision-making on Mega-projects: Cost–benefit Analysis, Planning and Innovation*. Cheltenham: Edward Elgar, pp. 239–62.

8 The public management of public–private partnerships

US city-level structures for brownfield clean-up and redevelopment

Rob Alexander

Introduction

This chapter presents the research design, implementation and results of a study that examined the extent to which non-elected local-level government managers impacted the outcomes of four 'brownfield' redevelopment public–private partnership projects in the US cities of Buffalo and Rochester, NY. In attempting to convert these environmentally contaminated properties into market-rate residential housing developments, these public managers encountered a range of process, programme and political challenges related to the various relationships formed with private, citizen and other governmental actors within the broader partnership. As such, this study examined the evolution of these PPPs through the theoretical lenses of organizational networks and institutional forces. This chapter, however, focuses upon the empirical development of a measure for PPP success that was used for selection of the case studies and how that measure shaped subsequent data analysis.

Background to study

Public–private partnership arrangements have occurred for as long as researchers and practitioners have contrasted 'public' and 'private' governance constructs (Hodge and Greve 2007) and study of such inter-organizational structures spans both policy and organizational theory research communities (Skelcher and Mathur 2004; Ghere 1996; Lowndes and Skelcher 1998; Googins and Rochlin 2000). Yet a comprehensive theory of PPP performance has defied researchers due to the diversity of contextual variables impacting performance and the implied contingencies. Despite this difficulty, the use of this term by elected officials and public managers continues to grow, particularly in US municipal governments and when discussing clean-up and redevelopment of contaminated properties.

In an era of rapid economic change, many post-industrial cities in the United States find themselves straddled with derelict fuel stations, old manufacturing facilities, chemical tank yards and empty lots lying underused and abandoned because of fears, real or perceived, that they are contaminated. Called 'brownfields', these properties symbolize economic despair, provide space for criminal activity, pose public health risks, affect real property values in adjacent areas and divert development efforts away from urban cores to greener spaces (McCarthy 2002; De Sousa 2005). In addition, brownfields represent underperforming property tax income. It is estimated that in the state of New York alone, over 7,600 brownfield sites in 14 major cities represent almost $200 million of lost tax revenue (US Conference of Mayors 2000, 2003, 2006).

Brownfield properties exist on a marketability continuum where strong market demand compels private actors to address projects at one end of the spectrum while weak market demand leaves projects at the other end untouched. In the middle lie threshold, or weakly marketable, sites where public actors must act in concert with private investors for property clean-up and redevelopment to occur (Davis 2002; Howland 2003). When private actors are unwilling to acquire the risk inherent in contaminated property redevelopment, public actors and public policy must intervene to address uncertainties and increase property marketabilities. Practitioners trumpet that the key to successful clean-up and redevelopment of these sites is effective 'public–private partnership' work.

Empirical evaluation of brownfield PPPs focuses upon the extent to which policy instruments designed for facilitating relationships achieve their intended purposes (Brachman 2003; Ball and Maginn 2005; Noble and Jones 2006). Less studied are the roles that individual public managers play in shaping project outcomes. While emphasis on PPP structures and financing is critical to understanding both outcome and accountability effectiveness, it is also important to consider the planning, designing and implementation tasks performed by public managers when these arrangements occur (Noble and Jones 2006; Williams 2002; Jones and Noble 2008). This is especially true as more evidence accumulates signifying the extent to which individuals impact outcomes of multi-organizational projects (Crosby and Bryson 2005; McGuire 2002; Waugh and Streib 2006; Peters 2000). It is for this reason that this study examines public management behaviours in brownfield PPPs through a network management lens.

Public management of PPPs as network management

In the United States, policy-makers and public managers at all levels of government refer to PPPs as an answer to resource-intensive challenges, particularly in regards to economic development. The idea is that, when the transaction costs of co-ordinating across organizational boundaries are minimized, both public and private partners experience outcomes that they would not have otherwise realized working alone (Herranz 2008). In the literature, researchers utilize the term 'public–private partnership' broadly when discussing inter-organizational relationships between government and private firms, and narrowly when describing these relationships as they occur in public–private infrastructure and economic development projects (Hodge and Greve 2007). In the broadest sense, PPPs are co-operative arrangements between public and private actors in which actors share risks to co-develop public products and services (Klijn and Teisman 2003), placing PPPs in the conceptual realm of inter-organizational networks. In the narrowest sense, they are formal policy designs establishing specific financing structures that enable risk-sharing between government and the private sector for tangible capital projects.

PPPs as network forms of organization

Understanding how brownfield projects function as cross-sector public management networks and how public managers influence these networks to produce outcomes requires a careful understanding of how network structures and the interpersonal behaviours of network actors interact over time. Woven together, these theories suggest that policy outcomes in brownfield networks stem from neither the proper arrangement of network actors nor the correct design of public policy nor the appropriate application of management strategies. Rather, outcomes are best explained by a combination of all three.

PPPs as multi-actor networks exhibit both functional and structural characteristics. At the functional level, Hodge and Greve (2007) identify five different types of PPPs, which include institutional co-operation; long-term infrastructure; public policy networks; civil society and community development; and urban renewal and downtown economic development. At the same time, Mandell and Keast (2007) describe multi-actor networks as ranging in form based upon degrees of interpersonal negotiation and commitment. The structural level, however, pertains to the quantity and quality of ties between the PPP actors. Theorists normally measure these ties as instances of information and resource exchanges but may also identify other linkages such as memberships, affiliations and personal commitments (Milward and Provan 1998). Generally, different patterns of network ties correlate with different patterns of information dissemination and resource exchange, which, in turn, impact decision-making and network outcomes (Dawes *et al.* 2009; Droege *et al.* 2003). Network ties may be quantified to produce measurements of centrality, density and cliques. These measures may, in turn, be viewed as variables that differentiate networks and their relative performances (Provan *et al.* 2007; Wasserman and Faust 1994).

Network structures are not static and evolve over time with different types of networks having different lifespans and, subsequently, different structural arrangements. Networks may be open-ended and long-term, as in the case of natural resource management collaboration (Lubell and Fulton 2008; Thomas 2003) or health and human service networks (Isett and Provan 2005; Milward *et al.* 2010; Provan and Milward 1995), or they may be short-term and focused on specific outcomes, as in the case of infrastructure projects. While few studies examine the significance of time-frame differences on network processes, projects exhibiting clear goals and a short lifespan tend to produce loosely coupled networks relying less upon maturing trust-based relationships and more upon arm's-length linking mechanisms (Mandell and Steelman 2003; Pryke 2005) to co-ordinate 'linear' sets of tasks that clearly follow one another.

The interests and motivations driving public and private organizations to establish network ties and engage in network functions derive from different institutional and organizational forces. In the private sector, firms choose to engage in networks when neither internalizing nor externalizing the project sufficiently addresses transaction cost concerns (Jones *et al.* 1997). In the public sector, the unique political, institutional and resource environments that demand transparency and democratic accountability exacerbate efforts to minimize transaction costs in the same way. As a result, public organizations primarily select network approaches when institutional, political and resource pressures induce them to do so. Researchers examining PPPs through a network governance lens must therefore pay attention to the different motivations of sector-based actors when explaining how PPPs perform (Becker and Patterson 2005; Hodge and Greve 2007).

Network management strategies for PPPs

Network management becomes necessary when the risks and uncertainties associated with multiple organizations coming together within a problem-solving arena impede decision-making. Klijn and Koppenjan (2004) describe three sources of policy network uncertainties based upon the relative lack of information and knowledge about causes and effects, lack of inter-network communication, and extent to which network actors come from different organizations in different sectors acting in different networks with their own rules and norms.

The literature describes two sets of strategies for managing these uncertainties. First, network managers may focus upon the interpersonal relationships between network actors, appealing to the psychological need for reciprocity by taking steps to generate trust and build social capital (Jeffries and Reed 2000; Berardo 2008). Second, network managers may shape the rules and norms governing behaviours in the network informally by regulating information and formally by adopting specific tools that alter the institutional environment (Oliver 1991; Koppenjan and Klijn 2004). McGuire (2002) and Herranz (2008) further bundle these behaviours into operational categories. These authors propose that management behaviours occur along the vectors of relationship maturity and degree of involvement in the relationship. However, not all management is strategic and researchers must also give attention to the impacts of more passive forms of management by partnership actors (Herranz 2008).

Brownfield redevelopment projects as PPPs

Conceptualizing PPPs as an inter-organizational network resonates with how brownfield clean-up and redevelopment projects requiring PPP structures unfold. With two different technical phases (clean-up and redevelopment), as well as the standard PPP phases of planning and implementation, these projects occur through the interactions of multiple stakeholders. These stakeholders include elected representatives, private developers, public managers, landowners, investors, citizens, activists, regulators and end-users (Dair and Williams 2006).

Brownfield projects are also characterized by distinct process phases during which different stakeholders may play more central roles than others. Phases begin with *site selection* and a *Phase I assessment*. Site selection involves the sifting through of a range of stakeholder preferences regarding economic development priorities, land-use planning, end use, and resource commitments by project leaders. Phase I assessments, then, provide a quick overview of the degree of contamination on the selected site as well as economic feasibility data regarding site redevelopment. If the Phase I assessment reveals levels of contamination requiring remediation, property owners conduct a much more detailed *Phase II assessment* to determine contamination details and the means by which it will be contained or removed. *Remediation* soon follows and *redevelopment* begins. Table 8.1 provides a conceptual model of brownfield projects as PPPs integrating stakeholder and phase characteristics.

Table 8.1 Stakeholder model of brownfield policy processes

Brownfield phase	Key stakeholders
Site identification	Citizens Elected officials Public managers (planners, engineers) Private property owners Insurers
Initial site assessment – Phase I investigation	Public managers Environmental engineers
Economic assessment and planning	Citizens Elected officials Economic development officials Developers Lawyers Public managers Insurers
Detailed site assessment – Phase II investigation	Environmental engineers Public managers
Project development and financing	Lenders Developers Clients
Clean-up execution	Environmental engineers Consultants and contractors
Redevelopment of site	Developers Construction companies Clients Public managers

Source: Derived from Dair and Williams (2006) and Dennison (1998: 142–7)

Examining brownfield PPP projects through the network management theory lens articulated above suggests that successful brownfield projects, with their short lifespans, clear project goals, and multiple expert domains, require highly central and stable formal structures to achieve successful outcomes. However, the entry and exit of project actors to and from the network across project phases challenges stability, suggesting that successful brownfield networks also exhibit high levels of multiplexity, or layers of ties between network actors. These ties ensure that, while project actors may exit the network after they have completed their primary task, ties remain to highly central actors enabling the transfer of relevant information.

A measure of 'success'

One challenge facing research about the degree to which public management behaviours impact PPP success is measuring, in an *ex post* manner, which brownfield PPP projects qualify as 'successful' and which qualify as 'unsuccessful'. In particular, defining project success across large numbers of diverse stakeholders directly involved with brownfield project processes posed several conceptual challenges for this study. To address this challenge, this study developed a success measure from existing brownfield theory and assessed the reliability of that measure against the independent opinions of experts in the field.

A review of the brownfield literature revealed a range of indicators for brownfield project success (Table 8.2) including both proximate and regional economic impacts, perceptions of fairness and process satisfaction, financial costs, and job creation (Bacot and O'Dell 2006; Wedding and Crawford-Brown 2007; Ganser 2008). To assess the extent to which these indicators were relevant to the sociopolitical context of this study (the state of New York), success data were collected through an online survey and a series of stakeholder interviews with New York-based brownfield experts as well as from the New York State Remediation Database, an online data source regarding all real properties remediated with assistance from the state of New York. Matching the empirical indicators with those found in Table 8.2 and aggregating the empirical data together created a success measure to be used for subsequent case selection.

The survey asked a purpose sample of brownfield experts to identify brownfield redevelopment projects they perceived as both successful and unsuccessful, why they thought so, the criteria they applied and the type of agency or organization that they represented. Each respondent listed as many success criteria as possible and then ranked the top five criteria in order of importance. They then repeated this exercise focusing on criteria that would cause them to perceive that a project was unsuccessful. These lists were compared to assess discriminant validities and a score was calculated for each criterion, enabling rankings based upon importance. A total of 28 surveys were completed, spanning public, private, citizen and civil society stakeholders at the local, state and federal levels.

The resulting data indicated that the perceived success of brownfield remediation and redevelopment projects by this sample required the application of the following three criteria in order of importance:

Table 8.2 Outcome indicators and brownfield project success (alphabetical)

Indicator	Definition for 'success'
Area-wide impacts	Positive social, economic and environmental impacts on broader community
Citizen support	Degree of citizen support for project processes and outcomes
Clean-up costs	Real costs for remediating property to levels appropriate for end use
Development costs	Real costs for constructing end use on remediated property
Funding	Perceived satisfaction of levels of public and private financial support
Impact of location	Perceived importance of property as economic development
New job creation	Number of full-time employees hired for the project
Planned end use	Perceived satisfaction with end use
Political support	Degree of elected official support at multiple levels of government
Property value impacts	Real positive change in adjacent property values
Return on investment	Real income generated per cost over predetermined time period
Use of time	Perceived efficiency of time between start and end of project

1. existing contaminations were addressed;
2. the project was strategically located to maximize impacts; and
3. the project had high political support from elected officials and citizens.

To increase the construct validity of the success measure, respondents were also asked to list criteria used to identify 'unsuccessful' projects resulting in the following list:

1. existing contaminations were not addressed;
2. the time and resource efficiencies of the project were low; and
3. the project was not strategically located for maximum community impact.

These two lists of criteria were combined to produce five variables that together formed the success measure used to enable case study selection (Table 8.3).

Research design and case selection

The research question framing this study focused upon the mechanisms and processes that link network management practices to project outcomes and required a comparative case study approach (Mahoney and Goertz 2006; Bennett and Elman 2006). Case selection subsequently utilized a 'most similar' case selection strategy (Seawright and Gerring 2008), selecting cases that varied on both the dependent and explanatory variables of interest but matched along all

Table 8.3 Operationalizing the dependent variable: brownfield project success

Outcome measures	Operationalization as success	Mechanisms of data collection
Time to completion (*time*)	Actual time to completion	Interviews, actual time measured
	Stakeholder satisfaction with time from initial site investigation to development or present	
Clean-up costs (*cost*)	Actual clean-up costs per acre	Interviews, actual costs
Implementation processes (*process*)	Stakeholder satisfaction with implementation processes	Interviews
Contamination abatement (*clean*)	Certificate of Completion or similar indication from appropriate regulatory authority	NYS DEC records Interviews
Area-wide impact (*impact*)	Reported increase in values of neighbouring properties	Interviews

other key explanatory variables. Doing so provided a set of case studies enabling effective comparison of factors influencing project outcomes.

The case selection process utilized highly specific decision rules to narrowly define a small population of eligible cases within the state of New York. The first stage involved identifying municipalities exhibiting similar real estate market strengths, municipal policy-tool use experiences, political support and degree of intergovernmental ties. The second stage entailed a full review of completed brownfield projects in each of these municipalities to find projects with similar end uses, sizes and levels of city government involvement and then collecting data for the success measure to develop a relative rating of the successfulness of each project within each municipality. These steps resulted in the selection of one successful and one unsuccessful brownfield project each in the cities of Buffalo and Rochester, NY (Table 8.4). Despite constraining the ability to generalize findings to a broader population of brownfield properties, narrowing the sampling frame in this manner increased the likelihood that analysis captured the explanatory effects of interest (Collier and Mahoney 1996).

It is important to note that the high success project in Buffalo shared the same physical property with the city's low success project. This fact meant that a strong path dependency existed between these two projects with the events resulting in the lower success having a direct impact on the subsequent higher success. While this may appear to create an internal validity problem, it is essential to recall that the purpose of this study was not to provide evidence for a causal relationship but to describe plausible causal mechanisms between social network structures and

Table 8.4 Comparison of selected cases

Variable	Buffalo low success (BLS)	Buffalo high success (BHS)	Rochester low success (RLS)	Rochester high success (RHS)
City	Buffalo	Buffalo	Rochester	Rochester
Success measure				
Clean-up	Incomplete	Complete	Partially complete	Complete
Time to completion	2002–3	2006–9	2003–present	1996–2004
Clean-up cost	$1.2 million		$605,000	$4.05 million
Process satisfaction	Low	High	Low	High
Economic impact	None	High	None	High
Relative success rank	Lowest	High	Low	Highest
Property ownership during remediation	City of Buffalo	City of Buffalo	City of Rochester	City of Rochester
Brownfield property size	4 acres		1 acre	6.85 acres
Proposed end use	Mixed market-rate Residential/affordable housing		Market-rate residential	Market-rate residential

project outcomes. As Bennett and Elman (2006) state, 'the selection bias critique does not apply in the same way to inferences drawn from within-case process tracing or causal process observations' (p. 461). Therefore, because three years and more than 60 per cent turnover occurred in the composition of network actors between projects, Buffalo Low Success (BLS) and Buffalo High Success (BHS) were treated as two different projects with regards to their management characteristics.

Semi-structured interviews, follow-up surveys for interview participants, public records obtained through freedom of information laws, and media reports from newspapers, blogs and professional journals provided data for each case. Network analysis and process-tracing techniques were then applied to assess not only public management behaviours within network structures but also the plausibility of additional factors explaining project outcomes (Bennett 2008).

Network structures within each project were measured by applying social network analysis (SNA) techniques to the data (Milward and Provan 1998; Tichy *et al.* 1979). These techniques used relational information between individual and organizational actors to define structural properties of each project network over time, particularly as they related to information exchanges (Wasserman and Faust 1994). Sociometric matrices indicating who exchanged information with whom were constructed using data from interviews, the post-interview survey and documents. Links were considered binary, symmetric, non-directional and non-weighted, allowing for only basic description of network structures utilizing the SNA software AGNA.

Coding interview and document data for all possible explanatory variables using TAMS Analyzer qualitative software enabled construction of the project contexts within which process-tracing techniques then mapped out how project outcomes came to be (Bennett and Elman 2006). Credibility of these stories was subsequently verified with key interview respondents by allowing them to comment on initial analyses.

Key findings

Initial analysis examined the differences in network structures both within and between each project. Network data drawn from within each project determined which individuals operated from highly central positions in the overall project network as well as how these centralities varied across individual project phases. These data then revealed several differences related to the different levels of success between each project that were then tied into the broader management story constructed through the interview and document data.

At the whole-project level, two key network structure patterns emerged (Table 8.5). First, public managers or citizen leaders occupied highly central project network positions in the higher-success projects while private actors played more prominent roles in the lower-success projects. Second, the more successful projects experienced greater overall project centralities than the lower-success projects.

Table 8.5 Network statistics and actor centrality by project

	Network statistics		Most central actors
	Freeman centrality	*Density*	*Three most central actors*
RHS	0.599	0.109	City Senior Environmental Manager Citizen Leader City Housing Manager
BHS	0.530	0.145	City Planning Director City Housing Manager City Environmental Manager
RLS	0.493	0.179	City Senior Environmental Manager City Environmental Manager Environmental Consultant
BLS	0.443	0.128	Environmental Consultant City Planning Deputy Director Community Lender

Findings derived from interview and document data indicate that the high levels of centrality exhibited by public managers in the higher-success projects was initially a function of the public initiation of each project. In RHS, citizen activists motivated city council members to direct public managers at the city to commence property acquisition and remediation processes. In BHS, the Director of the Office of Strategic Planning (OSP) and the mayor seized the opportunity to revitalize what had been a failed project (BLS) to build political approval. For both lower-success projects, private actors assumed central roles when organizational capacity deficiencies diminished the abilities of city officials to do so and when the private actors perceived an opportunity and made an effort to steer the project.

In the higher-success projects, project processes required high levels of technical environmental information and compelled each city's lead environmental managers to occupy central positions in each network early on in the project lifecycle. However, the centrality of these environmental managers soon changed due to different organizational capacities found in each city. In Rochester, the senior environmental manager was cross-trained in both remediation and redevelopment processes and was able to maintain this central position across non-environmental project phases for both the high- and low-success projects. As the city council president described, this project succeeded in large part because this public manager 'could put the project together'. In Buffalo, the city environmental manager limited his work to the remediation phases, falling out of the most central position after the remediation phases were complete. This was partly due to the lack of broader resources for environmental work within the City of Buffalo and partly due to the fact that, in Buffalo, city-led brownfield projects were housed in the Office of Strategic Planning and subsequent planning and redevelopment project phases relied upon actions taken by OSP managers.

The ties between overall network centrality and project outcomes for the more successful projects were both a function of, as well as a factor for, project success. For example, the fact that RHS and BHS achieved full redevelopment meant that a full set of PPP actors became engaged in project processes, increasing the number of possible individuals needing information from highly central actors. At the same time, the higher overall centralities of RHS and BHS enabled central public managers to more effectively exchange information with PPP network partners, increasing project efficiency and allowing completion of complex technical tasks.

However, these project narratives revealed that the relationships between total project centrality and project outcomes occurred for two different reasons. In the RHS case, high project centrality derived from high levels of PPP network stability and enabled strong, trust-based relationships to develop. Of the key actors in the project network, only a few dropped out of project processes before project completion. This enabled network ties to strengthen and mature over time and enhanced the centralized communication role performed by the senior environmental manager. The high centrality of the BHS project, however, did not come about due to network stability but rather because of a lack of it. A highly unstable resource environment and turnover in key project actors compelled the city's director of the Office of Strategic Planning to centralize project processes and compel compliance of project partners through more coercive means.

As a result, network management within project phases for RHS and BHS occurred in two very different PPP management environments. Table 8.6 illustrates these differences. Due to the higher levels of trust and the greater stability of relationships, RHS exhibited lower within-project phase centrality than BHS. This is consistent with multiple interview responses regarding RHS describing how, once the appropriate information became disseminated, project actors implemented their tasks and proceeded to the next phase. Conversely, BHS interview data revealed that progress within individual phases required the direct intervention of the OSP director in phase-specific project tasks, even when they fell outside of his normal task jurisdiction.

Applying network structure findings to analysis of management strategies reveals two means by which network management efforts in these PPP networks influenced both process-oriented and construction-based outcomes. First, as exhibited by RHS, when internal and external project factors remained stable, trust-based relationship-building strategies enabled expectation for reciprocal action to drive PPP partner behaviours, achieving high levels of process satisfaction. Second, when financial resources, partnership composition consistency and market stabilities decreased or destabilized, highly central public managers achieved project construction by leveraging political influence, as evidenced by the successful outcomes in BHS. However, the lower-success cases reveal that neither trust-based relationship management nor leveraging political influence is sufficient to achieve project outcomes when the project context becomes too unstable or uncertain.

Across the cases examined, stakeholders active in the RHS project exhibited the highest levels of process satisfaction and indicated that the resulting redevelopment was highly successful despite the project having the longest time-frame and the highest remediation costs. In interviews, PPP network actors indicated

Table 8.6 Network centrality data by project phase

	RHS	*BHS*
Assembly	0.708	N/A
EconAssess	0.683	N/A*
EnvAssess	0.675	0.964
CleanPlan	0.696	0.714
ConstPlan	0.662	0.866
Design	0.645	0.807
Cleanup	0.585	0.934
Const	0.587	0.742
Sales	0.854	0.670

* Based upon case selection rationale, property assembly and economic assessment occurred prior to the start of BHS.

that the levels of trust and reciprocity between them throughout each project phase coupled with the symbolism attached to cleaning up a nuisance in a residential neighbourhood maintained enthusiasm and optimism for the project through its completion and created a sense of unique accomplishment. As a representative of the private firms engaged in home building for the project stated in a 2008 interview, 'This project is probably a once in a life type of deal. Everything fell together at once. Timing wise, partnership wise, funding wise, all the way through, everything just meshed together.'

In the BHS project, while the project achieved redevelopment and created positive neighbourhood impacts, many network actors reported lower satisfaction with project processes. This was largely due to the OSP director's use of political force to compel the behaviours of PPP actors both within and outside city government, giving the perception that the director was not as much a team player as an individual with a specific agenda. The community lender whose funding proved crucial for the final construction phases described that the director 'wanted to bring a neighbourhood market-rate product into the city. Period! And there was not going to be anyone that was going to tell him to the contrary.' A member of the city's public works division agreed, stating that his office was essentially ordered to allocate time and resources towards the project despite not having budgeted for it. However, remediation occurred, houses were built, and homeowners quickly purchased each of the new homes.

However, the capacity to manage network relationships or the ability to call upon political resources is not sufficient to achieve brownfield PPP success. For example, the start of new home construction prior to adequate property remediation in BLS where political support for the project was high stemmed from inadequate communication between network members. This in turn led to PPP partners claiming high levels of dissatisfaction with project processes. On the other hand, actors in the failed RLS project expressed satisfaction with the interpersonal elements of project process but the project did not achieve full remediation or redevelopment. In this particular project, broader environmental and market uncertainties beyond the control of any individual PPP partner diminished the positive impacts of relationship development. Specifically, property contamination for RLS stemmed from both on-site and off-site sources, limiting the abilities of local public managers to fully remediate the property. In addition, RLS project processes occurred during the 2008 start of the financial lending crisis, hampering negotiations over project financing and preventing construction from commencing.

The public management lessons from this research have several implications for brownfield PPP projects. Despite the implied dual nature of a 'PPP', it is important to consider the entire network of actors necessary to move the project from phase to phase, particularly when each phase involves very different sets of technical tasks. Fundamentally, public managers must consider the broader contexts of the projects themselves when selecting management strategies. When stable relationships abound, focusing on building trust between network actors and leveraging expectations of reciprocal action helps to move the project forward. When internal capacities to participate in networked processes decrease, accessing political power compensates. However, when the broader economic, environmental and political contexts destabilize, PPP partners should reconsider project goals and alter outcome expectations. Effective network management may not be sufficient to overcome these challenges.

Challenges of comparative case analysis based upon perceptions of 'success'

Utilizing the language presented by Hodge and Greve in the opening chapter, the criteria used for the success measure in this study reflected the narrow definition of PPP success they derived from Jeffares *et al.* (2009). Hodge and Greve state that, under a narrow definition, PPP performance is 'concerned with the achievement of particular service or outcome targets' as opposed to 'consideration of the longer term relationship that might exist beyond the delivery of a particular project or programme'. By focusing upon specific project characteristics such as time to completion, costs and direct impact, the success measure utilized here failed to capture the embeddedness of each brownfield project in the larger social and environmental systems surrounding them, limiting the extent to which network structures and management data could be used to explain project outcomes.

Interviews with state and local environmental managers support the importance of expanding measures of success to include these contexts. Respondents in this study indicated that the highly technical nature of brownfield PPP projects creates incentives for city officials to reduce the transaction costs of starting new relationships by retaining project partners across multiple projects. Future research on the abilities of network-management strategies to bring about PPP success should therefore use measures for success beyond the boundaries of a single project into the broader realm of multiple projects implemented over time. However, this may create difficulties in research design when the unit of analysis ranges from the individual to the whole network.

The success measure used in this study also succumbed to the pitfalls of incorporating stakeholder opinions into the calculation. As articulated by Hodge and Greve, utilizing stakeholder opinions enables success to be self-defining by the stakeholders from whom researchers elicit opinions. Yet emphasizing 'process satisfaction' as a primary component of success opened the door for relational theories of network management to explain how different levels of success occurred. In this study, the comparative case design intended to moderate the impacts of self-definition by making success relative to a set of otherwise similar projects.

However, the extent to which PPP stakeholder opinions shape the resulting measures also depends upon which stakeholders become included in the measure in the first place, opening the door for selection bias. For example, focusing data-collection for a success measure on low-income citizens would likely generate different values for success than focusing data-collection on private development elites. Being comprehensive in this selection process becomes important, particularly if measures for success are to reflect conflicts between public, private and citizen stakeholders.

Finally, it is important to note that PPP researchers use success measures in multiple ways beyond the role of the primary dependent variable. This study, for one, utilized such a measure to select case studies for the assessment of the relative strength of a key independent variable of interest. Merely focusing upon questions of 'How do we measure the success of PPPs?' when wrestling with the conceptual difficulties of doing so narrows the multiple ways by which success measures inform our work.

Concluding comments

The comparative case analysis described in this chapter leads to several implications for researchers analysing brownfield PPP success. First, awareness and management of the broader actor network matters, particularly if project success includes measures of satisfaction with project processes. Such measures become more relevant when researchers examine PPP projects in the broader social context of agency relationships over time. Under the appropriate organizational capacity and market stability conditions, public managers who employ trust-based network-management strategies not only achieve desired project outcomes but also generate positive relationships that extend into the next project, impacting overall perceptions of success. Should conditions require the leveraging of political power to compel network actors into task compliance, outcomes may still be achieved, but at the cost of procedural dissatisfaction.

Nevertheless, the extent to which these findings hold depends on how PPP success becomes defined and used. It is important for theorists to continue to evaluate how real and perceived processes and outcomes of brownfield PPP projects can be combined and recombined to generate different success measures from different stakeholder perspectives. This research recommends that future success measures be not only consistent across each project examined but also inclusive of the broader social, economic and environmental systems in which projects are embedded. By grounding empirical study of PPPs in these contexts, stakeholder values regarding the projects examined become known, and more concrete metrics for the measurement of 'success' may be developed and applied to a broad range of uses in PPP research.

References

Bacot, H. and O'Dell, C. (2006) Establishing indicators to evaluate brownfield redevelopment. *Economic Development Quarterly*, 20(2): 142–62.

Ball, M. and Maginn, P. J. (2005) Urban change and conflict: evaluating the role of partnerships in urban regeneration in the UK. *Housing Studies*, 20(1): 9–28.

Becker, F. and Patterson, V. (2005) Public–private partnerships: balancing financial returns, risks, and roles of the partners. *Public Performance & Management Review*, 29(2): 125–44.

Bennett, A. (2008) Process tracing: a Bayesian approach, in H. Brady and D. Collier (eds) *Oxford Handbook of Political Methodology*. Oxford and London, pp. 702–21.

Bennett, A. and Elman, C. (2006) Qualitative research: recent developments in case study methods. *Annual Review of Political Science*, 9: 455–476.

Berardo, R. (2008) Generalized trust in multi-organizational policy arenas: studying its emergence from a network perspective. *Political Research Quarterly*, 62(1): 178–89.

Brachman, L. (2003) *Three Case Studies on the Roles of Community-based Organizations in Brownfields and other Vacant Property Redevelopment: Barriers, Strategies and Key Success Factors*. Washington, DC: Lincoln Institute for Land Policy

Collier, D. and Mahoney, J. (1996) Insights and pitfalls: selection bias in qualitative research. *World Politics*, 49(1): 56–91.

Crosby, B. C. and Bryson, J. M. (2005) A leadership framework for cross-sector collaboration. *Public Management Review*, 7(2): 177–201.

Dair, C. M. and Williams, K. (2006) Sustainable land reuse: the influence of different stakeholders in achieving sustainable brownfield developments in England. *Environment and Planning*, 38: 1345–66.

Davis, T. S. (2002) 'Defining the brownfields problem', in T. S. Davis (ed.) *Brownfields: A Comprehensive Guide to Redeveloping Contaminated Property*. Chicago, IL: American Bar Association.

Dawes, S. S., Cresswell, A. M. and Pardo, T. A. (2009) From 'need to know' to 'need to share': Tangled problems, information boundaries, and the building of public knowledge networks. *Public Administration Review*, 69(3): 392–402.

De Sousa, C. (2005) Policy performance and brownfield redevelopment in Milwaukee, Wisconsin. *The Professional Geographer*, 57(2): 312–27.

Dennison, M. S. (1998) *Brownfields Redevelopment: Programs and Strategies for Rehabilitating Contaminated Real Estate*. Lanham, MD: Government Institute.

Droege, S. B., Anderson, J. R. and Bowler, M. (2003) Trust and organizational information flow. *Journal of Business and Management*, 9(1): 45–59.

Ganser, R. (2008) Monitoring brownfield housing development: strengths and weaknesses of indicator based monitoring in the English planning system. *Journal of Environmental Planning and Management*, 51(2): 201–20.

Ghere, R. K. (1996) Aligning the ethics of public–private partnership: the issue of local economic development. *Journal of Public Administration Research and Theory*, 6(4): 599–621.

Googins, B. K. and Rochlin, S. A. (2000) Creating the partnership society: understanding the rhetoric and reality of cross-sectoral partnerships. *Business and Society Review*, 105(1): 127–44.

Herranz Jr, J. (2008) The multisectoral trilemma of network management. *Journal of Public Administration Research and Theory*, 18(1): 1–31.

Hodge, G. A. and Greve, C. (2007) Public–private partnerships: an international performance review. *Public Administration Review*, 67(3): 545–58.

Howland, M. (2003) Private initiative and public responsibility for the redevelopment of industrial brownfields: three Baltimore case studies. *Economic Development Quarterly*. 17: 367–81.

Isett, K. R. and Provan, K. G. (2005) The evolution of dyadic interorganizational relationships in a network of publicly funded nonprofit agencies. *Journal of Public Administration Research and Theory*, 15(1): 149–65.

Jeffries, F. L. and Reed, R. (2000) Trust and adaptation in relational contracting. *The Academy of Management Review*, 25(4): 873–82.

Jeffares, S., Sullivan, H. and Bovaird, T. (2009) Beyond the contract: the challenge of evaluating the performance(s) of public–private partnerships. Paper for the 13th IRSPM conference, April, Copenhagen.

Jones, C., Hesterly, W. S. and Borgatti, S. P. (1997) A general theory of network governance: exchange conditions and social mechanisms. *Academy of Management Review*, 22(4): 911–45.

Jones, R. and Noble, G. (2008) Managing the implementation of public–private partnerships. *Public Money and Management*, 28(2): 109–14.

Klijn, E. H. and Koppenjan, J. F. M. (2004) Institutional design in networks: elaborating and analysing strategies for institutional design. Paper presented at the Eighth International Research Symposium on Public Management, Budapest, 31 March–2 April.

Klijn, E. H. and Teisman, G. R. (2003) Institutional and strategic barriers to public–private partnership: an analysis of Dutch cases. *Public Money and Management*, 23(3): 137–46.

Koppenjan, J. F. M. and Klijn, E. H. (2004) *Managing Uncertainties in Networks*. New York: Routledge.

Lowndes, V. and Skelcher, C. (1998) The dynamics of multi-organizational partnerships: an analysis of changing modes of governance. *Public Administration*, 76(2): 313–33.

Lubell, M. and Fulton, A. (2008) Local policy networks and agricultural watershed management. *Journal of Public Administration Research and Theory*, 18(4): 673–96.

Mahoney, J. and Goertz, G. (2006) A tale of two cultures: contrasting quantitative and qualitative research. *Political Analysis*, 14(3): 227–49.

Mandell, M. P. and Keast, R. (2007) Evaluating network arrangements: toward revised performance measures. *Public Performance & Management Review*, 30(4): 574–97.

Mandell, M. P. and Steelman, T. A. (2003) Understanding what can be accomplished through interorganizational innovations: the importance of typologies, context and management strategies. *Public Management Review*, 5(2): 197–224.

McCarthy, L. (2002) The brownfield dual land-use policy challenge: reducing barriers to private redevelopment while connecting reuse to broader community goals. *Land Use Policy*, 19(4): 287–96.

McGuire, M. (2002) Managing networks: propositions on what managers do and why they do it. *Public Administration Review*, 62(5): 599–609.

Milward, H. B. and Provan, K. G. (1998) Measuring network structure. *Public Administration*, 76(2): 387–407.

Milward, H. B., Provan, K. G., Fish, A., Isett, K. R. and Huang, K. (2010) Governance and collaboration: an evolutionary study of two mental health networks. *Journal of Public Administration Research and Theory*, 20(suppl. 1): i125–i141.

Noble, G. and Jones, R. (2006) The role of boundary-spanning managers in the establishment of public–private partnerships. *Public Administration*, 84(4): 891–917.

Oliver, C. (1991) Strategic responses to institutional processes. *The Academy of Management Review*, 16(1): 145–79.

Peters, B. G. (2000) Policy instruments and public management: bridging the gaps. *Journal of Public Administration Research and Theory*, 10(1): 35–47.

Provan, K. G., Fish, A. and Sydow, J. (2007) Interorganizational networks at the network level: a review of the empirical literature on whole networks. *Journal of Management*, 33(3): 479–516.

Provan, K. G. and Milward, H. B. (1995) A preliminary theory of interorganizational effectiveness: a comparative study of four community mental health systems. *Administrative Science Quarterly*, 40(1): 1–33.

Pryke, S. D. (2005) Towards a social network theory of project governance. *Construction Management and Economics*, 23(9): 927–39.

Seawright, J. and Gerring, J. (2008) Case selection techniques in case study research: a menu of qualitative and quantitative options. *Political Research Quarterly*, 61(2): 294–308.

Skelcher, C. and Mathur, N. (2004) Governance arrangements and public service performance: reviewing and reformulating the research agenda. Paper presented at International Colloquium on Governance and Performance, University of Birmingham (15–16 March).

Thomas, C. (2003) *Bureaucratic Landscapes: Interagency Cooperation and the Preservation of Biodiversity*. Boston, MA: MIT.

Tichy, N. M., Tushman, M. L. and Fombrun, C. (1979) Social network analysis for organizations. *Academy of Management Review*, 4(4): 507–19.

US Conference of Mayors (2000) Recycling America's land, in *A National Report on Brownfields Redevelopment*, US Conference of Mayors, Washington, DC.

US Conference of Mayors (2003) Recycling America's land, in *A National Report on Brownfields Redevelopment*, US Conference of Mayors, Washington, DC.

US Conference of Mayors (2006) Recycling America's land, in *A National Report on Brownfields Redevelopment*, US Conference of Mayors, Washington, DC.

Wasserman, S. and Faust, K. (1994) Social network analysis: methods and applications, in M. Granovetter (ed.) *Structural Analysis in the Social Sciences*. Cambridge: Cambridge University Press.

Waugh Jr, W. L. and Streib, G. (2006) Collaboration and leadership for effective emergency management. *Public Administration Review*, 66(s1): 131–40.

Wedding, G. C. and Crawford-Brown, D. (2007) Measuring site-level success in brownfield redevelopments: a focus on sustainability and green building. *Journal of Environmental Management*, 85(2): 483–95.

Williams, P. (2002) The competent boundary spanner. *Public Administration*, 80(1): 103–24.

9 Beyond the contract

The challenge of evaluating the performance(s) of public–private partnerships

Stephen Jeffares[1], Helen Sullivan and Tony Bovaird

Introduction

Public–Private Partnerships are firmly established in public governance in the UK and internationally. Driven by a desire, need or requirement to deliver public services through some degree of co-operation, PPPs can take a variety of forms and are manifest in different ways in different territories. Indeed, the enormous permutations of partnership purposes, structures and processes have led Brinkerhoff and Brinkerhoff (2011) to counsel caution in transferring specifics from one setting to another, given the limited generalized applicability of any set of conclusions about PPPs. Decisions about the shape and remit of PPPs are influenced as much by national history and tradition as they are by immediate circumstances, as Hodge and Greve (2005) indicate, contrasting the 'corporatist-like' PPPs of Germany and Sweden with the role of private finance in English infrastructure projects. The resultant breadth of activity contained under the label 'PPP' can be unhelpful, particularly for comparative analysis and research.

In the UK where partnership activity is arguably most strongly embedded in public policy, the range of activities that may be labelled 'partnerships' can be equally confusing and unhelpful for the analyst or researcher. The 'New Labour' administrations (1997–2010) launched a range of 'partnership' initiatives including: arrangements between government bodies and private partners to finance and/or supply capital projects and/or services; policy partnerships involving a range of actors from the public/private/voluntary and community sectors in pursuit of specific policy outcomes, e.g. community safety; area-based partnerships, again involving actors from a range of sectors competing for funds to deliver 'regeneration' programmes of various kinds; and community or user partnerships, arrangements between public bodies and individuals or groups of service users or citizens to design and deliver interventions or services. Brinkerhoff and Brinkerhoff (2011) have produced a typology of partnerships in the international sphere that encompasses policy, service delivery, infrastructure, capacity building and economic development.

While the above may help to give an indication of the scope and scale of partnership activity in the UK and internationally, thus highlighting its significance to public policy-makers, the elasticity of the term is challenging for research, particularly evaluation research, which seeks to make judgements about the performance and 'added value' of partnership activity.

In response to this challenge, the growth of 'partnerships' in the UK has been matched by the production of partnership evaluation frameworks and toolkits, some academic, some practice-based. However, these partnership evaluation tools have tended to focus on specific policy areas, e.g. health and social care, or particular sectors, e.g. public sector, community and voluntary groups. Rather less is known about how to evaluate the performance of PPPs as much of the literature is focused on how to develop private–private strategic alliances (e.g. Cravens *et al.* 2000) rather than how to evaluate subsequent activity.

The purpose of this chapter is to identify and describe an approach to evaluating the performance of PPPs. Our starting assumption is that developing a bespoke approach is necessary, as PPPs have different sets of actors, motivations and purposes to those of other partnerships involving the public sector. The first section of the chapter sets out the challenge, outlining what we mean by PPPs – specifically, partnerships for public service delivery – and highlighting the performative challenges for these arrangements. The second section of the chapter explores the challenge of evaluation and considers the contribution of theory-based approaches to the evaluation of partnership performance. Drawing on Skelcher and Sullivan's (2008) work it proposes a theoretically informed framework for understanding partnership performance and offers an approach relevant to PPPs. The third section of the chapter identifies and compares a number of popular evaluative approaches and tools used in the evaluation of partnerships of different kinds and in different ways. Through an analysis of the questions used by these tools and frameworks in assessing partnerships we identify 12 common partnership principles. We then combine this analysis with our theoretically informed framework to illustrate the balance of coverage of existing partnership evaluations and to consider the implications of this for comprehensive and robust evaluation of partnership performance.

Public–private partnerships and service delivery – imperatives, emergent forms and questions of performance

There are many structures and vehicles available for the provision of public services, so in exploring their performance it is important to be specific. This chapter is concerned with partnerships between public and private for-profit entities for the purpose of the delivery of public services. It covers, in particular, joint ventures, public–private partnering contracts, Private Finance Initiative (PFI) and capital investment strategic partnerships. It therefore excludes in-house provision, consortium arrangements between two or more public agencies (e.g. procurement consortia of local authorities clubbing together to achieve economies of scale) and partnerships with third-sector organizations. It also excludes service outsourcing, where a public authority contracts an alternative service provider to provide certain services in place of that public authority.

There is a range of drivers for public authorities, particularly local authorities, to consider collaborative approaches to public service delivery – Dickinson and Nicholds (2012) point to organizational fragmentation, cost-effectiveness, prevention, personalization and place shaping as key drivers in the UK, while Hodge (2010) lists 15 different objectives that different stakeholders might typically have for PPPs in an international context. The cost-effectiveness driver in the UK has been a central force for partnership working, with powerful performance-management regimes in the public sector requiring public agencies to demonstrate that they are simultaneously meeting financial and policy-performance objectives. For many processes, particularly standard business or back-office processes, there has been a tendency in recent years to outsource the process to a third party, often a private for-profit provider. There are, however, alternatives to outsourcing a service area, including joint ventures, partnering contracts and capital investment strategic partnerships. (In addition, of course, a public agency may simply decide to offload the service, i.e. transfer it entirely to an external provider, without any subsidy or further involvement.) Drawing on a UK government publication (DCLG 2006), Table 9.1, below, spells out the three forms of Public–Private Service Delivery Partnership (PSDP), together with CLG's (Community and Local Government) view of their characteristics, drivers, challenges and limitations.

Clearly, all of these entities have differing implications for potential benefits, costs and risks. The decision to form a partnership rather than to outsource or off-load is both expensive and time-consuming and has potentially problematic continuing consequences. It exposes public authorities to opportunistic behaviour by their partners. The traditional transactional cost analysis of the calculus that lies behind decisions to choose a particular entity (Williamson 1975; Thompson *et al.* 1991) emphasizes the need to take into account the level of complexity and uncertainty attaching to the service specification (a negative driver to external-ize), the importance of the externalized service to the outcomes sought by the public authority, the market structure (particularly the likelihood of collusion if a contract is to be let), whether the assets needed by the external partner can be used partly to produce services for other clients as well (positive factor).

Public authorities may seek structures that privilege the voice of particular stakeholders, particularly politicians, through safeguards such as the need for committee authorization and scrutiny panels that ensure decisions cannot be rushed or 'difficult' partners bypassed. The operation of these safeguards can, in turn, annoy other stakeholders or even be perceived as a challenge to the 'part-nership' relationship. Most empirical attempts at transactional cost analysis have found it particularly hard to estimate the costs, and benefits, of these macro-level governance processes.

Each of the PPP types described in Table 9.1 requires a bridge between quite different cultures. In a joint venture (JV), for example, it is likely that those work-ing in the top management tier of the JV (usually top managers who originally came from each of the constituent partners) both help to create and are personally aligned to its culture – but major cultural differences may exist between these managers and those working in the wider organization and in the partner agencies

Table 9.1 Forms of public–private service delivery partnerships

Vehicle	Description	Drivers	Challenges and limitations
Joint venture	A newly established company owned by both the public authority and private company	Enables joint working, pooling of assets, pursuit of complementary objectives, pursuit of realizing operational potential	Risk of insolvency, time and cost of establishment, matching public and private cultures in one vehicle, loss of accountability to public
Public–private partnering contracts	Public authority selecting a partner to assist them in improving service delivery and contributing strategically Two types – either 'big bang' strategic partnership or incremental partnerships	Alternative to outsourcing where both parties directly participate in provision, more collaborative and less adversarial, access to private sector skills and resources, profit for private sector, reassurance for public authority from open-book finances	Private partner concerns over board structure, public partner concerns over accountability, more complicated and therefore more costly than outsourcing
PFI and capital investment strategic partnerships	A form of capital outsourcing but with partnering contract Public authority procures investment and services in relation to an asset with a design, build, finance and operate contract with a private provider	Public authority receives a ring-fenced subsidy, allows public authority to concentrate on mainstream service provision by delegating specific 'non-core' provision responsibilities (e.g. facilities) to private 'experts', transfer of provision and maintenance costs, realizing additional income from spare capacity, project benefits from commercial acumen, transferred staff retain benefits through TUPE	Public authority loses possession of capital facility for contract duration, financing structure is complex, costly and heavily legal-dependent, loss of difficult-to-replace staff expertise to the contractor, funding mechanism rather than partnering arrangement, VfM difficult to gauge, risk apportionment rather than risk sharing, inflexibility can inhibit continuous improvement.

Source: Adapted from DCLG (2006)

with which the JV has to interface. For example, the 'middle management' of the JV itself, or the professional, technical and clerical staff transferred, may experience significant 'cultural dissonance', while senior politicians may actively oppose the JV culture on ideological grounds (or oppositional politics) and both local politicians and the local media may stoke up hostility to it, e.g. because it is 'different to what we do here', or because of the profits it 'takes out of the services' or because of the high consultancy fees it pays. In partnering contracts, there is often little prior experience of cross-sector working, so that the willingness to trust partners with very different values, beliefs, attitudes and behaviours can be slow to develop. In PFI and capital strategic partnerships, the long-term nature of the deals can arouse hostility in stakeholders who fear inflexibility in the services provided. In each of the PPP types, a particular cultural gulf faces the private partner: it may have to sacrifice profit for a number of years in return for the long-term business arrangement with the public authority; it may have to accept behaviours, attitudes and relationships that it would not tolerate from its own internal employees; and it may experience a battering to its reputation at the hands of the local (and sometimes) national media.

The adoption and operation of PPPs of the kinds described above raises a number of important questions and issues for those charged with evaluating their performance.

Partnership performance

Partnership performance could be narrowly conceived as concerned with the achievement of particular service or outcome targets as set out in the partnership agreement (strategy, contract, business plan) and assessed in relation to other factors such as the cost of the partnership's operations. While we may describe this as a 'narrow' conception, this does not mean that it is a simple one; the challenges of data collection, verification and interpretation are likely to be significant, particularly if one is considering outcomes and in circumstances where the partners may be cautious about allowing access – even to each other – to all of the financial and service data they hold. Hellowell and Vecchi's (2010, 2012) detailed work on PFIs and PPPs in the UK and Italy provides evidence of just how challenging a task this is.

Alternatively, partnership performance may be more broadly conceived and include consideration of the longer-term relationship that might exist beyond the delivery of a particular project or programme, and the wider benefits to particular individuals or partner organizations or indeed to citizens and service users. Few of these ambitions are likely to be specified in the formal partnership agreements and it is possible that they will not be fully shared even amongst the partners, never mind with the intended beneficiaries or the wider public. Consequently the challenge for the evaluator is at least to define and refine these broader understandings of partnership performance, contextualize them and prioritize them alongside the service/outcome performance ambitions and then work out ways of collecting data to explore them. Boardman and Vining (2010: 181) advocate such an approach within the rubric of 'cost–benefit analysis' but then admit that not only would this be an ambitious approach, but also that they are actually not aware of any cost–benefit analyses of PPPs.

PPPs as politically loaded

PPPs are as much political as they are managerial entities. Their presence in a particular policy arena or local area evokes strong views, not least because the involvement of private for-profit firms in public service provision is still regarded with ideological distaste by many politicians, professionals and union members – and indeed by many other local actors.

Moreover, the establishment of a PPP is often preceded by a series of attempts at reform, sometimes labelled as 'modernization' or 'transformation'. Moving to such a different structure as a PPP is often a signal that more piecemeal approaches to reform have been judged to have been ineffective. However, this inevitably means that many protagonists and advocates of the previous reform approaches are sensitive to the implied criticism of their own performance represented by the new approach. They are therefore likely to deconstruct any claimed performance by the PPP in great detail, keen to focus on those aspects of performance that cast the PPP in an unfavourable light.

A further, often underestimated, source of resistance to a PPP is the suspicion that it may entail, in the long run if not in the short run, a loss of local jobs (and even a transfer of jobs to other parts of the country, which is often seen as even more unacceptable). Both staff and elected members are often very much against any innovative approaches that threaten job levels, and their attitudes to a PPP can be blighted by uncertainty over this potential outcome, since it often takes long periods before the level and location of actual job losses becomes clear. Since 'efficiency savings' are, at least in the long term, mainly created by finding ways of providing services with fewer staff, any PPP that emphasizes 'efficiency savings' as a key element of its future potential simply reinforces the suspicions felt by these stakeholders.

Other concerns that can result in hostility to PPPs include the belief that profits going to private partners are being 'leached' out of services at the expense of users, the suspicion that the private partners are attempting to get a 'foot in the door' in the council in order eventually to take over further services, political concern that there is less 'control' over the service since both parties have to adhere to the agreements made explicit in the contract, and local media suspicion of 'outsiders taking over local services at hugely inflated salaries'.

For supporters of PPPs the dice are loaded the other way and there are usually great expectations on PPPs for improvements in service delivery. The decision to invest in this new delivery agent is usually justified in a detailed business case that focuses on the promise of deliverable benefits. These can be spelled out in a range of ways, but they normally include significant attention to 'efficiency savings' on the one hand and improvements of service quality on the other, usually demonstrated in terms of performance indicators that are in national use (previously known in England as the 'Audit Commission PIs', now known as the 'national indicator set').

The performance of PPPs is therefore always likely to be contested because of its political context. For instance, consider the following expectations of performance:

- *contracted expectations* – typically cost savings, efficiencies, service level maintenance or improvement;
- *government expectations* in terms of the contribution of different arrangements to the 'performance' of an area, e.g. in terms of the contribution made to improved outcomes (assessed in England by Comprehensive Area Assessments until 2010);
- *private stakeholder expectations* – the shareholders and board members – typically including profit, reputation, enhanced expertise, access to public sector strategic thinking;
- *political/community expectations* – delivery on promises, sense of service improvement;
- *partner expectations* – close working relationships, sense of trust, enthusiasm, commitment, cross-sectoral learning;
- *financial expectations* – financial solvency and sustainability of the partnership, in some cases even the hope of major profits to eventually be shared between the partners;
- *cultural expectations* – partnership as an expression of the 'way things are done'.

The task for the evaluator then is not so much the search for 'the definitive answer' (as, even if achieved, it would not be accepted as such by all) but the search for an evaluation framework that allows for a range of questions to be asked and perspectives to be explored, and enables some understanding to be gained about the importance and contribution of 'beyond the contract' performance.

The policy emphasis on partnership working (across all sectors and policy areas) in the UK since 1997 generated considerable interest in and development of partnership assessment tools and evaluation frameworks (Sullivan and Skelcher 2002). The parallel emphasis on 'evidence-based policy-making' also acted to encourage evaluators (academic and otherwise) to engage more directly with policy-makers in applied evaluations and to explore new ways of undertaking evaluation appropriate to the complexities of partnership policy and practice (Barnes *et al.* 2005; Sullivan 2011). One important development is 'theory-based evaluation', well-known examples of which include 'theories of change' (Connell and Kubisch 1998) and realistic evaluation (Pawson and Tilley 1997). Theory-based or driven evaluation was developed to enable the assessment of the outcome of complex community interventions. It is based on the premise that performance should be understood in terms of the causal model held by policy designers, which could include all actors with a stake in the desired outcomes. This 'theory of change' links context to processes and activities, and ultimately to programme outcomes (Connell and Kubish 1998; Pawson and Tilley 1997). While theory-based evaluation emphasizes the significance of elaborating programme theories, i.e. articulating in some detail how and why a programme is expected to work, it also acknowledges the contribution of overarching theories of how the world works to actors' construction of particular programme theories

(Sullivan *et al.* 2002). In the next section of the chapter we consider the ways in which theory can help evaluators meet the challenge of evaluating the performance of public–private partnerships.

Theorizing performance

Skelcher and Sullivan (2008) suggest that the theory-driven approach to analysing collaborative performance provides an important tool for researchers and policy-makers. They begin with the question: How can we explain the different ways in which collaborations (public–private partnerships for our purposes) might be expected to perform? They argue that if it is possible to set out expectations about the main performance domains for public policy collaborations, and to specify the theory that could be used to explain performance in each domain, then the methodological problems of identifying metrics and attributing causality can be better specified.

For Skelcher and Sullivan the importance of the theory-driven approach for the analysis of collaborative public policy is that it proceeds from the causalities that connect different purposes to intended outcomes, so that the assessment or measurement of performance involves operationalizing a particular theoretical position (Skelcher 2008). This is the converse of the metric-driven approach to performance measurement widely used in the public sector where the focus is on identifying what can be measured, typically employing quantitative indicators, and then working backwards into the question of causal attribution. The metric approach is limited as 'the measures cannot be assumed to reflect the causal theory behind policy designers, and neither are the underlying assumptions or limitations of the set of measures explicit' (Skelcher and Sullivan 2008: 752).

Public–private partnerships of the kind we are exploring fit with Sullivan and Skelcher's definition of public-purpose collaborations: arrangements where the primary imperative is to realize benefits for the wider community rather than for special interests (Sullivan and Skelcher 2002). As such (and as we have argued above in relation to public–private partnerships) their performance has a particular salience in the wider political environment, as they reflect commitments made by politicians (who will be judged by the electorate), they involve the spending of public money (raising questions of efficiency and value for money) and the achievement of benefits for service users (raising issues of responsiveness and quality). Consequently, Skelcher and Sullivan argue, their performance can be analysed from a number of different theoretical perspectives, each of which asks different questions and explains different aspects of performance. They propose five different theory-driven approaches of five performance domains, covering the democratic, integrative, transformative, policy, and sustainability dimensions of partnership. These are linked to democratic theory, exchange and power-dependency theory, institutional theory, policy network theory, and discourse theory.

We have adapted Skelcher and Sullivan's approach by adding a sixth

Table 9.2 Performance domains and schools of theory

Performance domain	Focus	Relevant theory
Democracy	Does the partnership meet democratic principles?	Democratic theory
Policy	Does the partnership achieve its goals?	Network theories
Transformation	Does the partnership produce radically new ways of achieving outcomes (e.g. via path-breaking behaviours)?	Institutional theory
Connectivity	Does the partnership stimulate innovation through the interactions of actors?	Innovation theory Network theories
Coordination	Does the partnership achieve synergies of inputs, processes, outputs or outcomes?	Exchange theory Power-dependency theory
Coalitional (sustainability)	Is the partnership sustainable over time?	Discourse theory

Source: Adapted from Skelcher and Sullivan (2008)

performance domain in order to fit with the specific circumstances of PPPs (see Table 9.2). This draws attention to the particular focus on PPPs as transformative agents able to develop approaches to improving services and outcomes above and beyond what would have been possible through existing arrangements. It also highlights the significance attached to innovation as a product of the new connections and interactions of actors in PPPs. Finally it focuses on one particular aspect of co-ordination, the synergies generated through the adoption of the processes and practices of partnership.

In addition to offering insights into how the performance of PPPs may be considered analytically, the six performance domains could be articulated normatively to describe the features of a 'performing PPP' in pursuit of public purpose (see Table 9.3).

Table 9.3 The performing partnership

Features	Outputs
Innovative (connective performance)	Goals achieved (policy performance)
Resourceful (co-ordinative performance)	Goals exceeded (transformative performance)
Sustainable (sustainable performance)	
Principled (democratic performance)	

Of the six performance domains, policy, democratic and transformative performance are important but addressed in greater depth elsewhere. Much of recent UK research into performance measurement and management has focused on policy performance, and recently it has particularly focused on achievement of outcomes (e.g. Boyne *et al.* 2003; Bovaird *et al.* 2009; Sullivan 2009; Dickinson 2008). While less attention has been paid to evaluating democratic outcomes, there have nevertheless been a number of in-depth studies with this purpose (e.g. Skelcher *et al.* 2005; Cowell *et al.* 2009). Transformative performance has been the explicit goal of the UK 'modernization agenda', particularly in relation to service improvement (Martin 2009).

Where the co-ordinative, coalitional and connective performance domains differ is that collaboration is a prerequisite for all three, rather than simply a valuable element. These three partnership performance domains can be measured as follows:

- Coordinative performance measures are concerned with how well the partners are able to join up and develop common tasks and compatible goals, integrate strategies and achieve common purpose. The measures here are focused on the early emerging stages of a partnership as they begin to adjust to different ways of working and organizational and disciplinary cultures (focus on synergy, i.e. positive non-linear effects of aligning activities between the partners).
- Coalitional performance focuses more on sustaining the collaboration, that is the ability of the partners to sustain the coalition despite differences in interests and motivations. The measures here are focused on established rather than emerging partnerships. They highlight the extent to which relationships and behaviours in one period reproduce (or undermine) the circumstances favourable to the continuation (or damaging) of those relationships and behaviours in the next period (focus on cementing existing organizational ties and establishing new bonds).
- Connective performance focuses on the search for new forms of value-added through collaboration – the innovation that results from exploiting the dynamic and emergent properties of networks and complex adaptive systems (focus on outcomes that are specifically generated by the ways in which the partners interrelate with each other).

These three partnership performances are interrelated. Coalition performance is often linked with trust – in that the sustainability of a coalition results from trust. However, such trust is likely to emerge from the success of co-ordinative and connective performances, where the partners are acknowledging that the partnership has added value because their relations have transcended those entailed as mere signatories to a contract.

But how does this theoretically informed approach to evaluating the performance of PPPs compare with the evaluation frameworks that are in use in the field and what can we glean about the theoretical or other assumptions that underpin these frameworks? The next section considers this with an analysis of published evaluation frameworks.

The challenge of evaluation – a rapid appraisal of the existing approaches and toolkits

This section explores partnership evaluation toolkits and begins by recalling the policy context out of which they arose. While in the UK the Conservative administrations of the 1990s had encouraged partnership working in the public sector, New Labour went much further, promoting 'partnership' as a touchstone of its 'modernization' of public services. Public policy announcements consistently made reference to partnership either as an instrument of modernization or as a goal of modernization. Partnership was ubiquitous across policy areas as it was across tiers and spheres of governance.

As already indicated, partly as a consequence of this expansion of partnership activity, a new industry was born, as academics and organizational development specialists set about devising and developing new ways of assessing the contribution of partnership activity. In addition to the increased attention paid to theory-based evaluation approaches, both policy-makers and academics developed a greater appetite for formative evaluation (shaping programmes as they were implemented) and interactive evaluation (working with those involved in delivering the programme as part of the evaluation). These developments had a significant impact on the role and profile of evaluation inside and outside government, bringing in more academics to engage with public officials and involving academics and commercial consultants in new relationships with each other in evaluation consortia. Alongside these more traditional forms of evaluation, another form of evaluation – self-assessment toolkits – was also emerging. Self-assessment toolkits were designed to identify what was working well and what areas a partnership needed to address to 'perform or become 'effective'. Some included guidance on how to form a successful partnership, how to review activity and developments in the early stages and how to scrutinize those partnerships firmly established to assess their likely sustainability.

Despite this wealth of activity it is important to acknowledge that many of the 'partnerships' sponsored by the New Labour programme were principally about joining up what were seemingly fragmented organizational arrangements of key public services and outcomes. They less often focused on partnerships forged on contracts, such as a joint venture for the delivery of business processes or Information and Communication Technology (ICT). And yet these, too, are often framed as partnerships. Likewise, many of the evaluation frameworks and self-assessment toolkits that were devised in this period were done with particular partnership forms and/or particular policy areas in mind. This is not to say that they did not or could not have wider applicability, but it has to be recognized that modernization-era evaluation frameworks and toolkits were not designed for the ever-evolving hybridized PPPs. Consequently, it is important to examine these toolkits and frameworks in more depth to understand what types of performance they measure before gauging whether they are relevant for assessing the performance of PPPs.

The analysis that follows draws on a sample of mainly UK-based evaluation toolkits (inter- and intra-sectoral) uncovered during a literature review of the evaluation of partnership performance. These cover a number of policy areas, though a number are orientated to health. We do not make any claim that these tools are representative of the range of tools that exist, nor can we give any indication of how big the overall population of these evaluation toolkits is, and hence the size of our sample. For now our purpose in this chapter is to identify the types of partnership performance this sample of toolkits covers (and how this fits with our theory-based framework), the similarities and differences in coverage across toolkits, and the implications of this coverage for any future evaluation of partnership performance.

Although there are differences in scope and method, in essence most partnerships are assessed through the application of some form of evaluation frameworks, assessment tools or toolkits. The purpose of evaluation tools varies between measurement and intervention and they can be self-initiated or imposed, self-administered or engage a third party. As a catch-all, we will refer to them as performance tools. Although the performance tools differ in their area of focus and scope, they share, broadly, the same three characteristics, as shown in Figure 9.1. The model in Figure 9.1 depicts a tripartite picture of partnership performance tools akin to that of Sabatier and Jenkins-Smith (1993), with, at the deep core level, an underlying vision of a performing partnership that informs and is informed by second-order principles of partnership. The third layer consists of proxy measures (typically 'questions') that are formulated to assess whether or not the principles are actualized. We turn first to discuss the second-order layer of the model: the partnership principles and the implications for comparison.

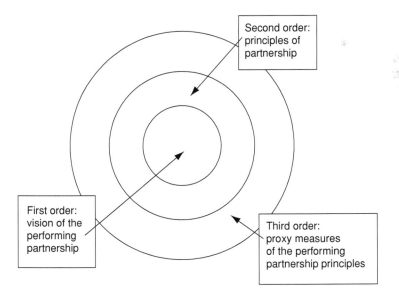

Figure 9.1 Vision, principles and proxy measures of partnership performance tools

Performance tools, explicitly or implicitly, introduce a series of categories, which they hypothesize as systemic aspects of partnership-working or partnership principles. These principles typically include a range of qualities such as trust, vision, leadership, communication and participation. Whether it is made explicit or not, the rationale underlying these partnership principles is an overall sense of the 'ideal' or performing partnership: a fantasy of the perfect partnership.

Below, we list principles and a set of questions extracted from the partnership toolkits we have identified (Figure 9.2). To begin, it is possible to divide the principles into those regarding the partnership processes and those regarding partnership structures or mechanisms.

- Purpose – clarity of purpose (Frearson 2002; Thorlby and Hutchinson 2002: A)
- Vision (Markwell *et al.* 2003; Shortell 2002; Hardy *et al.* 2003: 2; Johnston 2001; North-east Derbyshire 2005)
- Leadership (Shortell *et al.* 2002; Johnston 2001; Thorlby and Hutchinson 2002)
- Communication (Markwell *et al.* 2003; Thorlby and Hutchinson 2002)
- Information management (Markwell *et al.* 2003; Thorlby and Hutchinson 2002)
- Decision-making efficiency (Thorlby and Hutchinson 2002)
- Participation (Markwell *et al.* 2003; Thorlby and Hutchinson 2002; Smith and Beazley 2000)
- Public access (Skelcher *et al.* 2005)
- Human resource – valuing people (Markwell *et al.* 2003)
- Skills development (Markwell *et al.* 2003)
- Commitment (Markwell *et al.* 2003, Shortell *et al.* 2002; Hardy *et al.* 2003: 1, 3)
- Governance
- Internal governance and membership (Skelcher *et al.* 2005; North-east Derbyshire 2005)
- Social inclusion and equality (Bovaird and Loeffler 2007)
- Member conduct (Skelcher *et al.* 2005)
- Fair and honest behaviour (Bovaird and Loeffler 2007)
- Accountability (Skelcher *et al.* 2005; North-east Derbyshire 2005)
- Transparency (Bovaird and Loeffler 2003)
- Relationships (Markwell *et al.* 2003)
- Social capital (Markwell *et al.* 2003)
- Trust (Hardy *et al.* 2003: 4; Johnston 2001)
- Management arrangements (Thorlby and Hutchinson 2002; Shortell *et al.* 2002; Hardy *et al.* 2003: s5; Johnston 2001: 4)
- Financial control (Markwell *et al.* 2003; Thorlby and Hutchinson 2002)
- Efficiency and effectiveness (North-east Derbyshire 2005)
- Evaluation and review (Markwell *et al.* 2003; Frearson 2002: D; Johnston 2001: 3; North-east Derbyshire 2005)
- Programmes monitoring (Markwell *et al.* 2003; Hardy *et al.* 2003: s6)
- Learning and sharing (North-east Derbyshire 2005)
- Strategic development (Markwell *et al.* 2003)
- Programme planning (Markwell *et al.* 2003)
- Programme delivery (Markwell *et al.* 2003)
- Flexibility (Markwell *et al.* 2003)
- Partnership values (Thorlby and Hutchinson 2002)
- Sustainability (Bovaird and Loeffler 2003)

Figure 9.2 Examples of principles embedded within partnership performance tools

Yet we know from previous experience how empty, vague and slippery terms such as 'trust' or 'leadership' can be. It follows that superficially similar partnership assessment toolkits could, in fact, be expressing very different visions of partnership performance.

To illustrate the challenge of comparing these tools by the second-order principles alone, consider the following examples. The 'smarter partnerships' tool by Johnston (2001) advocates the importance of leadership as a partnership principle. Under this principle the first question asks partners to what extent they agree/disagree with the view that in their partnership, 'partners share a common vision of the difference they want to make and the direction to take' (Johnston 2001). So here we may assume an endorsement for partnership working where the purpose of partnership is clear, agreed and realistic. Compare this with Shortell's list of principles and questions where, in the category of 'vision', the question asks to what extent the partnership 'has a clear vision for the partnership' (Shortell *et al.* 2002). Again, this appears to share the sentiment that the purpose of the partnership is clear, agreed and realistic. And yet, also under the category of 'vision', Shortell includes the question whether 'the partnership is in agreement on strategies to pursue and to achieve priorities' (Shortell *et al.* 2002). Here the programme theory appears to have a different emphasis, one that is less about clarity and more about alignment of policies. For a third tool, 'The working partnership', the author includes, as a principle 'leadership', with a sub-principle of 'vision', and has as a question within this theme: 'Do senior leaders of partner organisations support partnership working in dealing with local issues?' (Markwell *et al.* 2003). Rather than vision as alignment or clarity, here the programme theory for successful partnership appears to value local connections and commitment. This example of how three tools probe the principles of vision and leadership illustrates the limitations of comparing second-order principles alone.

It is therefore important to understand and compare the various programme theories or underlying intent of the tools and also to probe how these different toolkits operationalize the principles they embody, in order to reveal the deeper assumptions behind these programme theories. In particular, embedded within the toolkits are what are referred to in Figure 9.1 as 'proxy measures' of the performing partnership. In qualitative evaluations, the proxy measures are found in the themes of the interview guide or the first-level codes of a transcript coding framework. In questionnaire-based evaluation tools the proxy measures are found in the questions. The questions are carefully phrased to explore second-order principles such as trust or leadership.

Consequently, there is a need to compare the performance tools not by their second-order principles (trust, leadership) but by their third-order proxy measures (questions). This will allows us, through careful coding, to expose the workings of the underlying programme theory.

To be able to compare models satisfactorily we began by comparing the proxy measure questions of eight commonly cited partnership assessment toolkits, 319 questions in total. We chose these as they appeared to represent the range of toolkits and frameworks we had accessed and also offered coverage (between them) of a range of dimensions of partnership performance. Toolkits considered included:

- Thomson and Goodwin (2005) – PPP-EV model
- Skelcher *et al.* (2005) – Governance Assessment Tool
- Shortell *et al.* (2002) – Partnership Management Capability Index
- Hardy *et al.* (2003) – Partnership Assessment Tool
- Frearson (2002) – Partnership Self-assessment Toolkit
- Johnston (2001) – Smarter Partnerships
- Thorlby and Hutchinson (2002) – Working in Partnership
- Markwell *et al.* (2003) – The Working Partnership

While these eight toolkits are particularly well founded and widely cited, this sample of toolkits is inevitably partial, so our analysis at this stage aims to be illustrative of range, rather than comprehensive.

We coded the toolkit questions iteratively to generate a set of codes. In naming codes we chose single-word or hyphenated titles that reflected the key argument or point of the question. For example, 'alignment' or its more specific discussion of alignment of performance management was recorded as 'alignment – perform-ance'. As is common with this form of coding, the early stages of the process results in many new codes, but by the end of the sample, a point of saturation is reached. It was a process of consolidation. From the 319 toolkit questions, we initially generated 212 codes (see Appendix 1). In a second 'pass' of the codes, we consolidated these into 51 codes, and a third pass resulted in just 12. The 12 codes are composite partnership principles and provide a checklist of different dimensions of partnership performance. The 12 composite partnership principles are a partnership where there is/are:

1. clear, aligned and realistic purpose;
2. availability of appropriate financial and human resources;
3. clarity of motivations, roles, capabilities and contributions;
4. sufficient organizational processes and procedures that foster collaboration;
5. alignment of partners and policies;
6. commitment, ownership and responsibility of partners towards the partnership;
7. participative and empowering partnership;
8. a culture of collaboration, trust and openness;
9. presence (and awareness) of cultural transformation, synergy, efficiencies or exchange;
10. definition of success and monitoring and reporting of its performance;
11. continual engagement with others, developing and learning; and
12. clear attribution of benefits, risks and blame.

We do not claim that our set of codes was definitive or exhaustive. However, importantly, these codes are validated, in that they have been refined in empirical testing by at least one study (usually multiple). The principles have been built up from the first-order proxies (the questions) rather than being simply stated in the abstract by partnerships or derived by toolkit authors. This approach allows for a more systematic comparison of which partnership characteristics need to be evaluated. It allows us to do two things:

- to demonstrate the difference between generalist and specialist tools. For example, the Governance Assessment Tool focuses on just four of our 12 categories whereas Markwell *et al.* (2003) attempts to understand breadth rather than depth with 10 of our 12 categories.
- to quantify both the overt and tacit preoccupations of the tools. For example, the Governance Assessment Tool quite clearly has an interest in democratic performance whereas the Working Partnership has a strong emphasis on participation that perhaps can be linked back to the emphasis on the founding National Health Service body that funded its creation (Figure 9.3 depicts these in graph form).

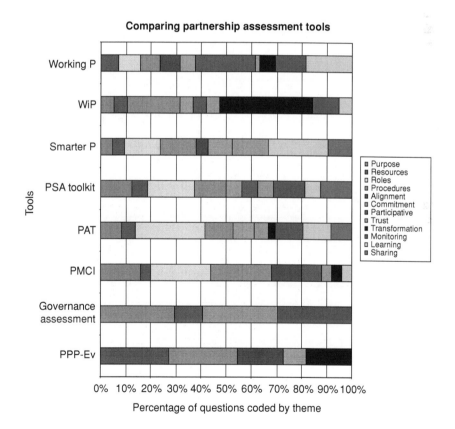

Figure 9.3 Toolkits, questions and themes

This form of analysis goes beyond the claim of individual partnership tool authors that their principles are comprehensive and the questions equally weighted. When considered comparatively, both implicit and explicit preoccupations of the toolkits are surfaced and their degree of comprehensiveness can be compared.

This analysis therefore offers a means to assess the applicability of partnership performance tools for PPPs. It has asserted the importance of judging a performance tool not by its (explicit author-derived) principles but by the content of its proxy measures. From this it is possible to begin to compare the performance challenges facing PPPs and the potential contribution of established performance assessment tools.

Crucially, however, this process has as a second implication for assessing partnership performance, which concerns how we describe, conceptualize and theorize 'performance' in partnership. To explore this we return to our theoretically derived partnership performance domains outlined in Table 9.2 and analyse the questions in the eight partnership evaluation toolkits in relation to the different theoretical domains of partnership performance (see Figure 9.4).

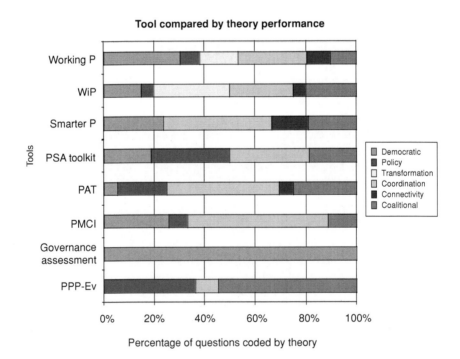

Figure 9.4 Toolkits, questions and theories of performance

The results show considerable variation in the coverage of the toolkits. Two toolkits provide some (though uneven) coverage of all six performance domains. The Partnership Assessment Tool covers five domains excluding the transformational domain; this is interesting give the ubiquity of the tool in health and social care partnerships in the UK. Three toolkits cover four of the performance domains, though have only three in common (co-ordination, democratic and coalitional). Unsurprisingly, the Governance Assessment Tool maps exclusively onto the democratic domain. By contrast the PPP-Ev tool has no coverage of this domain.

We indicated earlier that the co-ordinative, coalitional and connective performance domains were rather different to the other domains as in these cases partnership was a prerequisite for their manifestation. Assessing the toolkits on this basis we find that they do rather well with seven toolkits covering coalitional and co-ordinative performance, though only four cover connective performance. One obvious conclusion from this initial analysis is that if partnership performance is to be evaluated comprehensively then the tools to be used should provide coverage of all of these domains.

Conclusion

Public–private partnerships for service delivery are increasingly used by the public sector in seeking service improvement and efficiency savings across a range of service areas. Whilst there is an abundance of partnership evaluation toolkits and frameworks for developing private–private strategic alliances, the literature is relatively silent when it comes to approaches and instruments for assessing the performance of public–private partnerships. We have argued that public–private partnerships engaged in the pursuit of public purpose are required to consider 'performance' in a range of ways and that a theory-based approach can provide the requisite scope and shape to a multidimensional assessment of performance.

This chapter has undertaken an analysis of the questions asked in popular partnership evaluation tools and frameworks and identified 12 composite partnership principles, which in their totality could be interpreted as constituting a vision of an 'ideal' partnership. We then mapped these principles onto the proposed partnership performance domains of a theory-based approach, which we identified as democracy, policy, transformation, connectivity, co-ordination and coalitional (sustainability). This mapping has illustrated the balance of coverage of different performance domains, identifying those aspects of performance that receive most and least attention. It suggests that, regardless of their origins, partnership assessment tools may be of use in assessing public–private partnerships, providing they offer sufficient coverage of the performance domains of concern to the evaluators, the public–private partnership and/or the commissioners. However, to provide a comprehensive and robust evaluation of public–private partnership performance, the full range of performance domains needs to be taken into account, which is not the case for most of the toolkits we have examined here.

If the challenge issued by Hodge (2010: 105) is to be met, namely that 'improved conceptual frameworks are now needed in order to undertake comprehensive evaluations [of PPPs]', then the analysis presented here of a small sample of partnership assessment tools, mainly meant for the UK context, needs to be undertaken for a wider set of toolkits designed for assessment of public–private partnerships in the international context.

Note

1   Address for correspondence: Dr Stephen Jeffares, School of Government and Society, University of Birmingham, Edgbaston, B15 2TT. S.R.Jeffares@bham.ac.uk

Appendix 1: Coding

12 partnership performance principles and the initial codes (n=212) drawn from a sample of 319 partnership toolkit questions.

1. Purpose is clear, aligned and realistic

Clear vision; Shared vision; Agreed mission/priorities; Clear objectives; Smart objectives; Clear purpose; Programme Management (7 codes)

2. Availability of appropriate financial and human resources

Experience; Financial resources; Member conduct; Investment in people (4 codes)

3. Clarity of motivations, roles, capabilities and contributions

Agency clarity; Resource skill clarity; Role clarity; Security (4 codes)

4. Sufficient organizational processes and procedures that foster collaboration

Administrative support; Appropriate; Communication; Conduct; Constitution; Contribution recognized; Democratic decision-making; Due process; Focused; Harmonious; HR induction; Leadership/well-managed; Loyalty/commitment; Organizational processes and clear procedures; Productive; Resilient; Role defined; Solvent; Sustainable; Viable (20 codes)

5. Alignment of partners and policies

Aligned – relevance; Alignment; Alignment – partner; Alignment of HR policies; Alignment of processes; Alignment/government; Alignment – local (7 codes)

6. Commitment, ownership and responsibility of partners towards the partnership

Senior commitment; Organizational commitment; Ownership of objectives by those responsible; Commitment – endorsement and resource; Commitment – enjoyment; Commitment – attendance; Commitment – enthusiasm; Commitment to community development (8 codes)

7. Partnership is participative and empowering

Respected by community; Ethical; User involvement; Participative; Consultative; Democratic representation; Objectives – emancipation; Participative; Participative/giving account; Participative/accountability; Participative/empowerment; Participative/inclusive; Participative – delegation (13 codes)

8. Culture of collaboration, trust and openness

Public awareness; Public access; Conduct; Welcoming; Inclusive; Member access; Trust; Communication; Collaborative ethos; Respectful; Consensual/mature; Trust; Freedom of speech (13 codes)

9. Presence (and awareness) of cultural transformation, synergy, efficiencies or exchange

Cost-effective; Achieving objectives; More choice; Reduced costs; Collective voice; Seamless service; Improved quality; Improved coverage; Improved user outcomes; Cultural transformation and awareness; Knowledge exchange; Recognize difference; Cultural transformation (13 codes)

10. Defines success, monitors and reports its performance

Reporting; Scrutiny; Governance; Reporting; Goals/purpose; Goals; Review; Performance measures; Monitoring performance; Monitoring risk; Alignment – monitoring performance; Learning organization/accountability (12 codes)

11. Partnership is continually engaging with others, developing and learning

Consultative; Networking; Reflexive; Monitoring – shared; Review; Change management; Striving; Learning; Open to change; Evaluation; Conflict resolution; Inter-partnership collaboration; Investment in people; Knowledge exchange; Learning organization (15 codes)

12. Clear attribution of benefits, risks and blame

Accountability; Communication; Benefits shared; Communication achievements; Mutually accountable; Benefits shared fairly (6 codes)

References

Barnes, M., Bauld, L., Benzeval, M., Judge, K., Mackenzie, M. and Sullivan, H. (2005) *Building Capacity for Health Equity*. London: Routledge.

Boardman, A. E. and Vining, A. R. (2010) Assessing the economic worth of public private partnerships, in Hodge, G., Greve, C. and Boardman, A. E. (eds) (2010) *International Handbook on Public–Private Partnerships*. Cheltenham: Edward Elgar.

Bovaird, T., Downe, J. and Martin, S. (2009) *Reforming Local Government: Impacts and Interactions of Central Government Policies from 2000 to 2006: Final Report of the Meta-evaluation of the LGMA*. London: Communities and Local Government.

Bovaird, T. and Loeffler, E. (2003) Evaluating the quality of public governance: indicators, models and methodologies. *International Review of Administrative Sciences*, 69(3): 313–28.

Bovaird, T. and Loeffler, E. (2007) Assessing the quality of local governance: a case study of public services in Carrick, UK. *Public Money and Management*, 27(4): 293–300.

Boyne, G., Farrell, C., Law, J. and Powell, M. (2003) *Evaluating Public Management Reforms: Principles and Practice*. Buckingham: Open University Press.

Brinkerhoff, D. W. and Brinkerhoff, J. M. (2011) Public–private partnerships: Perspectives on purposes, publicness, and good governance. *Public Administration and Development*, 31: 2–14.

Connell, J. P. and Kubisch, A. C. (1998) Applying a theory of change approach to the evaluation of comprehensive community initiatives: progress, prospects and problems, in Fulbright-Anderson, K. *et al.* (eds) *New Approaches to Evaluating Community Initiatives. Volume 2: Theory, Measurement and Analysis*. Washington, DC: The Aspen Institute, pp. 15–44

Cowell, R., Ashworth, R., Skelcher, C., Bovaird, T., Downe J. and Chen, A. (2009) *The State of Local Democracy: The Impact of Policy Changes on Accountability and Public Confidence*. Report to CLG. Cardiff: Cardiff Business School.

Cravens, K., Piercy, N. and Cravens, D. (2000) Assessing the performance of strategic alliances: matching metrics to strategies, in *European Management Journal*, 18(5): 529–541.

DCLG (2006) *Structures for Service Delivery Partnerships: Technical Notes*. London: Department for Communities and Local Government.

Dickinson, H. (2008) *Evaluating Outcomes in Health and Social Care*. Bristol: Policy Press.

Dickinson, H. and Nicholds, A. (2012) The impact of joint commissioning, in Glasby, J. (ed.) *Commissioning for Health and Wellbeing*. Bristol: Policy Press.

Frearson, A. (2002) *Partnership Self-assessment Toolkit: A Practical Guide to Creating and Maintaining Successful Partnerships*. Leeds: East Leeds Primary Care Trust.

Hardy, B. Hudson, B. and Waddington, E. (2003) *Assessing Strategic Partnership: The Partnership Assessment Tool*. London: ODPM/Nuffield Institute.

Hellowell, M. and Vecchi, V. (2010), Are Italian healthcare organisations paying too much for their public private partnerships? *Public Money and Management*, 30(2): 125–32.

Hellowell, M. and Vecchi, V. (2012) An evaluation of the projected returns to investors on 10 PFI projects commissioned by the National Health Service. *Financial Accountability and Management*, 28(1): 77–100.

Hodge, G. (2010) Reviewing public private partnerships: some thoughts on evaluation, in Hodge, G., Greve, C. and Boardman, A. E. (eds) *International Handbook on Public–Private Partnerships*. Cheltenham: Edward Elgar.

Hodge, G. and Greve, C. (eds) (2005) *The Challenge of Public–Private Partnerships: Learning from International Experience.* Cheltenham: Edward Elgar.

Johnston, D. (2001) *Smarter Partnerships: Making the Most of Partnership Working Employers of Local Government & EDUCE Ltd.*

Markwell, S., Watson, J., Speller, V., Platt, S. and Younger, T. (2003) *The Working Partnership.* London: Health Development Agency.

Martin, S. J. (2009) *The State of Local Services: Performance Improvement in Local Government.* Report to Communities and Local Government. Cardiff: Cardiff Business School.

North East Derbyshire District Council (2005) *Partnership Development and Evaluation Handbook.* Chesterfield: NE Derbyshire DC.

Pawson, R. and Tilley, N. (1997) *Realistic Evaluation.* London: Sage.

Sabatier, P. and Jenkins-Smith, H. (eds) (1993) *Policy Change and Policy-Oriented Learning: Exploring an Advocacy Coalition Approach.* Boulder, CO: Westview Press.

Shortell, S. M., Zukoski, A. P., Alexander, J. A., Bazzolli, G. J., Conrad, D. A., Hasnain-Wynia, R., Sofaer, S., Chan, B. Y., Casey, E. and Margolin, F. S. (2002) Evaluating partnerships for community health improvement: Tracking the footprints. *Journal of Health Politics Policy and Law*, 27(1): 49–91.

Skelcher, C. (2008) Does governance perform? Concepts, evidence, causalities and research strategies, in Hartley, J., Donaldson, C., Skelcher, C. and Wallace, M. (eds) *Managing to Improve Public Services.* Cambridge: Cambridge University Press.

Skelcher, C., Mathur, N. and Smith, M. (2005) The public governance of collaborative spaces: discourse, design and democracy. *Public Administration*, 83(3): 573–96.

Skelcher, C. and Sullivan, H. (2008) Theory driven approaches to analyzing collaborative performance. *Public Management Review,* 10(6): 751–77

Smith, M. and Beazley, M. (2000) Progressive regimes, partnerships and the involvement of local communities: a framework for evaluation. *Public Administration*, 78(4): 855–78.

Sullivan, H. (2011) 'Truth' Junkies – using evaluation in UK public policy. *Policy and Politics*, 39(4): 499–512.

Sullivan, H. (2009) *The State of Governance of Places: Community Leadership and Stakeholder Engagement.* Report to Communities and Local Government. Cardiff: Cardiff Business School.

Sullivan, H., Barnes, M. and Matka, E. (2002) Building collaborative capacity through 'theories of change': early lessons from the evaluation of health action zones in England. *International Journal of Theory, Research and Practice,* 8(2): 207–26.

Sullivan, H. and Skelcher, C. (2002) *Working across Boundaries: Collaboration in Public Services.* Basingstoke: Palgrave.

Thomson, C. and Goodwin, J. (2005) *Evaluation of PPP Projects Financed by the European Investment Bank. Synthesis Report.* Luxembourg: European Investment Bank and Yescombe Consulting Ltd.

Thompson, G., Frances, J., Levacic, R. and Mitchell, J. (1991) *Markets, Hierarchies and Networks: The Coordination of Social Life.* London: Sage and Open University.

Thorlby, T. and Hutchinson, J. (2002) *Working in Partnerships: A Sourcebook.* London: New Opportunities Fund.

Williamson, O. E. (1975) *Markets and Hierarchies.* New York: Free Press.

10 A theory-driven approach to public–private partnerships

The dynamics of complexity and control[1]

Koen Verhoest, Joris Voets and Kit Van Gestel

Introduction

Public–private partnerships are hot in the public sector, but PPP research remains weak in its theoretical and conceptual capacity (Hodge and Greve, first chapter of this book; Pollitt 2005; Skelcher 2005). A major gap, in our opinion, is the lack of theoretical and conceptual work on the actual governance of PPPs, and the relation between complexity and control in particular.

This paper builds on a five-year research project (2007–11) focused on the way public partners try to control specific PPPs and how this affects the performance of those PPPs, using case studies in Flanders, Belgium. We explore which theoretical perspectives (including inter-organizational co-operation, trust, control mechanisms and neo-institutional economics) provide the best insights and explanatory power, and integrate these theoretical perspectives in a conceptual framework (first section). The chapter deals with two questions in particular: how do public partners control different phases of a PPP, and how is this control (dependent variable) affected by elements of complexity (independent variable)? The chapter also brings in empirical evidence, namely a comparative case study concerning two DBFMOs[2] of local sports infrastructure (second section). The paper concludes with lessons learned, and critical reflections on the value of these concepts for future PPP research (third section).

Conceptual framework

Because long-term contracts are complex and risky undertakings, governments hoping to achieve the theoretical benefits of long-term contracting with a private partner are confronted with daunting management and governance challenges (Bloomfield 2006: 409). Since our knowledge about the specific factors that contribute to PPP governance and project success or failure is still limited (Bloomfield 2006; Hodge 2004), we introduce a new conceptual framework (Van Gestel *et al.* 2012) to help fill that gap. This framework tries to capture the entire cycle of the process of a PPP, to improve our understanding of how the governance of PPPs affects their performance. The framework consists of five components – complexity, government capacity, governance or control mix, trust,

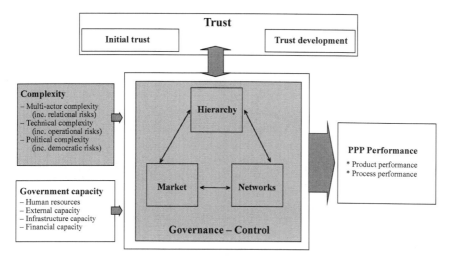

Figure 10.1 Conceptual framework (see also Van Gestel *et al.* 2012)

and performance – and their relations (see Figure 10.1). We now discuss the complete theoretical framework. We also illustrate the relevance of the framework by using empirical material from two cases. However, in this part we limit our focus to the two boxes referring to 'complexity' and 'governance-control' (marked in grey) in order to illustrate how complexity may affect the control mix in PPPs.

Antecedents of governance: complexity and government capacity

We distinguish two antecedent variables that determine the control mix used in a public–private partnership. The first variable is the complexity of the actor constellation, the tasks and the objectives of the envisioned future PPP project and its environment. This concept refers to key project characteristics such as the scope, budget, policy objectives, number of actors involved, and the risks connected to them. Risks are important, because complexity and uncertainty[3] are closely related to the presence of risks (Das and Teng 1998), and a higher complexity (and uncertainty) is usually associated with an increased risk (Sagheer and Iyer 2006). The second antecedent variable is 'government capacity', namely the capacity of the government to organize and engage in a PPP.

Complexity

Complexity refers to the level in which within a system there is variety (distinction) of parts as well as dependency (connection) between parts, making predictions about how the system will evolve more difficult. Complexity increases when the degree of heterogeneity and interdependencies increases (Edmonds 1996; Weaver 1948). The complexity of the environment affects the governance of public–private partnerships. By linking the types of risks identified in the literature (Grimsey and Lewis 2002; Das and Teng 1996; Ng and Loosemore 2006; Ducatteeuw 2005; Lewis 2001) to complexity, we can analyse complexity along three dimensions (Van Gestel *et al.* 2009): multi-actor complexity, technical complexity and political complexity.

Multi-actor complexity encompasses actor-related elements commonly used in network literature (see Voets 2008 for an overview): the number, nature and goals of the actors concerned, their resources, and their interdependencies. The number of actors is, for instance, relevant: the higher that number and the more conflicting their goals (all other things being equal), the more complex a PPP becomes.

Technical complexity refers to the extent to which selection and allocation criteria can be defined clearly, results can be defined *ex ante*, and the project is pioneering/unique or building on standardized approaches, as well as the extent to which private partners have to make substantial transaction-specific investments without having a use of it in other PPPs (also relevant in terms of transaction costs), the range of players around in the market, and to what extent the scope of the PPP is relatively straightforward or multifunctional.

Political complexity refers to the degree to which the objectives and tasks of the envisioned future PPP is salient in political terms. We expect this to be an important element that affects governance, as a high level of political complexity (e.g. competition of political parties, supportive or protesting societal stakeholders) is expected to lead to a different governance strategy by governments than in the case of a low level of political salience.

Government capacity

The second antecedent is the capacity of government to organize and engage in a PPP. We expect that this capacity also determines how a PPP is designed and controlled. This variable builds on the four dimensions of Christensen and Gazley (2008) of organizational capacity. The first dimension, 'human resources', captures the available experience, knowledge base, quantity of personnel and management qualities available. The second dimension, labelled 'external capacity', includes the social support, quality of relationships, co-ordination and access to information. The third dimension is 'infrastructure', referring to organizational structure and organizational culture. Finally, the 'financial' dimension is defined here as the possible budgetary constraints towards the project.

Governance – control

As shown by Figure 10.1, the crux of the conceptual framework considers how specific PPP projects are governed – defined here as 'control'. Control encompasses the mechanisms and instruments used by government to intentionally influence the decisions and behaviour of other governments or private partners in order to achieve government objectives (Verhoest *et al.* 2004). Translated to the context of PPPs, White (1991: 189) defines control as the general mechanisms and more specific sets of instruments that public actors use to consciously influence the behaviour of other public and private actors in the PPP to achieve the public actors' goals.

In the literature, three fundamental mechanisms of governance in social life are defined, namely hierarchies, markets and networks (Kaufmann *et al.* 1986; Thompson *et al.* 1991; O'Toole 1997; Bouckaert, *et al.* 2010). An interesting debate among scholars is which mechanisms and instruments are used or prevalent in PPPs. Teisman and Klijn (2002), for instance, argue that PPP can be linked to the trend toward network forms of governance, in which public actors take their interdependencies with other actors into account and try to solve governance problems through co-operation rather than through central steering and control. In their view, PPP can be seen as a network arrangement, where 'relational contracting' is more important than market exchange or hierarchy. In contrast, based on Dutch case studies, Eversdijk and Korsten (2008) argued that such a logic of commitment is in fact a myth. Governments, they claim, still put emphasis on the separation of risks by using strong and tight contracts (being market instruments). In our earlier research on PPP in Flanders, we found elements to believe that governments make use of different governance mechanisms that all fit into the well-known trinity of hierarchy, market and networks (Osborne 2002; Lowndes and Skelcher 2002).

We therefore consider the three mechanisms as a useful typology to analyse control efforts within the public sector, but these mechanisms are too general to apply to empirical research. We make them more tangible in the form of control instrument typologies. In cybernetics, the control system contains three subsystems: an *ex ante* sub-system of planning and target setting; an *ex nunc* and *ex post* measurement and monitoring sub-system; and an *ex post* sub-system of evaluation, audit and feedback. We use a control instrument typology that is based on existing typologies of regulative, economic and communicative instruments and developed further by Verhoest and Bouckaert (2005) and Bouckaert *et al.* (2010). Considering their central position in the conceptual framework, we now discuss the three main mechanisms in more detail.

Hierarchic governance instruments

Hierarchic control is closely related to the bureaucratic mechanism, which refers to the principle of the Weberian bureaucracy based on (arbitrary) rules about available inputs, required processes, and procedures.

Hierarchy entails a number of typical features. First of all, control is top-down. Actors that are being controlled are considered relatively passive objects. Secondly, authority is the interaction pattern. Rules and commands are the basis of planning in a normative power relation, whereas supervision is the basis of management control. In terms of sanction (positive and negative), rewards and punishment are used. Finally, conflicts are resolved through authority, which is exercised by the controlling government (Bouckaert *et al.* 2010).

These features can be translated into a typology of hierarchic control instruments that focus typically on unilateral control by government of input used and processes conducted by the private partner in the PPP. Table 10.1 lists hierarchical governance instruments, used in practice, like the use of *ex ante* approval rights (e.g. obligations for the private partner to get *ex ante* approval from the public partner before increasing tariffs), detailed *ex ante* rules and procedures (e.g. mandatory disclosures), or extremely detailed output specifications (e.g. defining the exact materials to be used by the private partner for construction), set by the public partner in the PPP.

Market-oriented governance instruments

The general assumption of the market mechanism is that actors base their behaviour on the price within a competitive market, and contractual exchange relations based on that price. The main difference between the market mechanism and bureaucratic mechanism is that there are no detailed *ex ante* rules set by superiors that direct implementation processes. The norms are set by the market in the form of a market price, which is formed by the interaction of supply and demand on the market or which is contractually agreed (Vosselman 1996).

The market mechanism is, moreover, based on a horizontal interaction relation between equal and mutually independent actors (Bouckaert *et al.* 2010). The governance instruments used here are often formulated in terms of a principal–agent relationship. To reduce the opportunistic behaviour of the agent, the principal–agent theory points to three strategies. The first strategy is monitoring, which means that the principal can observe, monitor and evaluate performance of the agent. Monitoring thus reduces the information asymmetry between principal and agent. Secondly, bonding implies that the principal can incorporate *ex ante* safeguards to prevent the agent taking actions that oppose the interests of the principal. The agent can also set up an internal assurance systems of its own in order to convince the principal that he is acting in a responsive way. A third strategy involves rewards and transfer of (typically operational) risks. The principal builds in performance-based sanctions and rewards to stimulate the agent to align his objectives with those of the principal. Transfer of risks also decreases the incongruence of goals.

These features can be translated into a typology of market governance instruments, where governance typically is focused on output and transaction. Considering the fact that PPPs are generally based on competitive bidding processes and contractual agreements between public and private partners, the market mechanism plays an important role within the governance strategy towards the private actors. Table 10.1 presents a list of market-based governance instruments, like transfer of risks (e.g. starting payments upon delivery puts the risk of late completion by the private partner), hard performance norms, monitoring and incentives, set in the contract (e.g. amount of the availability fee, being dependent on the quality and availability of infrastructure) and degree of competition (e.g. benchmarking of the service delivery to the market during the term of the contract).

Network governance instruments

The third governance mechanism identified in the literature is the network mechanism (Powell 1996).

The first feature is that interactions are based on reciprocity. Trust, collaboration and loyalty are key concepts in networks. Secondly, the network mechanism is based on the idea that actors are able to identify complementary interests. This leads to resource exchanges between actors that are based on interdependent relations, trust, loyalty and reciprocity (Kickert *et al.* 1997). Next, the third feature is the equal status of the government amongst other actors in the networks. Government does not hold a hierarchic position *vis-à-vis* other actors, in the sense that it cannot force the other actors directly to behave in a certain way. Nevertheless, government is a special actor because it has a monopoly over a number of resources, like the use of force and legislative powers, enabling it to cast the shadow of hierarchy (Scharpf 1994). Therefore, policy, as the fourth feature, is developed jointly in a network by interdependent partners. The fifth feature is that the network mechanism involves a specific set of management strategies (Kickert *et al.* 1997) in which success is not necessarily measured in terms of goal achievement but (also) in terms of satisfaction of participants about the process itself and whether joint solutions for problems can be agreed upon. Finally, conflicts are typically solved using the reputation of network members, rather than sanctions and the like. Network governance typically focuses on relational processes and trust. Table 10.1 presents an overview of specific network governance instruments, like frequent contacts and collaborative procedures (e.g. the establishment of a structural steering group where representatives of all partners meet to discuss progress) and advising or co-decision-making (e.g. joint decisions on entrance fees for infrastructure visitors).

Besides the formal presence of control instruments, we are also interested in the actual control that takes shape in real-life interactions between actors in the PPP (Verhoest *et al.* 2004). So, on the one hand, we use the typology of instruments (see Table 10.1) to disentangle and classify the formally present control arrangements. On the other hand – and this is where current PPP research often fails – we study the level of the actual interactions between actors. The formal instruments are relevant as they provide formal grounds for control, but their presence says little about their actual use in day-to-day practice. A PPP contract might encompass a wide set of formally stipulated control instruments that are not actually used in the real-life interactions between the public and private actors.

Since hierarchy, market and network are ideal-types, which are never to be found in their pure form, we study the mix of these three types of control instruments used in the PPP (Parsons 1995) in terms of their mutual interaction, affecting variables and overall impact of the mix on performance of PPPs.

Table 10.1 Three main sets of control instruments for PPP governance

Hierarchical instruments	Market instruments	Network instruments
Veto power by the public actor (e.g. to veto tariff increases by the private actor)	Competition and hard contractual agreements	Network management (including culture and relations)
Ex ante authorization and approval by the public actor	Hard performance norms and frequent performance monitoring	Mutual control by convincing and goals sharing
Right to annul decisions made by lower public bodies or private actors	Transfer of risks	Frequent (personal) contacts, extensive consultation and collaborative procedures between partners
Ex ante detailed rules, standards, directions/ regulations and procedures (e.g. detailed step-by-step plans), which are set unilaterally by the public actor	Performance audit provisions (auditing internal control systems) Restricted mediation provisions and quick recourse to litigation for settling disputes	Control through persons, based on social control, reputation, legitimacy etc.
Direct instructions by the public actor	Mutual contact between actors restricted to contractually-set monitoring moments	Substantial co-decision-making
Supervision and punctual inspections of primary processes (i.e. primary supervision)	Secondary supervision (audit on internal control mechanisms)	Horizontal control and involving stakeholders and peers in the process, like: user panels; user representation in governing boards; visitations (e.g. to benchmark each other's control systems)
Line item-budgeting, which authorizes expenditures at a very detailed level (decreasing autonomy to allocate money differently)	Market-oriented financing (performance-based financial incentives, e.g. finances dependent on visitor numbers)	
	Performance-based rewards and sanctions	
	Benefit sharing	
	Benchmarking (financing dependent on performance in comparison to similar projects in the market)	

Trust

'Trust' is another essential building block to understand the governance of PPPs. Trust is widely studied in the context of inter-organizational co-operation (Zaheer *et al.* 1998; Rousseau *et al.* 1998) and PPPs in particular (Edelenbos and Klijn 2007). A Dutch survey involving 207 practitioners signalled trust as one of the most important factors for a successful PPP (ibid.: 30). In our various contacts with practitioners, trust between partners was indeed stressed as a key factor in

PPP. We define trust as behaviour by one actor in a transaction with another actor that is inspired by a willingness to accept vulnerability by the first actor based upon positive expectations about the behaviour of the latter actor in the face of risk and uncertainty (Oomsels and Bouckaert 2012; see also Choudhury 2008; Kramer *et al.* 1996). The extent to which one actor trusts the other actor refers to a positive expectation about his future behaviour, based on a perception about his ability, benevolence and integrity in a relational transaction (Oomsels and Bouckaert 2012; Colquitt *et al.* 2007). Ability refers to the skills, competencies and other characteristics that allow a counterpart to have influence in some domain. Benevolence is the belief that an actor wants to do good for reasons that are not completely egocentric, and integrity refers to adherence to a set of values and principles that are acceptable to the trustor. When we refer to trust in the empirical part of the paper, it refers to all three bases of trust in an actor.

In organizational studies, 'trust' can be discerned (Sako 1998); either as a determinant of governance or as a governance mechanism in itself (Ouchi 1980; Adler 2001). We do not consider trust a separate governance mechanism, and also make a distinction between the network mechanism and trust. Network governance differs from trust in the sense that we consider trust to be an attitude of one partner towards other partners, whereas network governance entails the specific instruments and actions aimed at reducing disagreements and goal differences (such as discussion platforms and co-decision procedure).

The relationship between trust and formal control is a key topic in the literature on inter-organizational relationships (Vlaar *et al.* 2007: 408). There is insufficient space to discuss the different insights in much detail, but, essentially, trust matters in two ways, based on a time perspective.

First, trust plays a role prior to or during the design of the formal control instruments. Powell (1996), for example, claims that the absence of 'natural' conditions for the development of trust – like confidentiality based on past experience or on the similar characteristics of those involved – inter-organizational partnerships tend to be more strongly dependent on formal and institutional rules, which are also more expensive and time-consuming to apply (Costa and Bijlsma-Frankema 2007: 398). As such, the presence/absence and level of initial trust will be considered as an influencing factor towards the application of certain governance mechanisms.

Secondly, we study the actual trust developed during the PPP process and how governance affects the level of trust. Trust can be seen as an expression of appreciation towards the PPP process. In this sense, when an actor has developed a high trust towards other collaborating actors or the PPP as a whole, this suggests that the governance mix in the PPP functions well.

By distinguishing between trust as a context factor for ('initial trust'), and effect of ('trust development'), PPP governance, we can highlight the dynamics between trust and governance to explain why the PPP performs, or not. We now turn to performance as the final component in the framework.

Performance of PPPs

In the end, the black box of 'governance', influenced by antecedent factors and trust, is expected to have an impact on PPP performance. We assume that governments, in the end, try to control PPPs to achieve (better) performance. Based on the abundant performance literature we distinguish between two dimensions: 'product performance' and 'process performance' (Voets *et al.* 2009; Bult-Spiering and Dewulf 2006).[4]

Product performance refers to the production process where inputs are converted into outputs and results – it is task-oriented in terms of getting things done. In research on PPPs for infrastructure development, the latter is considered most important: we want to know whether the partnership meets the policy objectives and performance standards that were agreed at the outset of the PPP. Public–private partnerships are successful only if they are effective and create added value when compared to a conventional outsourcing (Bult-Spiering and Dewulf 2006). Product performance can further be divided into financial and substantive performance. Product performance can be studied once a PPP is in its operational or execution phase.

However, because PPPs are multi-actor arrangements, process performance is also an important dimension. Process performance refers to the actual co-operation in the partnership and the way in which the 'product' of the PPP (e.g. the infrastructure to be built) is realized. Process performance means that the processes in the public sector should be based on, and judged by, values such as honesty or fairness – it is process-oriented in terms of how things get done. Process performance is characterized by high dynamics: within a specific PPP, the extent to which certain elements, such as willingness to co-operate and trust, come into play can vary considerably over time (Bult-Spiering and Dewulf 2006: 37). Process performance is of particular relevance to study PPPs that are not yet in their operational or execution phase.

A dynamic perspective – introducing PPP phases

As PPPs are dynamic processes, interaction between the above-mentioned variables should be analysed from a dynamic perspective, in order to understand how the control mix changes, for what reason and with what effects. We distinguish four phases: the initiation phase, the public structuration phase the selection phase, and the implementation phase[5] (see Figure 10.2).

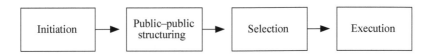

Figure 10.2 PPP phases
Source: www.vlaanderen.be/pps

We also use the four phases for case description, but cluster them for case analysis. Because the first two phases involve public actors only, we analyse the public–public relations in one public–public phase. In the third and fourth phases, the focus shifts to the public–private interactions, joined into the public–private phase.

Case analysis

To understand how control takes shape in a PPP, and to flesh out how complexity comes into play, a comparative multiple case study design is used. In the research project, we used different sets of cases with varying degrees of complexity, at different governmental tiers, at different phases of the PPP, with varying performance, and different types. This allows for cross-case comparisons, based on key variables of the conceptual framework. Because of word limits, we only briefly discuss a comparative case study of two contractual PPPs with the same focus (pool infrastructure), both involving similar actors (two local governments and a private consortium), and involving a DBFMO contract. Data were drawn from official documents (contracts, calls for bids etc.), grey material (personal notes, e-mails etc.), and 10 semi-structured interviews per case with the public and private actors involved in the PPPs, as well as observers.

Introducing the cases

Each case involved two neighbouring local governments (similar in size, population and budget) that faced high costs to renovate their old pools in the late 1990s. In each case, the involved local governments opted for an intercommunal infrastructure, which would be built and operated by private partners in order to provide a better and more cost-efficient pool. Overpelt and Neerpelt created the pool infrastructure 'Dommelslag' through a PPP with a consortium of private partners. Similarly, Schoten and Brasschaat engaged in a joint project with private partners for the construction and exploitation of a pool called 'Elshout'. Dommelslag opened in 2003 as the first pool infrastructure in Flanders designed, built, financed, maintained and operated using a PPP. All stakeholders (local governments, pool users and private partners) considered it a success. Elshout opened in January 2006 and is also considered relatively successful.

Complexity and control in the public–public phase

How do elements of complexity influence the institutional design and the use of specific control instruments and governance mechanisms in the public–public phase?

As to the multidimensional complexity for both cases in the public–public phase, we limit ourselves to highlight complexity features that affect the control mix. The multi-actor complexity in both cases differs with regard to the robustness of the governing coalition, which was substantially stronger in the case of

Dommelslag. In this case, Neerpelt and Overpelt had the same government coalition holding a vast majority in both local councils. In the case of Elshout, the same Christian Democratic Party was in coalition in both municipalities, but with different coalition parties. This implied that the political party that was the coalition partner in Brasschaat was in opposition in the local council of Schoten, and *vice versa*. A second aspect of multi-actor complexity, which differed among the two cases, was the kind of stakeholders and the alignment of interests among those stakeholders. Again, complexity was higher in the case of Elshout, with a strong difference in culture between the swimming clubs of Schoten and Brasschaat. Technical complexity was similar between the two projects, as they involved similar pool infrastructures and similar technical expertise. However, a relevant difference is that Overpelt and Neerpelt had to find a new location, while Brasschaat already owned a plot of land suitable for the pool infrastructure. This put Brasschaat in a dominant position *vis-à-vis* Schoten. Also, the political complexity in the case of Elshout proved to be considerably higher than in the case of Dommelslag. In the case of Dommelslag, both stakeholders and local councils were feeling a strong sense of urgency, as well as consensus that collaboration between both municipalities was the best way to proceed. In the case of Elshout, both the suggested location of the pool in Brasschaat and the specificities of the swimming pool were the subject of intense debate and opposition among the stakeholders and within the local councils. In contrast to the case of Dommelslag, strong and aggressive political opposition in the local councils in Brasschaat and Schoten made it very hard to find consensus, leading to an *ad hoc* coalition shift in the case of Schoten in order to get the collaboration approved.

Based on a very detailed analysis of single control instruments reported elsewhere (Van Gestel *et al.* 2009), we now discuss briefly for both cases the observed mix of control instruments and the influence of the level of complexity on this mix.

In Dommelslag, network-like instruments, although being 'closed' in kind, are dominant. The political and administrative actors involved in Dommelslag had a common long-standing history of interaction, reducing the relational risks significantly. Because of a low level of political complexity, the governing coalitions in both municipalities managed to keep discussions within the coalitions. This elitist and closed network-like way of working was possible because of vast majorities in the municipal councils and weak opposition parties. To save time, in both municipalities the mayor, as a political heavyweight, took the lead, assisted by administrative expertise.

The co-operation between the two municipalities was formalized in the Intermunicipal Service Association Pelt, which is a jointly-owned entity, vested in public law. But the elitist and closed manner of decision-making did not change. The municipal councils approved, *a posteriori*, the decisions made by the key players without any discussion. The joint purchase of the necessary grounds was done via this inter-municipal association, which also became the primary vehicle to interact with the private sector.

Given the technical complexity, the municipalities decided to use a 'concession of public works' (*concessie van openbare werken*) to structure the contractual PPP. This form of concession enabled both local governments to formulate clear requirements concerning the desired output and co-operation. The most important task was the drawing up of the specifications, a process in which there was a limited consultation of the stakeholders as users of the future swimming pool. The detailed output specifications, which were integrated in the call for bids, affected the dynamics in the public–private phase, as it restricted the freedom of the private candidates to be innovative in their bidding proposals (see below).

In the case of Elshout, the relatively higher level of multi-actor complexity hampered a successful application of network-like instruments. Because of the weak historical links between both municipalities (compared to Dommelslag), the outcomes of the negotiations between the two municipalities, were contractualized in a 'framework agreement' intended to reduce the relational risks. The negotiations preceding the agreement were relatively harder and characterized by more distrust, illustrating a recourse to more market-like control between both public partners.

Because the involved political actors feared conflicts because of a broad involvement of stakeholders and the desire of public actors to make quick progress, the public actors opted for a different legal procedure compared to Dommelslag. By using a 'domain concession' (*domeinconcessie*) they were not allowed to define extensive *ex ante* specifications in the call for bids, hence avoiding an intense deliberation process with stakeholders and opposition. Moreover this form of concession allowed the project to profit from an advantageous VAT regime, which helped to keep the price of the project manageable for both local authorities.

Brasschaat owned a plot of which Schoten wanted to buy a share. Therefore, the two local authorities could choose the most simple type of inter-municipal co-operation (an interlocal association). This association would advise Brasschaat, as the sole owner and concession giver, about the choice of a suitable private candidate. Schoten, however, wanted guarantees and compensation for agreeing to a pool on Brasschaat-owned territory, resulting in the above-mentioned detailed framework agreement. In Schoten, the decision to establish the interlocal association was taken by an *ad hoc* majority in the municipal council. Once the framework agreement was signed and some initial trust was built, there was improved ground for more network-like control.

The political complexity had a great effect on the institutional design and control mechanisms. Because of the societal, party-political and intergovernmental salience, the municipal councils were closely involved in the process and much attention was paid to convince them to approve all actions. In this way, all political parties were engaged in the project, giving them less ground to oppose the project later on.

At this time, the most important task was composing the conditions for the 'domain concession', done in mutual consultation in the body of the interlocal association, and which involved both municipal councils. Due to the restrictions

Table 10.2 Primary and secondary control mechanisms used during the public–public phase in the relationship with different actors in the cases of Dommelslag and Elshout

| | Dommelslag | | Elshout | |
	Primary	Secondary	Primary	Secondary
Between political coalition partners in both local authorities	N (closed)			M
In relation to political opposition in municipal council	H		N (open)	
In relation to private stakeholders	H	N	H	
In relation to private contractors	M	H	N	M

Note:
H – hierarchical processes dominant
M – market processes dominant
N – network processes dominant

of this instrument, the outcome was a rather vague blueprint for the project, namely that the grounds had to be used to construct and operate a pool infrastructure. Consequently, the private candidates were almost entirely free in designing their proposals, making public actors more dependent on the quality of the incoming tenders.

Table 10.2 summarizes the control mechanisms used during the public–public phase in both cases, and clear differences are observable. In Dommelslag, Neerpelt and Overpelt already featured close and friendly contacts between the leading officials in both (similar) governing coalitions before the PPP. This pre-existing network clearly facilitated the interactions during the public–public phase, making the process of drawing up a joint project a relatively (closed) network-like process, based on trust and reciprocity. Where Dommelslag clearly combines a closed network approach between the core actors, other actors were dealt with in a more hierarchical, unilateral way. In the case of Elshout, this positive history between the two governments was not present before the PPP. They were more distrusting, and negotiated hard with one another, making it a more market-like setting because exchange was the main interaction pattern. Because of a lack of good relations between political actors in both municipalities, high political salience and strong opposition, emphasis in this case was on market-like negotiations and, later, on more open network-like mechanisms.

Complexity and control in the public–private phase

The conclusion of the public–public phase marks the beginning of the public–private phase, where the PPP project continues in a new configuration. The public actors in the respective municipalities were collaborating through the created intercommunal bodies and the private partners entered the arena. This new constellation brought up new aspects of complexity, summarized in Table 10.3.

The major difference between the complexity in both cases, besides the different public structuring, was the characteristics of the private partners. In Dommelslag, a loose consortium of private companies with limited experience was selected, increasing the operational and relational risks. In Elshout, the selected consortium was more robust, experienced, and had a sturdy financial profile. However, one private partner had a fundamentally different idea (and culture) about the exploitation of pool infrastructures, affecting the relational and operational risks in a negative way. Finally, the political complexity in both cases disappeared somewhat into the background.

The starting point of the public–private phase in terms of control was the specifications in the call for bids (*lastenboek*) and the tender procedures drawn up by the public partners in the previous phase. In both cases this document was the basis for the tendering and future co-operation between the public and private partners. In Dommelslag, the 'concession of public works' made it possible to define many and detailed unilateral provisions. In Elshout, the 'domain concession' required much more additional negotiation once the partner was selected.

In Dommelslag, contacts between public and private partners were channelled through the service association Pelt. The specifications established by the latter were an important source of control, involving a number of obligations regarding the construction and exploitation of the future swimming pool. The 'concession of public works' enabled the municipalities to create strong competition between the private candidates while retaining strong control over the content of the negotiations. Further negotiations were conducted with the preferred bidder in a steering group (joining representatives of both parties) as a relatively 'closed' network-like instrument. The results were written down in the concession agreement (being a typical market instrument).

The steering group continued to exist after the opening of the pool infrastructure, acting as an informal discussion platform. The contract stipulated that after the construction phase the parties should meet twice a year, but in practice the frequency was much higher, up to one meeting each month. One possible explanation is the dominant network-like controlling culture of the public actors. However, another explanation might be that the unstable and inexperienced position of the private partners at the beginning of this phase required close involvement of the public partners.

The departure of the private constructors and the directors of the exploitation firm during the public–private phase weakened the consortium's financial basis. In addition, distrust appeared when one private partner wanted to co-operate with a rival consortium. Network-like control mechanisms alone were not sufficient to sort things out. Therefore, the public partner used the legal weapon of putting the private consortium into default (*'ingebreke stelling'*), thus using market control instruments present in the contract. These problems were, however, fixed a few months later, and public–private trust was gradually restored.

The political complexity shifted from the issue of a swimming pool to issues

Table 10.3 Complexity in the public–private phase

		Dommelslag	Elshout
Multi-actor complexity	*Government*	Intermunicipal Service Association Pelt (body with legal personality)	Interlocal association Brasschaat–Schoten (body without legal personality)
		Board of directors (small and close group)	Board of representatives from every political party
			Gives binding advice to Brasschaat
	Private partners	Three candidates in tendering procedure	Likewise
		Winner 'S&R Pelt' (consortium of several companies (constructors, architect, maintenance firm, exploitation firm – loose connection between partners))	Winner 'Sportavan' (consortium of three big companies (constructor, maintenance and exploitation))
		Unexperienced	Experienced
		Constructors wanted to leave the after the delivery of the swimming pool	The exploitation firm has a different opinion to the other partners
		Maintenance firm wanted to co-operate with a rival consortium	One partner forced out of the consortium – Sportavan becomes Sportoase (remaining partners take up exploitation responsibility
	Stakeholders	No structural involvement	Involvement in selection of partners
Technical complexity	*Scope*	Pool infrastructure with three basins, recreational elements, wellness facilities and cafeteria	Likewise + fitness facilities and multifunctional cafeteria
	Budget	Total investment €7.5 million by private partner	Total investment €14.3 million by private partner
		Yearly endowment €1 million to private partner	Yearly endowment €1.25 million to private partner
	Risk	5% Overpelt – 50% Neerpelt	60% Brasschaat – 40% Schoten
		Operational risks	Operational risks
		Demand risk	Demand risk
		Failure private partner	Failure private partner
Political complexity (salience)	*Society*	Entrance fee for the recreational user considered too high	Likewise
			Democratic risk (lack of support by opposition and stakeholders)
			Free-rider problem (users' neighbouring municipalities)

about service and price levels. One year after the opening, the private partner unilaterally raised the entrance fee, which was allowed by the contract. The public actor was dissatisfied, not because of the increase itself but because they were not consulted in advance (although such prior consultation was not required according to the contract). The public actors expected that the private partner, in the network-like atmosphere of trust and mutual consultation, would have discussed this with them beforehand. The public actor suspended the steering group meetings for some months, using this pressure instrument to obtain the inclusion in the contract of a consultation procedure for raising the prices. So the public actors used both network- and market-like instruments in this phase towards the private contractors.

In Elshout, societal stakeholders (end-users) were not actively involved in the public–public phase but were granted a role during the appraisal of the private candidates in different working groups. In this way, the municipalities could counter criticism that stakeholders were not sufficiently heard.

The 'domain concession' implied that the municipalities in Elshout were more limited in their *ex ante* control instruments: concrete provisions on the construction and exploitation of the future swimming pool could not be defined, making them highly dependent on the quality of the incoming tenders. The public actors negotiated an additional 'exploitation agreement' after the selection of the private candidate and approval of the 'domain concession' to make more detailed agreements, leading to a double contract structure to exercise control.

During this second negotiation process, the exploitation company of the consortium proved to have a different view on running the infrastructure than did the public partners. In addition, the exploitation company was not very keen to bear any operational risks. This created major distrust between both parties. The public partner used hard negotiations (a market-oriented control mechanism) by playing its role as sponsor to force the exploitation company out of the consortium: 'The deal would go on without the exploitation company or the deal would be off,' as one politician put it.

Another issue was access of citizens of other municipalities. One municipality gave its inhabitants a discount to go swimming in the old pools of Brasschaat and Schoten, leading to cheaper prices than for the population of the latter. Both municipalities were concerned that such a situation in the new infrastructure would increase societal salience in their communities, solving the issue through network-like control to convince the private partner to implement a more advantageous tariff for their own inhabitants (i.e. illustrating collaboration-oriented behaviour).

During the construction and exploitation phase, the two municipalities took a more distant approach to the project, as supervisors, leaving the realization of the project very much in the hands of the private partner. The different contracts created a wide set of control and monitoring instruments, but they were barely used.

By giving the private partner much discretion in maintaining and operating the infrastructure, but preserving the possibility for supervision and ultimate decision power, public partners had the feeling of trust in the co-operation and progress of the project.

As stated above, the use of different legal instruments in the two cases had complications for the opportunity of *ex ante* control. Nevertheless, the analysis of the ultimately signed contracts in both cases indicates that, in the end, only some differences appear between Dommelslag and Elshout in terms of content of the contracts. One major difference is the degree of interpretation of the swimming pool concept, which granted much more discretion to the private partner in the case of Elshout. Another important difference relates to the area of information and consultation structures (more focused on in Dommelslag compared to Elshout). In the contract of Dommelslag, in formal terms, consultation and information supply is stressed more than in the Elshout contract, while the latter stresses supervision and control. In Elshout, this supervision and control is, however, not applied so strictly (e.g. external monitoring of accountancy) as the agreements might indicate, because public actors trust the capacity and expertise of the private partner. In contrast, the actual consultation and information supply in Dommelslag are stronger than formulated in the agreements.

Linking the public–public and public–private phase

In the selection phase, control varies between both cases (see Table 10.4). In Elshout, more emphasis is put on market-like control. A possible explanation is the use of the 'domain concession', which restricts municipalities in their *ex ante* control. This made them more dependent on what the market offered them in the field of pool facilities. In Dommelslag, by using a 'concession of public works', the municipalities could formulate more *ex ante* requirements.

Table 10.4 Primary and secondary control mechanisms used in the public–private phase in the relationship with different actors in the cases of Dommelslag and Elshout

	Dommelslag		Elshout	
	Primary	Secondary	Primary	Secondary
Between political coalition partners in both local authorities	N (closed)		N (open)	
In relation to political opposition in municipal council	H		N (open)	
In relation to private stakeholders	H		N	
In relation to private contractors in tendering	M	H→N (closed)	M	(N)
In relation to private contractors in implementation	N (closed)	M	M	(N)

Note:
H – hierarchical processes dominant
M – market processes dominant
N – network processes dominant

In the actual negotiations in both cases, the emphasis lay primarily on market-like control. The preferred bidder was selected and the public and private partners became more or less equal partners at the negotiation table. The end of this phase was the contract. Within this broader setting of market negotiations, in the case of Dommelslag, relations with the private partners evolved from more unilateral to dense network relations. In the case of Elshout, stakeholders and political opposition were strongly involved in the selection of the private partner, whereas in Dommelslag processes remained quite closed for stakeholders and political opposition.

Moreover, the option in Dommelslag to use 'concession for public works' enabled them to exercise detailed control on the substance of the PPP, while the option in Elshout to use 'domain concession' left them with little control during the selection phase, except the need to construct a pool infrastructure on that plot of land. As a result, the contracts and negotiations in Dommelslag were very intense at the beginning of the public–private phase, while the contracts and negotiations in Elshout were less intense and needed to be complemented later in the public–private phase by a number of other documents to achieve the desired results.

In the execution phase, both sides become full partners. The control mechanisms used by the public partner were both network- and market-like. In Dommelslag, the accent lay especially on network control. A first possible explanation might be the dominant control culture within the municipalities. A second possible explanation might be that the unstable situation in Dommelslag, in terms of the make-up of the private consortium, required a close involvement of the public partners at the beginning of this phase. In Elshout, the emphasis lay mainly on market-oriented control. The public partners considered their task as being a more general one; namely, ensuring that a pool infrastructure was present (as opposed to Dommelslag, where public partners were also much more interested in the actual substance of that infrastructure). In Elshout, the public parties stuck to their supervisory role, and the private actor was trusted to know best how to develop and operate a pool complex. The negotiated contract and the risk-sharing remained the most important (underlying) control instrument. In general, clearly also in the public–private phase, the control patterns differed between both cases, and this difference seemed to be influenced by the complexity of the multi-actor, technical and political environment. In Dommelslag, the public partners evidently used market instruments to select and contract a private consortium while unilaterally setting a wide set of *ex ante* requirements that the bidder had to meet. However, they continued in a (closed) network-like fashion, involving many and close contacts with the private consortium, emphasizing good personal relations and trust and also meeting frequently. The public actors clearly wanted to have a high degree of control over the substance of the PPP. Consequently, they opted for a legal procedure that allowed them to do so. In contrast, after a market negotiation, which was very open to stakeholders and political opposition, the Elshout case showed how public actors took a more distant position, letting the private partners decide about substance – as long as a pool infrastructure was to be built.

Hence, in Elshout, the public–private interactions were much more business-like, much more formal and limited to a couple of meetings per year.

Conclusions

What then have we learned about the way public partners control the different phases of a PPP (i.e. the public–public phase and the public–private phase), and the impact of complexity?

Complexity vs control

We find that the control mix is indeed affected by complexity, both in the public–public phase and in the subsequent public–private phase. Although the cases studied share features of complexity, leading to a number of similar control instruments, some variations in complexity help to explain differences in the control mix. For example, similar political coalitions with vast majorities, a strong historical tradition of collaboration and strong interpersonal relations, weak opposition parties, relatively simple technical requirements and a low societal salience allow governments to use more closed network-based and hierarchical control approaches, compared to instances where multi-actor, technical and political complexity is much higher.

Different uses of control instruments

Another conclusion is that the threefold control instrument typology is useful, but should be developed further. Although we related the single control instruments to one control mechanism, it becomes clear that single control instruments can be used in different control logics. By focusing on their actual use, we have shown that they make up more of a continuum (e.g. more market-, more hierarchy-, or more network-like) than absolute categories. Contracts for instance can be framed in a market-like fashion (e.g. can be enforced in court, are very detailed, are frequently monitored, have a range of sanctions etc.), but also in a network-like spirit (e.g. are only gentlemen's agreements, are relatively simple and not highly detailed, have a joint monitoring, weak or no sanctions etc.). The contracts in both cases illustrate this: in Dommelslag, the contract emphasized instruments of information and consulting, while in Elshout the contract mainly contains instruments of monitoring and control.

Formal content of control vs actual behaviour of partners

Our analysis also shows a difference between the formal content and presence of control instruments on the one hand, and the actual behaviour partners develop on the other hand. A clear example is the way in which the governments in the Dommelslag case react during the public–private phase to the unilateral, but contractually allowed, rise of prices by the private consortium.

This example shows that while the private partner might behave and act within the stipulations of the formal market-based control instruments used (i.e. the contract), the public actors may have different expectations about the appropriate behaviour of the private partner (i.e. expectation of more network-like behaviour). Consequently, the public partner may respond with actions outside the formal control instruments (i.e. unilateral suspension of the steering group meetings).

These findings spark our interest in the actual control that takes shape in interactions between actors in the PPP. It is the combination of the formal and informal picture that we aspire to develop further to enrich the PPP research.

Control cycles through phases

Another conclusion is that the phase approach is valuable to understand control in the PPP, as control instruments, mechanisms and practices in one phase, for instance, present institutional constraints in the following phase.

From the analysis of the public–public phase, we learn that even while the public actors are positioned horizontally, the actual interaction is different.

It is also shown that the different outcomes of the public–public phases in both cases leads to a different interaction process in the public–private phase. The way the specifications in the call for bids are drawn up as the end product of the public–public phase, and the choice for a certain type of legal procedure (i.e. the choice for 'concession for public works' versus 'domain concession') to enter the public–private phase, clearly affects the dynamics of negotiation in the public–private phase.

We conclude that while the conceptual framework needs to be developed further in a number of directions discussed above, it proves a valuable basis to study PPP governance.

Finally, it is clear that we are not able to unlock the full potential of (these components of) the conceptual framework in the case studies discussed in this chapter. We accept that the relevance of the components will become clearer after analysing additional case studies, as they bring in more differences in terms of complexity features. We are only at the beginning of an interesting journey in developing theories on PPPs.

Notes

1   This chapter is based on research conducted within the frame of the Policy Research Centre on Governmental Organization in Flanders (SBOV II – 2007–11), funded by the Flemish government. The views expressed herein are those of the author(s) and not those of the Flemish government.
2   Design, Build, Finance, Maintain, Operate.
3   In many scientific articles the concepts of complexity and uncertainty are inextricably linked (Pitch *et al.* 2002; Comfort 1999). In our study we consider uncertainty as a main source of the 'complexity' of a specific project (Klijn 2007). The more uncertainty, the more complex the project.

4   We do not use their third dimension, named 'regime performance' (Voets *et al.* 2009), because we assume that the PPPs we study are not expected to provide a kind of a back-up system for government, for instance in times of crisis.
5   Because we focus on PPPs involving infrastructure development (as they are the most common type – see Eggers and Startup 2005), the execution or operational phase can be divided further into two different sub-phases. The first sub-phase refers to the building of the infrastructure itself; the second sub-phase is maintaining and/or managing the infrastructure.

References

Adler, P. (2001) Market, Hierarchy, and Trust: The Knowledge Economy and the Future of Capitalism. *Organization Science*, 12(2): 215–34. Online publication date: 1 April 2001.
Bloomfield, P. (2006) The Challenging Business of Long-term Public–Private Partnerships: Reflections on Local Experience. *Public Administration Review*, 66(3): 400–12.
Bouckaert, G., Peters, B. G. and Verhoest, K. (2010) *The Coordination of Public Sector Organizations: Shifting Patterns of Public Management*. Basingstoke: Palgrave Macmillan.
Bult-Spiering, M. and Dewulf, G. (2006) *Strategic Issues in Public Private Partnerships: An international perspective*. Oxford: Blackwell Publishing.
Choudhury, E. (2008) Trust in Administration: An integrative approach to optimal trust. *Administration and Society*, 40, 586–620.
Christensen, R. K. and Gazley, B. (2008) Capacity for Public Administration: Analysis of Meaning and Measurement. *Public Administration and Development*, 28(3): 265–79.
Colquitt, J. A., Scott, B. A. and Lepine, J. A. (2007) Trust, Trustworthiness, and Trust Propensity: A Meta-analytic Test of their Unique Relationships with Risk Taking and Job Performance. *Journal of Applied Psychology: An International Review*, 92, 909–27.
Comfort, L. K. (1999) Taking Complexity Seriously: Policy Analysis, Triangulation, and Sustainable Development. *Journal of Policy Analysis and Management*, 18(1): 181–84.
Costa, A. C. and Bijlsma-Frankema, K. (2007) Trust and Control Interrelations. New Perspectives on the Trust Control Nexus. *Group & Organization Management*, 32(4), 392–406.
Das, T. K. and Teng, B.-S. (1996) Risk Types and Inter-firm Alliance Structures. *Journal of Management Studies*, 33(6): 827–43.
Das, T. K. and Teng, B-S. (1998) Between Trust and Control: Developing Confidence in Partner Cooperation in Alliances. *The Academy of Management Review*, 23(3): 491–512.
Ducatteeuw, S. (2005) *Riskmanagement bij grote projecten*. Brussels: Politeia.
Edelenbos, J. and Klijn, E.-H. (2007) Trust in Complex Decision-making Networks: A Theoretical and Empirical Explanation. *Administration & Society*, 39: 25–50.
Edmonds B. (1996) What is Complexity?, in Heylighen, F. and Aerts, D. (eds) *The Evolution of Complexity.* Dordrecht: Kluwer.
Eggers, W. D. and Startup, T. (2005) *Closing the Infrastructure Gap: The Role of Public–Private Partnerships*. Deloitte Research.
Eversdijk, A. W. W. and Korsten, A. F. A. (2008) De bestuurskundige mythe van verbindend PPS-management – de Tweede Coentunnel als illustratie, in

Bestuurswetenschappen. The Hague: Sdu Uitgevers, pp. 29–56.

Grimsey. D. and Lewis, M. K. (2002) Evaluating the Risks of Public–Private Partnerships for Infrastructure Projects. *International Journal of Project Management*, 20: 107–18.

Hodge, G. (2004) The Risky Business of Public–Private Partnerships. *Australian Journal of Public Administration*, 63(4): 37–49.

Kaufmann, F. X., Majone, G. and Ostrom, V. (eds) (1986) *Guidance, Control and Evaluation in the Public Sector.* Berlin: de Gruyter.

Kickert, W. J. M., Klijn, E.-H. and Koppenjan, J. F. M. (1997) *Managing Complex Networks.* London: Sage.

Klijn, E.-H. (2007) Managing Complexity: Achieving the Impossible? *Critical Policy Analysis*, 1(3): 252–77.

Kramer, R. M., Brewer, M. B., and Hanna, B. A. (1996) Collective Trust and Collective Action: The Decision to Trust as a Social Decision, in Kramer, R. M. and Tyler, T. R. (eds) *Trust in Organizations.* Thousand Oaks, CA: Sage Publications, pp. 357–89.

Lewis, M. K. (2001) R*isk Management in Public Private Partnerships*. Centre for Globalization and Europeanization of the Economy, University of Gottingen.

Lowndes, V. and Skelcher, C. (2002) The Dynamics of Multi-organizational Partnerships: An Analysis of Changing Modes of Governance, in Osborne S. (ed.) *Public Management: Critical Perspectives.* London: Routledge and Kegan Paul, pp. 302–23.

Ng, A. and Loosemore, M. (2006) Risk Allocation in the Private Provision of Public Infrastructure. *International Journal of Project Management*, 25: 66–76.

Oomsels, P. and Bouchaert, G. (2012) Managing Trust in Public Organisations: A Consolidated Approach and its Contradictions. Paper presented at the IRSPM conference, Rome, 11–13 April.

Osborne, S. P. (2002) Managing the Coordination of Social Services in the Mixed Economy of Welfare: Competition, Cooperation or Common Cause?, in Osborne, S. *Public Management: Critical Perspectives.* London: Routledge and Kegan Paul, pp. 253–72.

O'Toole, L. (1997) Treating Networks Seriously: Practical and Research-based Agendas. *Public Administration Review*, 57(1): 45–52.

Ouchi, W. G. (1980) Markets, Bureaucracies, and Clans. *Administrative Science Quarterly*, 25, 129–41.

Parsons, W. (1995) *Public Policy: An Introduction to the Theory and Practice of Policy Analysis.* Cheltenham: Edward Elgar.

Pitch, M. T., Loch, C. H. and De Meyer, A. (2002) On Uncertainty, Ambiguity and Complexity in Project Management. *Management Science*, 48(8): 1008–23.

Pollitt, M. (2005) Learning from UK Private Finance Initiative Experience, in Hodge, G. and Greve, C. (eds) *The Challenge of Public–Private Partnerships: Learning from International Experience.* Cheltenham: Edward Elgar, pp. 207–30.

Powell, W. (1996) Trust-based Forms of Governance, in Kramer, R. M. and Tyler, T. R. (eds) *Trust in Organizations: Frontiers of Theory and Research.* London: Sage Publications.

Rousseau, D. M., Sitkin, S. B., Burt, S. B. and Camerer, C. (1998) Not so Different After All: Across-discipline View of Trust. *Academy of Management Review*, 23, 393–404.

Sagheer, M. and Iyer, K. C. (2006) Risk and Uncertainty Assessment in PPP Infrastructure Projects: Need for a Systems Dynamic Framework. Proceedings of the 6th Global Conference on Flexible Systems Management, 20–22 December, organized by Asian Institute of Technology, Bangkok.

Sako, M. (1998) Does Trust Improve Business Performance?, in Lane, C. and Bachmann, R. (eds) *Trust within and between organizations.* Oxford: Oxford University Press, pp. 88–117.

Scharpf, F. (1994) Games Real Actors could Play: Positive and Negative Co-ordination in Embedded Negotiations. *Journal of Theoretical Politics*, 6(1), 27–53.

Skelcher, C. K. (2005) Public–Private Partnerships and Hybridity, in Ferlie, E., Lynn Jr, L. E. and Pollitt, C. (eds) *The Oxford Handbook of Public Management*. Oxford: Oxford University Press (ch. 15).

Teisman, G. and Klijn, E.-H. (2002) Partnership Arrangements: Governmental Rhetoric or Governance Scheme?, *Public Administration Review*, 62(2): 197–205.

Thompson, G., Frances, J., Levacic, R. and Mitchell, J. (1991) *Markets, Hierarchies and Networks. The Coordination of Social Life*. London: Sage.

Van Gestel, K., Voets, J. and Verhoest, K. (2009) *Samen in bad? PPS bij gemeentelijke zwembaden. Een vergelijkende analyse van twee cases,* Leuven: Steunpunt Bestuurlijke Organisatie Vlaanderen.

Van Gestel, K., Voets, J. and Verhoest, K. (2012) How Governance of Complex PPPs Affects Performance. *Public Administration Quarterly*, 36(2).

Verhoest, K. and Bouckaert, G. (2005) Machinery of Government and Policy Capacity: The Effects of Specialization and Coordination, in Painter, M. (ed.) *Challenges to State Policy Capacity: Global Trends and Comparative Perspectives*. Basingstoke: Palgrave Macmillan, pp. 92–111.

Verhoest, K., Peters, B., Bouckaert, G. and Verschuere, B. (2004) The Study of Organizational Autonomy: A Conceptual Review. *Public Administration and Development*, 24(2): 101–18.

Vlaar, P. W. L., Van den Bosch, F. A. J. and Volberda, H. W. (2007) On the Evolution of Trust, Distrust, and Formal Coordination and Control in Interorganizational Relationships: Toward an Integrative Framework. *Group & Organization Management*, 32(4): 407–29.

Voets, J. (2008) Intergovernmental Relations in Multi-level Arrangements: Collaborative Public Management in Flanders. Doctoral dissertation. Leuven: K. U. Leuven – Faculteit Sociale Wetenschappen – Instituut voor de Overheid.

Voets, J., Verhoest, K., Troupin, S. and Van Gestel, K. (2009) Les PPP en Belgique: un état des lieux, in Rouillard, C. (ed.) *Public–Private Partnerships and Reconfiguration of the State: Challenges and Issues for Democratic Governance*. Quebec: Les Presses de l'Université Laval.

Vosselman, E. G. (1996) *Ontwerp van 'management control' systemen. Een economische benadering*. Deventer: Kluwer Bedrijfswetenschappen.

Weaver, W. (1948) Science and Complexity. *American Scientist*, 36(4): 536–44.

White, H C. (1991) Agency as control, in *Principals and Agents: The Structure of Business*, edited by Pratt, J. W. and Zeckhauser, R. J.. Boston, MA: Harvard, pp. 187–212.

Zaheer, A., McEvily, B. and Perrone, V. (1998) Does Trust Matter? Exploring the Effects of Interorganizational and Interpersonal Trust on Performance. *Organization Science: A Journal of the Institute of Management Sciences*, 9(2): 123–42.

11 Conclusions

Rethinking public–private partnerships

Carsten Greve and Graeme Hodge

Introduction

'PPPs are dead!' One keynote speaker to a recent European conference announced (Konvitz 2012). This provocative exclamation certainly drew attention – but is it actually true?

We began this volume on rethinking public–private partnerships by asking whether the era of PPP had now essentially passed us by; and this question still haunts our conclusions. Some of the crucial issues currently relevant for PPP have been raised, and subsequent discussion is likely to see intense debate. There are a wide variety of ways the term 'partnership' can be conceived, and today there is consensus that conditions have been changing for partnerships in the wake of the global financial crisis. There is also now a fresh sense that there are new strategies for organizations and individual actors involved in PPPs. So where does this leave us? And how might PPP fit into the turbulent times ahead? Our concluding remarks in this chapter address these questions by focusing on three issues: (1) the meanings and interpretations that cause us to rethink PPPs, (2) the turbulent times in which PPPs are now placed, and (3) the strategies that countries, organizations and individual actors may follow in future. Each of these issues is now tackled in turn.

Rethinking public–private partnerships

This volume has sparked discussion on how we think about PPPs. PPPs are part of the broader New Public Governance (NPG) framework in public administration and management noted by Osborne (2009). In the first chapter we distinguished between PPPs as project, organization, policy or governance tool and symbol and we noted that each of these ways of understanding PPP exists within a particular context and culture. Some chapters of the volume have understandably focused on projects: Sturup on mega-projects in Australia, Connoly and Wall on PFI projects in the UK, Reeves on infrastructure projects in Ireland, Alexander on brownfield projects in the US, and Verhoest *et al.* on infrastructure sporting facility projects in Belgium. As Sturup notes, mega-projects are first and foremost projects that need to be initiated and completed by a certain deadline. A second theme of chapters involved examining PPP organizations: Ysa *et al.*, for example, focus on a case organization in Spain. Other chapters have, thirdly, viewed PPPs through policy lenses: Connoly and Wall, and Hellowell and Vecchi write about policy dimensions of financing PPPs. Clearly, PPP policy is here closely intertwined with how the UK nowadays finances its public sector activities, the quality and content of advice given to Parliament by various actors, and the powerful hold that the City of London's finance sector seems to have over Parliament.[1] Jeffares *et al.* focus on performance and evaluation policy for PPPs. A fourth theme in this volume is the examination of PPPs as a governance tool, or a way of governing the relationship between the public sector and the private sector. This was the focus of Amirkhanyan and Pettijohn's chapter on the role of the non-profit sector in the delivery of public services. Many chapters also discussed the particular context and culture shaping PPP ideas and practices: Amirkhanyan and Pettijohn's discussion on the role of non-profits in the US public service context; several indirect discussions concerning the particular role of the City of London as a finance centre of the world; and discussions on how the PPP idea was imported from one context (most often the UK) to others such as Australia, Belgium and Ireland.

Thus PPPs are most frequently discussed as projects, but increasingly, questions are being asked about broader matters of organization, policy and the contextual and cultural relationship between the public sector and the private sector as we govern. Ideally, PPP theory needs to take all of these lenses into account. Clearly, each individual disciplinary area has a deep vein of specific literature: on project management (and improving practices); on organizational behaviour (including relevant hybrid forms); on policy (and working across sectors); on governance and collaboration; and on context and culture (where much is written on different varieties of capitalism and assessing capitalism versus more socialized systems). Approaching PPPs theoretically in each of these ways is of course fully legitimate in scholarly terms. But infrastructure PPP is as political a phenomenon as it is a sophisticated technical task – and there is no point in trying to grasp bigger discussions on capitalism versus more socialized systems if the purpose is construed as better optimizing a particular PPP project. The real need now is to more strongly and explicitly integrate theoretical thinking. What is suggested in the present volume is that from an intellectual point of view, it is beneficial at the very least to understand at what theoretical level one is approaching the PPP phenomenon. Likewise, there is a need to be more aware of how PPP is already operating at policy and governance levels, as well as the narrower project and organizational levels, and to better connect these discussions. Perhaps the most obvious example is the UK PFI policy, which has been seen as the most 'advanced' policy on PPPs worldwide. The policy has been adjusted throughout the last two decades, and is now facing a challenge due to the financial crisis as well as banking credibility and legitimacy crises inside the UK. It was the policy and ideas about the public sector and private sector governing together, however, that led to the materialization of more than 700 projects and organizations in the 1990s and the 2000s. And it did, for a time, bring a degree of political success for UK governments.

There are a number of focused theories already in use which could potentially lead to better understanding PPPs. Accordingly, theories on finance is a crucial arena. To assess the financial implications of long-term infrastructure projects (LTICs), the chapters by Connoly and Wall and by Hellowell and Vecchi both apply a financial lens to their analysis. Whether it is the new financial alternatives trialled since the GFC (nominated by the former), or concerns over consistently excessive financial returns to investors (nominated by the latter), finance is central to infrastructure PPP. More importantly, there is more work to be done in theorizing financial and economic performance of PPPs as they contribute to ongoing infrastructure operations as well as economic development. Theories of power and discourse are also important. Sturup's analysis of mega-projects focused on the theory of governmentality inspired by Foucault. Interestingly, Sturup argued that the 'problem' of PPP did not lie in our understanding of the technology, but in the distortions inherent in the application of the PPP technology – the art of governing mega-projects. Her analysis looked at governing through the use of technologies to build on particular rationalities and produce knowledge. This approach is well suited to illustrate how PPP projects play a crucial part in politics and how we become enrolled in, and then stand in awe of, mega-projects. Theories on non-profit-sector partnerships are also relevant at a time when the UK's big society ideal lingers. Amirkhanyan and Pettijohn give a fascinating *tour de force* on the problematic challenges that occur when non-profit sector partnerships begin to have an impact. They show how the non-profit sector has long been intertwined with both the public and the for-profit sector, and illustrate some of the core dilemmas that evolve when the non-profit sector gets too close to the public sector.

Theories on performance and evaluation also continue to stay relevant. Chapter 9 by Jeffares *et al.*, for example, points to the need for greater focus and systematic attention towards the performance and evaluation of PPPs. They suggest how the performance debate and our notions of what matters in assessing PPP can progress by using a more theory-based approach to evaluation questions. Reeves also engages in discussion on value for money and accountability for PPPs. His analysis of VfM as a mechanism for accountability in Ireland indicated significant shortfalls that now need to be overcome. Whilst there is much official evaluative documentation on PPPs, a substantial part of this comes from the UK National Audit Office, and in contrast to its early timid and almost impotent commentaries, the contemporary stance of this Office seems to have been far more independent and sceptical since the GFC. The evaluation perspective of Jeffares *et al.* therefore lays important groundwork for a more sustained and holistic approach to evaluating the worth of PPP.[2] Lastly, theories on innovation and management are fundamental for future productivity growth. Some chapters in this book view PPPs from an innovation theory perspective where the strategic actions of key actors become important. This is especially evident in the chapter by Ysa *et al.*, who see the public–private mix as perfect for innovation, with the additional need of success factors such as high-standard public leadership (including proactive networking and entrepreneurship) in the face of real exposure to risks. Alexander, as well, views PPP as an inter-organizational network arrangement where both the public and private sector can win. His case analyses again showed the importance of good public leadership in the partnership process. In particular, he referred to boundary-spanning managers and the evolving literature on that topic in public management and administration.

This edited volume shows how different theories at various theoretical levels can contribute to understanding PPPs. The theories span from advanced finance theories and those wrestling with more abstract ideas on power and discourse, to theories on the role of the non-profit sector, as well as more targeted theories on performance, evaluation, complexity and control, and innovation and management. While it may not be sensible to embrace all of the theories used in this volume in one framework, there are certain links that could be explored further. For example, the link between the theories of finance and the theories on performance, evaluation and (complexity and) control. The key challenge here is to grasp how financial instruments and the broader policy on financing infrastructure through private finance can relate to the more concrete evaluations of PPP performance. Along these lines there is a need to understand the complexity of challenges PPPs face and the subsequent performance and control systems. Many interconnections between these literatures have not yet been drawn, and evaluations, where they do exist, are typically of low veracity.

A second link to be explored is that between the theories that try to understand the power relations in projects and organizations, and those that focus on innovation and management. Innovation and new ways of managing may be limited if there are certain interests connected to the larger projects. Power relations can, of course, also be discussed in terms of the policy of inviting private finance into projects.

A third link to be explored is that between the theories of innovation, management and performance and the theories of the role of the non-profit sector. This relationship was discussed in Chapter 6 on the non-profit sector, but there could be more concrete links between management activities and innovative strategies occurring at management level, as well as the possibility for managers to change the institutional relationship between the public and the non-profit sector.

Amirkhanyan and Pettijohn quote Boris for saying: 'the interactions between government and non-profit organizations in civil society is complex and dynamic, ebbing and flowing with shifts in social and economic policy, political administrations and social norms' (Boris 2006: 3, quoted in Amirkhanyan and Pettijohn Chapter 6). Non-profits work with a particular community group rather than the median voter and are becoming more professional. Partnerships with non-profit organizations rely more on qualitative methods and self-reporting data, and non-profits change when they have a contract to fulfil.

Which theories are missing in these chapters? There are of course many different theories that could come into play in a discussion of PPPs. The law perspective is perhaps not so dominant in the present collection of chapters, but the legal perspective is discussed in many other works on PPPs, at least in terms of commercial law. Longer historical perspectives on the evolution of PPPs are also not so visible as our focus has turned more to recent turbulent times. A recent discussion on how turbulent economic times also existed historically is discussed at length by Roberts (2012).

Turbulent times

There is no doubt that PPPs are going through turbulent times. As an official from the OECD phrased it:

> The financial crisis has been tough on PPPs. The lack and high costs of credit stymied plans for new projects and the refinancing of those already under way. Moreover, the operational PPPs such as transportation projects and airports, which depend on drivers paying tolls and airline companies paying landing fees have watched revenues dry up as travelers have cut back on spending.
>
> (Hawkesworth 2010)

At a societal level, too, there has been much interest in PPP, but with a renewed air of scepticism around business motives rather than trust. In the UK, for example, parliamentary committees have inquired into the lessons learned from the PFI programme to date (House of Commons Committee of Public Accounts 2011) in the midst of several high-profile cases of banking indiscretions by executives, and a loss of confidence that financial professionals acted in the interests of their clients. The feeling of the population has been that whilst there is a need to rebuild business confidence and strengthen the finance sector, there is equally a huge need for trust to be rebuilt between citizens on the one hand and both the business sector and government on the other.[3]

From a business perspective, while the number of deals was up 11 per cent worldwide from 2010 to 2011, PricewaterhouseCoopers noted deals tending away from Europe towards Asia Pacific. Moreover, financing is moving from traditional banks towards state support and development banks, including the European Investment Bank (PricewaterhouseCoopers 2012). Spain has been the largest market in Europe outside the UK, and with Spain, Italy, Greece and other EU countries having debt clouds hanging over their heads, the turbulent times seem set to continue. Indicators from the OECD as well as leading global consultancy organizations confirm our sense that such governments have long lived beyond their means, taking politically expedient decisions whilst hiding behind accounts that lacked both transparency and accuracy.

As Connoly and Wall demonstrated in Chapter 2, there are risks connected to rising interesting rates, credit being unavailable, exchange-rate depreciation, and slump in domestic demand that may slow down the whole economy. Risk transfer is a key part in the story of PPPs, but whilst risk should, in principle, be allocated to the organization most likely to shoulder it, it is, in practice, far more complicated. Indeed, the global financial crisis seemed to turn existing beliefs and assumptions about risk and responsibility on their heads. Governments took over risk management from many private sector companies as the crisis set in. Government's role in managing systemic risk was rediscovered, and the tendency for markets to be gamed for personal gain by elites was relearned.

This edited volume has given some indication of how turbulent the times are for PPPs. Chapters in this volume showed – with references mainly to the situation in the UK – governments took over financial engagements in PPP projects, new financing deals had to be struck, and the question of regulating profits from PPPs became topical. Interestingly, therefore, some UK projects essentially became 'public–public' partnerships as the Treasury took on the core responsibility for the financing of the projects. There was a shift in finance sources from banks to insurance companies and pension funds, and, as Hellowell and Vecchi showed, governments have since struggled with how to regulate the profits generated by PPPs and how to institutionalize a robust regulatory regime for them. The debate on regulatory reform is well known from the experience with privatization of public enterprises and with infrastructure companies more generally. Hellowell and Vecchi point out, however, that a similar discussion might now be relevant for PPPs. And whilst this is not the first time that such an issue has been raised in the context of PPP (see for example Hodge 2005[4]), it is now, at long last, formally on the public agenda. As Reeves points out, much debate in Europe has centred on the interpretation of risk sharing and the Eurostat (European Union's statistical office) decision – but risk sharing in PPPs assumes that risks can be transferred to the organizations that are most competent to handle that risk. It also assumes that risk sharing is real, with a quantitative commercial hard edge, rather than a fragile system of trust that can be easily dissolved. As has been evident during recent turbulence, not only have governments sometimes stepped in to cover the risks that the private sector were supposed to handle for individual project deals, but governments have also stepped in to rescue the global finance system as a whole because of systemic risk resulting from abuse and personal greed. Under these circumstances, simplistic notions of 'risk sharing' re-emerge as highly controversial at best and naive at worst. Whatever the outcome, those who have trumpeted risk as the key ingredient of the PPP framework have been left with red faces.

Turbulent times have also given rise to a wider point on the role of government in both the economy and in society more generally. Much of the PPP literature has been assuming that PPP was part of a larger 'modernization' or 'transformation' era in public policy as Jeffares and colleagues point out in their chapter. But with turbulent times likely to persist, concerns over 'modernizing' have paled into insignificance alongside more fundamental issues of market rescues, ongoing economic instability and corrupt practices by banking and newspaper executives. One central lesson from the various recovery efforts made around the globe is that the government's role in terms of short-term financial stimuli as well as its more medium- and long-term roles in economic development have all been rediscovered and legitimized. As a consequence, governments may well have a substantial and semi-permanent presence in the economy in future years in many countries. Economic theories, however, have not counted on an active government.

Keynesian economics are still being largely scorned (except by select economists such as Paul Krugman of the *New York Times*), but few politicians and scholars have contemplated the perspective of a long-term presence of the government in the economy. In any event, the performance of PPPs is set to continue to be highly contested because of its inherent political context.

The issues have been well played out in the European Union's recent discussions about how to influence governments to become more involved in the economy. The European Commission has begun to use the PPP concept as a governance symbol in addition to the project and organization dimensions. In a 2011 speech to supreme audit institutions in Europe, Elias Messaoudi of the European Commission stated that:

> in the past, the Commission has laid the ground for more focus on PPPs (Green Paper, communication in 2005) but dealt with PPPs in a narrow sense. Nowadays the Commission adopts a horizontal approach including all relevant policies with a view to a consistent and coordinated response.

In the US, the government also took over banks and financial institutions. It was not with the aim of keeping them in the public realm, although that has been the practice for some banks and companies. Government intervention should therefore not be viewed as something extraordinary, but as a key feature in the 'new normal' conditions that characterize our economy today.

It is also likely that, even amidst turbulent times, lessons from the global financial crisis will not amount to a transmogrification of our collective awareness and sensitivity to public interest matters, but a hardening of personal attitudes and prejudices for or against private sector involvement in matters of public interest. In this light, a definitive answer on how to evaluate PPPs in a technical, optimal way is probably elusive, as Jeffares *et al.* note, leaving the real task as agreeing on an evaluation framework that addresses the legitimate concerns of the involved stakeholders.[5] Government's broader role in society will also see the rehearsing of old debates about the strengths and weaknesses of all sectors, too. Importantly, it may open up fundamental issues on the nature of what in the past have been well-accepted assumptions concerning values. For example, new debates about exactly what is public and what is private (when it comes to excessive CEO salaries or 'private' contract information, for example) may occur. New debates about the nature of chasing economic growth while income inequality deepens also suggest that the value of economic efficiency (and capital growth) may not continue to monopolize values such as fairness and equity. It is also likely that governments will rediscover that citizens expect them to have a proactive role in managing social issues and intervening in markets where the public interest is at stake, rather than standing aside and watching actors in imperfect markets playing games. In other words, citizens expect government to govern. Recent UK debates have seen this fundamental point being rediscovered with accusations that Treasury officials had essentially forgotten their public roles and had failed on multiple fronts. House of Commons Committee of Public Accounts

(2010), for example, reviewed the Treasury's response to the global credit crisis and observed that 'the Treasury failed to use its Infrastructure Finance Unit...to promote a downward trend in the cost of private debt finance', and the government 'did not use its negotiating position with the banks to assist PFI lending' while at the same time 'the taxpayer was providing unprecedented support to the banking system'. More recently, too, Stewart (2011) quoted Margaret Hodge (Chair of the Committee of Public Accounts Review into Lessons from PFI) who accused Treasury of being 'dreadfully complacent' whilst City investors made bumper profits from taxpayers by buying up PFI contracts and taking the proceeds to offshore tax havens (Stewart 2011). Perhaps it is little wonder that this UK review reported that 'at present, PFI deals look better value for money for the private sector than for the taxpayers' (House of Commons Committee of Public Accounts 2011).

Many of these debates will form the heart of new tensions as we progressively try to rise above political lobbying and technocratic hubris and 'democratize finance', as Engelen *et al.* (2011) put it. Consistent with the ideas are the calls to pay greater attention to building a more transparent regime for PPPs, as Reeves argues in his chapter. There is concern that the balance has tipped in favour of confidentiality in PPP contracts, but transparency could ensure a 'buy in' for the actors involved in establishing a PPP, according to Reeves. There is an increasing awareness of the potential of a more systematic transparency approach for PPPs (Greve and Hodge 2012).

Strategies and implications

Can PPPs be a response to turbulent times? What kind of strategies might key actors employ in trying to position and manage PPPs? Strategies are here understood in broader terms relating to government and private sector organizations' approaches to future developments, and as organizational and managerial strategies that individual actors may try to pursue.

There are a number of strategies that could be used. A sample might include abandonment, scepticism, marginal changes, *status quo*, reconfiguration, and branding.

Abandonment: Governments and private sector organizations can decide to give up on PPPs. PPPs may have peaked in policy terms. Governments can choose to relegate the PPP phenomenon to a time capsule of a few recent decades, which might be tempting for some governments around the world. The UK government has, nevertheless, upheld its support for PPPs, albeit in a more toned-down version.

Scepticism: Scepticism has perhaps always been warranted when government money is on the line and long-term deals are on the table. Governments may in the future be more hesitant to get into larger infrastructure projects using private finance. Some countries do not even have the option of obtaining private finance. The scepticism might be institutionalized in government decision-making so new PPP projects or organizations are required to go through several new decision points before being realised.

Marginal changes: There may only be marginal changes made to the many PPP projects already underway. The amount of political capital so far invested in the PPP brand in places such as the UK, Australia and Canada suggest that there will be real hesitation before completely abandoning a policy project. The trend of creating PPP projects may indeed also move to the Asia Pacific and away from Europe (as PricewaterhouseCoopers seemed to suggest), with the look and feel of projects themselves only experiencing marginal changes.

Status quo: Maintaining the *status quo* might be an aspiration for some politicians, but it seems an unlikely scenario for the future. The *status quo* involves being content with the current number of PPP projects and existing policies – and this seems to run counter to the desire of organizations and politicians whose natural bent is to promise renewal, progress and growth. The interest in PPPs from both governments and business groups has been massive, and governments are still searching for ways to build new infrastructure projects. Governments are also experimenting with new ways of collaborating with the non-profit sector, as Amirkhanyan and Pettijohn show.

Reconfiguring PPPs: A sizeable number of PPP projects may undergo reconfiguration if they have not done so already. In the UK, the reconfiguration is already happening for many long-term infrastructure contracts. The PricewaterhouseCoopers comment above indicates that reconfiguration is also taking place geographically, with the action moving away from Europe and towards the Asia Pacific. One way in which such a reconfiguration might occur in future is through concepts such as 'growth bonds', an idea being floated in the UK where citizen savings are offered tax breaks and risks are underwritten by government (Wright 2012). Another way is to trial new mechanisms for financing the initial construction phase of a project (through, say, a mini-perm-type arrangement, government bonds or short-term government finance) in tandem with longer-term pension or insurance companies to take on the long-term contract. Whilst there is no magic, easy path along this route (see Clark *et al.* 2011 and Orr 2009, for instance), there is much interest in making it work and a range of options ought, logically, be seriously considered. Clark *et al.* (2011), for example, view insurance companies, pension funds and sovereign wealth funds as all having the ability to invest over inter-generational timespans and thus a unique competitive advantage in infrastructure markets. They foresee a reconceptualization of the field and, ultimately, 'a new era of infrastructure investing'.

Increased PPPs and expanded branding: Some of the chapters in this book suggest that PPPs are still important and that their role could be expanded in future years. Partnerships between government and organizations in the non-profit sector seem likely to surge. In a number of challenging policy areas, PPPs also seem to be an option that governments or private sector organizations do not want to be without. Brownfield projects and new ways of collaborating in the health sector are both examples of this. The European Commission is an example of an organization that tries to use PPPs in a branding exercise for strengthening the role of government in the economy.

Theoretically, more attention is turning to the practice and actions of individual actors in their management strategies, as pointed out by Ysa *et al.* and Alexander. As Klijn (2008) reminded everyone, 'it's the management, stupid', and there needs to be increased attention on managers who, in practice, are the actors who make PPPs work. Calls for more attention on management are, however, framed by the macro developments in finance and economy.

The role of public managers is singled out in Ysa *et al.*'s chapter. They take for granted the larger institutional framework of PPPs and then examine what drives PPPs forward. They point to the role of public managers in making innovative activities. Public managers need to be given leeway to collaborate and engage in inter-organizational settings. The implication for research is that we should not only pay attention to structure and institutions but also to managers' strategies as they make their way in collaborative negotiations. A like-minded conclusion can be drawn from Alexander's detailed study of brownfield development projects in the state of New York. Here, public managers (non-elected, local-level government managers) negotiated with many different stakeholders in private sector organizations, local government, and the affected citizens. Alexander's perspective shows the key role played by active engagement by these non-elected local-level government managers as they strived to transform the brownfield development projects. He focuses on the management of the broader network of stakeholders that were crucial in the development process. This process was also about trust-building that could be used in future projects, showing that management strategies do not only have immediate results to strive for, but also that they should be seen in a long-term perspective. Both Spanish and New York cases point the way to more studies that go into detailed analyses of managers' strategies and choices in PPPs.

One further issue seems relatively certain in the end: the quest for rethinking PPPs is set to continue through turbulent times, and there are going to be new ways of exploring the relationship between the public sector and the private sector, which will include the formation of partnerships. The concept of PPP is being debated and expanded continuously, and can benefit from incorporating notions of projects, organizations, policy, governance tool and political-cultural attributes. Today's turbulent times have shaken up the PPP landscape, and for particular types of PPPs, such as long-term infrastructure contracts, the future in some ways hinges on how and if these projects can attract adequate and robust finance. For other types of PPP, there seem to be many societal challenges where innovative types of partnerships are in demand. Larger questions are also being addressed in the future role of the government in the economy. This question must be seen in the reconfiguration of markets and projects that are currently taking place. Theoretically, there is a move towards a desire to understand actors' motives and strategies in more in-depth ways. Turbulent times have put a question mark over PPP projects and have triggered a process of rethinking – but the reflex to form partnerships in the light of societal challenges seems bound to persist in one form or other. PPP concepts are clearly being presently rethought. And, interestingly, it is the multidisciplinary insights that are bringing new life to help understand the future of PPPs.

So the PPP phenomenon is not dead. But equally, new forms of PPP will need to evolve with a renewed sense of 'democratized finance' if they are to be seen as successful, particularly as the legitimacy of old partnership forms is increasingly challenged. Many debates concerning the fundamental role of government as well as new debates questioning previous assumptions on just what is private and what is public will no doubt flourish. Integral to these discussions will be better assessment of 'who' has been getting 'what' out of PPPs to date. Politicians choosing to ignore these lessons and to take the traditional narrow advice of specialists from single disciplines such as finance or economics alone will do so at their own peril.

Notes

1   PJCCFS (2012) notes that the financial industry has been uniquely able to defy governments or ignore government regulation. Historical examples from the growth of the City of London showed patterns of quite open defiance and set the context for contemporary behaviours in the financial sector.
2   We might note the work of Hodge (2010) here as well.
3   In the UK, the City (i.e. the financial sector) has been recently described as 'a massive cesspit' needing to be cleaned up (Wright *et al.* 2012), following high-profile scandals involving LIBOR rate setting, misleading sales of pension products and excessive bank charges (Moore 2012). The Governor of the Bank of England, Sir Mervyn King, put it more simply, characterizing the behaviour of leading banks as 'deceitful manipulation' (Winnett 2012).
4   Note that the notion of a strong regulatory agency taking on the independent role of governing long-term contracts was suggested in 2005. It was also acknowledged that 'this part of the PPP debate [wa]s yet to receive any serious public discussion, let alone be resolved'.
5   A recent call by Weaver (2010) for a theoretically based framework for implementation more generally could also be relevant for PPPs.

References

Clark, G., Monk, A., Orr, R. and Scott, W. (2011) *The New Era of Infrastructure Investing.* Electronic copy available at: http://ssrn.com/abstract=1837813

Engelen, E., Eturk, I., Froud, J., Johal, S.., Leaver, A., Moran, M., Nilsson, A. and Williams, K. (2011) *After the Great Complacence: Financial Crisis and the Politics of Reform*, Oxford: Oxford University Press.

Greve, C. and Hodge, G. (2012) Public–Private Partnerships: Observations on Changing Forms of Transparency. Paper to the Transatlantic Conference on Transparency Research, Utrecht University, 7–9 June.

Hawkesworth, I. (2010) Public–Private Partnerships: Making the Right Choice for the Right Reasons. *OECD Observer*, no. 278.

Hodge, G. A. (2005) Governing the Privatised State: New Accountability Guardians. Paper presented at 'Accountable Governance: An International Research Colloquium', Queen's University, Belfast, 20–22 October.

Hodge, G. A. (2010) Reviewing Public–Private Partnerships: Some Thoughts on Evaluation, in *International Handbook on Public–Private Partnerships*, edited by Hodge, G., Greve, C. and Boardman, A. Cheltenham: Edward Elgar, pp. 81–112.

House of Commons Committee of Public Accounts (2010) Financing PFI Projects in the Credit Crisis and the Treasury's Response. Ninth Report of Session 2010–11, HC553. The Stationery Office.

House of Commons Committee of Public Accounts (2011) Lessons from PFI and Other Projects. Forty-fourth Report of Session 2010–12, HC1201. The Stationery Office.

Klijn, E.-H. (2008) It's the Management, Stupid. Inaugural lecture, Erasmus University of Rotterdam.

Konvitz, J. (2012) Keynote Address to the European Consortium for Political Research, Standing Group on Regulation and Governance, Exeter, June.

Messaoudi, E. (2011) Public–Private Partnerships: The Implementation of the Commission's Communication. Presentation to European supreme audit institutions, Bonn, Germany, February.

Moore, J. (2012) Diamond's Not Forever. . . As He'll Soon Discover. *The Independent*, 30 June.

Orr, R.J. (2009) Pensions and Infrastructure: The Path to Common Ground. Working Paper 51, Collaboratory for Research on Global Projects, Stanford University, May.

Osborne, S. (ed.) (2009) *The New Public Governance?* London: Routledge.

Parliamentary Joint Committee on Corporations and Financial Services (2012) Statutory Oversight of the Australian Securities and Investments Commission, Canberra, March.

PricewaterhouseCoopers (2012) World Overview of PPP Markets. Presentation to the OECD, 26 March. Available at www.oecd.org/gov/budget/ppp

Roberts, A. (2012) *America's First Great Depression: Economic Crisis and Political Disorder after the Panic of 1837.* Ithaca, NY: Cornell University Press.

Stewart, H. (2011) Investors 'Using Tax Havens to Cash In on PFI Contracts'. *The Guardian*, 1 December.

Weaver, K. (2010) But Will It Work? Implementation Analysis to Improve Government Performance. *Brookings Issues in Governance Studies*, no. 32, February. Washington, DC: Brookings.

Winnett, R. (2012) Banking Scandal 'As Big a Threat as Deficit'. *The Daily Telegraph*, 30 June.

Wright, O. (2012) Osborne's Latest Plan: Ask Britain's Savers for Money. *The Independent*, 6 June.

Wright, O., English, S. and Armitage, J. (2012) Cable: The City is a Massive Cesspit. *The Independent*, 30 June.

Index